PITINO

MY STORY

PITINO

MY STORY

RICK PITINO

WITH SETH KAUFMAN

DIVERSION
BOOKS

Diversion Books
A Division of Diversion Publishing Corp.
443 Park Avenue South, Suite 1008
New York, New York 10016
www.DiversionBooks.com

For more information, email info@diversionbooks.com

First Diversion Books edition September 2018.
Hardcover ISBN: 978-1-63576-562-5
eBook ISBN: 978-1-63576-563-2

Printed in the U.S.A.
SDB/1809
1 3 5 7 9 10 8 6 4 2

I dedicate this book to my wife, Joanne, who has endured so much heartache and pain—you are my champion.

I also dedicate it to my five incredible children: Michael, Christopher, Richard, Ryan, and Jacqueline.

CONTENTS

FOREWORD

IN THE SPRING of 1986, I had just finished a mediocre first season as the Varsity Basketball Coach at McQuaid Jesuit High School in Rochester, New York. Stu Jackson and Herb Sendek, the two full-time assistant coaches at Providence College for Rick Pitino, stopped by McQuaid to talk to me about my best player, Greg Woodard. From that brief meeting came my biggest professional break. Coach Pitino hired me as his graduate assistant coach.

Graduate assistant coaches' salaries and job requirements are very different today from what they were in 1986. Back then, Providence College provided me a small stipend and free tuition. However, after a week or so on the job, I realized that I would have no time to go to classes. The workload and the 24-hour-a-day commitment Coach expected left no time for classes or homework. I bypassed getting my Master's in Education from Providence and instead got my Doctorate in Basketball from Coach Pitino.

That 1986–87 season will be forever remembered in Rhode Island for our Final Four run led by Billy Donovan and Coach. Billy was as valuable a college basketball player as there has been since the institution of the 3-point shot, and no coach has ever maximized a team's limited ability like Coach Pitino did that year.

But the Final Four is not what I remember most about that glorious season. I'll always remember the process that led to the winning. At that point, there was no 20-hour-a-week limit on practice time, nor was there a required day off for student-athletes as there is now. Our team committed to the plan Coach Pitino laid out: An hour of practice before breakfast in the morning, an hour of individual instruction for our players during breaks in the academic day, followed by a three-hour team practice in the afternoon. Then it was dinner, study hall, and one hundred free throws to end the day.

Day after day. Week after week.

The Friar players voluntarily committed to a process that gave them their best chance at success. No team ever deserved to win more than that team. No coach ever extracted more from less.

Coach Pitino was a demanding, confidence-boosting visionary. When the 3-point shot was introduced, he understood immediately how to maximize its potential and how to create quality 3-point shots while also defending the line. The strategy gave us a margin of error against more talented teams. He ushered in the pick-and-roll offensive attack that is so prevalent today. At the time, the Bob Knight motion offense dominated the game, and we were the only team around relying on that pick-and-roll set. His match-up zone press was unique, and we played fast with one of the slowest teams in the country.

I'm proud of our success. But I'm equally proud that we achieved all of it the right way! I saw up close that you could demand great effort on the court, care deeply about the players' off-the-court development, and still win big at a place like Providence, a school that had struggled badly since joining the Big East Conference. And I saw that you did not have to compromise your integrity or cut corners to get the results necessary in major college basketball.

Since that 1986–87 season, I have followed Coach Pitino's teams closely. We never worked together again, but the investment he made in me as a young coach has brought about a loyalty that will never be shaken and will never be broken. He won big at Providence, rebuilt the

New York Knicks on their way to an Atlantic Division title, brought the University of Kentucky back to glory, had some bad lottery luck with the Boston Celtics, and finally came back to the state of Kentucky and built a power at the University of Louisville—highlighted by their NCAA championship and multiple Final Fours. Unfortunately, so many people now forget so much of what Coach accomplished and all those he has positively impacted. Instead, most focus on how and why he left Louisville.

That's where this book—*Pitino: My Story*—comes into play. After months of enduring speculation, rumors, innuendo, and shocking headlines that attacked his professional integrity, Coach Pitino gets to tell his side of the story in an unvarnished fashion. It's his time to set the record straight, and then it's up to you to decide who and what you believe.

I will always be grateful and indebted to Coach Pitino for giving me a chance to pursue my dreams in coaching. Now I urge you to give Coach Pitino the same chance he gave me many years ago. Read his story and decide for yourself. Thirty-two years ago, he taught our team at Providence College to dream big dreams and then put in the work to achieve those dreams. Now my dream for Coach is for some brave college athletic director to read this book and believe in Coach the way our Providence team believed in him, and give him another opportunity to do what he does as well as anyone who has ever coached basketball—win big and help the young men that play for him develop their full potential as players and people.

—JEFF VAN GUNDY
NBA Analyst
Former Head Coach of the
Houston Rockets and New York Knicks

PROLOGUE

I WAS TALKING about leadership when the scandal that would destroy my career came crashing down.

Some ironies are more painful than others. That one hurts.

David Novak, the former CEO of fast-food giant Yum! Brands Corp., was in my office at the University of Louisville on the morning of September 26, 2017. He had come by to tape a forty-five-minute talk for a podcast devoted to honing leadership skills. I locked my office door to ensure we wouldn't be interrupted. As a guy with a pretty good track record of helping players and assistant coaches get to the next level, I had a few thousand thoughts to share. Predictably, forty-five minutes stretched to more than two hours.

Suddenly, my longtime executive assistant, Jordan Sucher, unlocked the door. Jordan essentially coordinated everything in the Louisville basketball office—from my schedule to team travel to what each assistant coach was up to. I always considered him pretty unflappable. But I could see he was upset.

"Coach, we have to end this," Jordan said. "There's a major problem."

I was surprised by the urgency in Jordan's voice. I think David was, too, because when I turned to apologize for abruptly ending our talk, he was ready to leave: "We've got enough here for the podcast. Don't worry about it."

Jordan directed me to our conference room. Kenny Klein, our director for media relations, and John Carns, our compliance director, were there. Everyone looked grim.

"What the hell is going on?" I asked.

"They picked up two of your assistant coaches," Kenny said.

"Who's *they*?"

"The FBI."

"The FBI? What are you talking about?"

"The FBI picked up Kenny Johnson in the parking lot right outside. And they picked up Jordan Fair at the airport."

LOL I was still totally in the dark. "What's this about? Why did they get picked up?"

"Some type of sting operation."

Sting operation? I tried to stay calm. For the last year and a half, I had *LOL* been a broken record to my staff. "Follow every single NCAA recruiting requirement. Do not even walk across the street when there's a red light!" That was my mantra to my assistant coaches who handled a lot of the recruiting work. The NCAA had been crawling all over Louisville basketball as part of a compliance investigation, and I continually urged my staff to follow every letter of every law in the rule book.

So missteps on our part seemed impossible. Over and over, I had demanded my staff adhere to NCCA recruitment guidelines.

Kenny Johnson came into the office and said the FBI had questioned him for ninety minutes.

Less than an hour later, the FBI came to question me.

A special agent asked if I wanted a lawyer present. I said, "No. There is no reason for an attorney. I've got nothing to hide."

"Are you aware of what's going on?"

"Absolutely not."

They didn't spell out the thrust of their investigation to me, but I realized from their questions it had something to do with recruiting violations. They asked if I knew a marketing executive at Adidas named Jim Gatto. I said yes. They asked about our relationship. They asked me questions about Brian Bowen, a top high school player who had committed to our program. They asked me questions about Bowen's family. They asked me questions about a guy I barely knew named Christian Dawkins, who was, last I heard, the general manager of an AAU basketball team. They asked me if I knew that one of my assistants, Jordan Fair, had allegedly been in a Las Vegas hotel room meeting with Dawkins and an AAU coach named Brad Augustine to discuss a recruit.

I made it clear I had nothing to do with any recruitment misstep and barely knew any of the people they mentioned other than my assistant coaches and Gatto.

After about ninety minutes, the FBI left. I called up Jordan Fair and I ripped into him.

"What the hell were you doing in a Las Vegas hotel room? I told you when you left, to make sure that you don't even jaywalk!"

He said, "Well, I was at a bar with my friend. And I said, let's have a beer before you head to Orlando. Then all of a sudden, this guy, Christian Dawkins, says, 'Let's go up to the room.'"

"What were you doing with Christian Dawkins? You don't even know him."

"I met him when Bowen visited. Took his number and we've been talking back and forth."

"About what?"

"Nothing. It's just small talk. Recruiting."

"Son, you're in big trouble. You tried to take shortcuts. You didn't follow instructions." And that's the last I ever spoke with him.

LOL

As the day wore on, my head continued to spin. Now I knew the Department of Justice was working on an investigation and that money from Adidas, which sponsored the University of Louisville athletic teams, was said to be involved. But I had no clear idea how broad the investigation was or if charges were going to be brought and who, exactly, was in the line of fire.

Much of this has yet to be fully adjudicated, but that day, the Department of Justice made national news—reported by print and television outlets across the nation—by issuing three complaints filed by the U.S. Attorney in New York's Southern District Court alleging wrongdoing by ten people, including four assistant coaches—Auburn's Chuck Person, Oklahoma State University's Lamont Evans, USC's Anthony Bland, and Arizona's Emanuel "Book" Richardson—and player agent Rashan Michel. (These complaints have been made available on justice.gov.) One of the complaints targeted Gatto, an Adidas consultant named Merle Code, Dawkins—described as "a business manager"—Augustine, and Munish Sood, "a financial manager." The complaint alleged the men conspired to commit wire fraud by "concealing bribe payments to high school players and/or their families in exchange for the student-athletes' commitment to play basketball" at two different programs—"University-6 and University-7."

The complaint also noted that the name of an allegedly all-powerful college coach—dubbed Coach-2 in the legal document—had surfaced in taped conversations. And Augustine, the AAU coach, was even taped making a vulgar reference to Coach-2, claiming the coach had enormous pull with Adidas. Additionally, an FBI agent said phone records revealed Coach-2 and Gatto, the Adidas executive, had three telephone calls around the time Brian Bowen committed to Louisville.

Press reports identified the mysterious University-7 as the University of Miami and University-6 as the University of Louisville.

As for Coach-2? That was me.

I was not charged with any wrongdoing, but to many people who read the complaints or just heard about them—I had been implicated. They didn't consider that two people actually being charged—Dawkins and Augustine—dragged my program and name in the mud in hopes of generating cash and connections, or as the U.S. v. James Gatto et al Complaint put it, "for obtaining money and property." To the general public, the ten people named in the complaint weren't the story. It was me; I was in big trouble.

. . .

In many ways, recruiting in college basketball has become as competitive as the games themselves. It stands to reason. College basketball is a multi-billion-dollar business. The better your team does, the more money your school will make. And the better your recruiting class is, the better your team will do. So let's complete the circle: the better your recruiting class is, the more money your school is likely to make.

LOL

That's why programs invest in recruiting. And that's why some programs cheat. They try to incentivize recruits into coming to a certain school by offering perks that are against NCAA recruiting rules.

This has been going on for the last fifty years. But now, according to the charges leveled by the DOJ investigation, the money is bigger than ever. That's the big news. High school athletes—or their families—are allegedly being offered as much as $150,000. This is a huge jump from a few decades ago, when a fancy lunch, a promise of a summer job, $200, or maybe even a thousand bucks was the price paid to land a player.

As I heard it, back in the 1950s and 1960s, the enticements were mostly to help families to travel to games, so parents and siblings could see their son or brother play. Some coaches arranged for that. It was low level and it was rare. The money came from boosters. Or a coach with access to petty cash. I believe there are very few big-time programs that try to skirt the rules. Why? Well, it's almost the inverse logic of why programs would cheat: teams now make so much money that it doesn't make sense for them to risk getting caught.

So, when I read the Department of Justice complaint, I was shocked—and not just about how negatively they painted me and my program. It seemed like everyone was getting paid off. Agents were paying assistant coaches ten grand to steer players to them. Families were getting $50,000 to guide their kids to certain schools. AAU coaches were taking money, supposedly to pass on to family members. And a guy working for Adidas—who used to work at Nike—allegedly was caught on tape discussing how to submit fake invoices to generate the cash to pay some of these huge recruiting bills. Incredible.

C. Dawkins

How did recruiting get to this point?

LOL

How did it manage to drag me down?

I believe the same amount of cheating goes on today as it did fifty years ago. And I maintain it is less than 10 percent of the entire industry. But there are so many more factors that have entered the equation and have led to abuses. The game is now flooded with money. I will examine the evolution of how that flood began in greater detail in a subsequent chapter. But the short version is this:

Three shoe companies—Nike, Adidas, and Under Armour—have a collective market value *$170 billion* as of June 2018. These companies have complex marketing strategies, but they are primarily focused on obtaining endorsement deals with superstar athletes. These deals are crucial to driving sales. In order to make these deals, the sneaker companies rain hundreds of millions of dollars annually on a number of marketing channels.

They pay money to grassroots basketball teams—often referred to as AAU teams. They sponsor leagues for these teams, which feature the top high school basketball players in the country. Since these young players are potential stars, sports agents use people called "runners"—essentially low-paid employees whose mission is to secure prospects for agents. To do that, these runners try to connect and woo AAU coaches, their players, and the players' families. An elite player—one who makes it to the NBA—can generate millions of dollars for an agent. So you can understand why an agent or runner might try and bend rules to win a prospect's future business.

Meanwhile, shoe companies are also spending an estimated $500 million annually to sponsor college athletic programs, and men's basketball teams are their primary concern. These schools are considered shoe company satellite franchises by their benefactors.

I've used very broad strokes to describe the big money relationships at work here. But don't worry, I'll provide more detail soon.

I'm going to share the story of my life in basketball. I've spent more than forty years coaching and motivating, teaching and competing, winning and celebrating. And, yes, recruiting—year after year after year. By telling my story, including the strangest, most disheartening events of my career—which involve conspiracy, false accusations, and abuses of power—I hope to reflect on my evolution and the evolution of the college game itself. I hope to examine not just where it's been and where it's going, but where it should go and how to get there.

That big trouble everyone thought I was in? It was ugly. My reputation's been destroyed. But at this point, I can't get in any *more* trouble. *LOL* So let's get busy. Buckle up. This is going to be a wild ride.

PITINO

MY STORY

1

A FIVE-STAR BEGINNING

Howard Garfinkel changed the way college basketball coach-

es recruited by showcasing high school phenoms like Michael

Jordan, Moses Malone, and Patrick Ewing.

He also changed my life.

▼

DEFENSE. I'VE ALWAYS prided myself on the way my teams have played it over the years—an infamous and intense full-court press. I like to think of it as a relentless, focused assault on our opponents, one that involves precision positioning and maximum conditioning, and one that, ideally, leads to offense.

But when my name was tied to the headline-grabbing Department of Justice investigation, I was knocked off my game.

And when the powers that be at the University of Louisville subsequently fired me for what they falsely claimed was "just cause"—forcing me from the school I'd devoted sixteen years of my life to promoting and improving—I was literally knocked *out* of the game.   *LOL*

From the moment it was revealed that my name had come up in an FBI investigation into corrupt basketball recruiting practices, hundreds of reporters, headline writers, and talk radio hosts, all eager to do what they are paid to do and break stories, pronounced me guilty.

They ignored, as we'll see, my previous, very public stance on the undue influence of sneaker money in college and AAU basketball. They rarely, if ever, sought out my assistant coaches for a second opinion. And many of them repeatedly failed to correctly decipher the information in the DOJ statements.

LOL But hey, why let facts get in the way of a good story?

No wonder I was off my game.

To outsiders looking in, I can see how I might easily appear to be a villain. Only two years earlier, my program became embroiled in a tawdry scandal when one of my assistants, acting completely on his own, hired strippers and prostitutes to perform for recruits. Now, with the US Attorney's complaint, I was "caught"—totally tangentially—in a second recruiting debacle. If I only read the headlines, I would think I was a bad guy, too.

But the Department of Justice—which ultimately lit the fuse that blew up my career—has never actually said I'm guilty of anything. I haven't been indicted and no one who worked on my Louisville staff *LOL* has been indicted, either. They just consider me, as a US Attorney told my legal team, "collateral damage."

Funny stuff, right?

So it's finally time to play defense.

This isn't to say that I'm a saint or that I'm infallible. We all have to live with things we regret, and I will point out my mistakes later, but I've never cheated the game and I've never cheated in the game.

My story is complicated and crazy. But let's start at the beginning, when basketball was nothing but fun. Then I'll share the good, the bad, the ugly, and the ridiculous.

This time defense isn't about precise positioning or wearing down an opponent.

It's about telling the truth.

HOW IT ALL STARTED

If I attempted to diagram my career the way coaches sketch plays on a whiteboard, it would probably end up looking like a wild, abstract drawing with lines crisscrossing all over the place. I may have developed a reputation for meticulous attention to detail and contingency planning over the years, but my own personal career trajectory has been filled with unexpected, improvisational moves. I've left jobs in two different cities and returned years later when new opportunities beckoned. I bounced between the college game and the pros. There was a time I was sure I'd be working at Penn State. And at one point, I was minutes away from signing a contract to coach Michigan. Back in 1987, if you told me that I would ever leave Providence, I would have said you were nuts. And until my wife called me a lamb—something I'll explain later—I never seriously considered moving to Louisville.

But the first and best move I ever made—the move that set my whole career in motion—was one that, at the time, I didn't even consider a career move. It was guided by one thing and one thing only: My love of the game of basketball.

In 1966, I was a freshman on the junior varsity squad at St. Dominic High School in Oyster Bay, Long Island, and we traveled to Friendship Farm Basketball Camp, run by Jack Donohue outside New York City. It was a big deal. Donohue had coached Kareem Abdul Jabbar—known as Lew Alcindor at the time—at Power Memorial Academy in Manhattan. Respected Archbishop Molloy basketball coach Jack Curran was working the camp and there were lots of All-American college ball players helping out, too. Each of these collegiate stars worked as a bunk counselor. As fate would have it, the bunk for St. Dominic's players drew the short straw. We didn't have a big-name All-American athlete supervising us.

Instead, we got a bunk counselor who looked more like Woody

Allen than Jerry West. He was short, wore big glasses, walked around with a copy of the *Racing Form* under his arm and a cigarette in his mouth. His name was Howard Garfinkel, and he was a basketball scout.

This strange guy had the bunk next to me. We would go to bed and wake up with the stench of Chesterfield cigarettes swirling in the air, because the first and last thing he'd do every day was light up a smoke. Whenever he pulled out his pack of cigarettes inside the bunk, we'd all yell at him and throw things at him, but he ignored us and puffed away.

On the third day of camp, we decided to teach Garf—everyone called him Garf—a lesson. Right before lunch, a bunch of us took every stitch of clothing he owned out of the bunk, went into the woods, and the tallest kid on the team hung the wardrobe up on tree branches. When Garf noticed his clothes were gone, he immediately started cursing and screaming at us: "Where's my clothes!?"

I finally took pity on him and led him to the woods—and he flipped out again when he realized he couldn't reach his clothes. I grabbed a stick and used it to liberate his shirts, pants, and underwear. And because of this, even though I was one of the perps who took his clothes, he thought I was the good kid in the group. The next morning he woke us all up with his cigarette smoke and a chant. "Let's go, Pitino! Let's go, Pitino!"

That was the start of a great friendship.

At the end of the session, Garf said to me, "Look, Pitino, I run a basketball camp, too. You're going to get your butt kicked, but you should come."

Like so many teens, I fantasized that maybe one day, I'd be a pro. And like thousands of high school jocks, pretty much the only thing I ever wanted to do was play my favorite sport. So I convinced my parents to pay for a session at Garf's Five-Star Basketball Camp. It was the summer of 1967. I was a few months shy of turning fifteen when they

4

signed me up and, completely unwittingly, helped me make what would be the most influential decision of my entire life.

I really didn't know all that much about Howard Garfinkel at the time, other than he was a kindhearted crank who loved basketball. But he was already a New York basketball legend, famous for his years as a Big Apple "bird-dog"—a high school basketball scout who would help identify and recruit talent for some of America's biggest college teams.

Garf's Five-Star Basketball Camp would soon become a basketball Mecca. College coaches from every major program would make a summer pilgrimage to evaluate the best schoolboy players on the East Coast. But in its early years, this was not the case. Legend has it the first session only had twenty-two campers. When I showed the next year, there were maybe 150 players.

GARF
FIVE
STAR

I don't think any of us campers realized we were participating in what was essentially ground zero of one of America's greatest basketball laboratories. Instead of scientists, our lab was populated by counselors who turned out to be bona fide basketball geniuses. My first year at Five-Star, the head coach—the title of the lead instructor who organizes the camp staff—was Bob Knight, the soon-to-be coach of Indiana University who would go on to win over nine hundred games. At the time, he was moonlighting from his regular job coaching Army. The profession wasn't quite as lucrative as it is now, and so Coach Knight was one of a long line of notable talents who spent summers as the camp head coach, a list that includes future NBA coaches Hubie Brown, Chuck Daly, and Mike Fratello.

Coach Knight came up with the idea of training stations—thirteen areas on the court where players would focus on one specific area of the game and just drill, drill, drill. For a basketball junkie like me, this was heaven. I refined my dribbling, my bounce passes, my footwork on defense, my one-on-one moves. Everything. I played basketball ten hours a day. I got stronger. I got faster. And my basketball IQ probably doubled. But, true to Garf's original prediction when he first invited me to camp, I did get my butt kicked. Many of the other campers were more talented than I was.

That motivated me to return to the camp at Honesdale, Pennsylvania, before my junior year of high school. One of my goals was to show Garf that I was a hell of a basketball player. This time my parents only had to pay for half the session because Howie hired me to work as a waiter in the camp dining hall. By now I was more aware of just what Five-Star was. I knew that our coaches were some of the best minds in the game. I also knew Howie published *High School Basketball Illustrated*, which some college coaches regarded as a recruiting bible. This insight made me want to excel even more at the camp. I had heard other campers were getting scholarships—including my St. Dominic teammate Tom Riker, a future first-round NBA pick, who signed with South Carolina University—and I wanted one, too. So I listened hard to what was being taught, determined to absorb every lesson and then put it to use on the court. I wasn't a nerdy kid, but in a sense, I was a basketball nerd. I would study opponents to learn their tendencies. I would practice jab steps, spin moves, and going to my left when I had the ball, striving to be equally adept with either hand. And as for those hands, where were they on defense? Up. Always up. Still, I was not a dominant player. But I felt I had held my own.

I came back to camp the following year more focused than ever. I would be going into my senior year at St. Dominic, where I would be named team captain, and I wanted to make an impression over the summer to help me land a scholarship somewhere. Thanks to my Five-Star education and all the drilling and practicing, now I understood and saw the game with a speed and ease I hadn't had two years earlier. And the result of all my hard work, all the drilling and refining moves, started to show up on the court. I averaged 32 points a game that summer and I was named the MVP of the camp all-star game. That was a

6

great moment for me. I had finally gotten the recognition I wanted from Garf.

LURED BY DR. J

During my senior year at St. Dominic, I also started getting invitations from coaches to go on campus visits, and I went to seventeen schools. *Wow* The most memorable trip I went on was with Al Skinner, a forward from Malverne, Long Island. We both had really strong senior years, and we went to visit the University of Massachusetts at Amherst. At the time, UMass had a sophomore sensation named Julius Erving. Julius was developing a national reputation, but since he was also from Long Island, he was already famous to Al and me for his tremendous scoring ability.

During the trip, the Amherst campus was in upheaval. Students were taking over buildings, pressing for more racial equality and protesting the war in Vietnam. I remember the coaches trying to shield us from the unrest, but we told them it was no big deal. We had seen similar protests at other schools we visited. At any rate, both Al and I decided we wanted to play together with Julius. So we committed to the school.

Freshmen weren't allowed to play on the varsity team in those days, but Al and I would practice against Julius every day for an hour when the freshman team would play against the varsity as a sort of scout team.

A high-flying forward, Julius's dunking prowess was already well known on campus—even though the NCAA did not allow dunks in *LOL* games. The man soon to be known across America as Dr. J would put on a slamathon during pregame warm-ups. This was, for its time, revolutionary, above-the-rim stuff. And because the games were played in a five-thousand-seat arena with first-come, first-served seats, huge lines would form before game time, and fans would pack our freshman games. Everyone wanted to witness Julius putting on an aerial display the likes of which had not been seen before.

Al and I both joined the varsity the next year, and expected to play with Julius. Unfortunately for us, the newly formed ABA announced it would allow players to enter the league without finishing college, and Julius went pro when the Virginia Squires came calling.

That was a disappointment, but I loved my time with the Redmen—who are now called the Minutemen. Al and I became close friends as well as teammates. Al was a prodigious scorer and rebounder, while I held down the starting point guard duties. We won the Yankee Conference two years in row and made it to the NIT twice, which at the time was still a prestigious event, so prestigious that in 1970 Al McGuire at Marquette turned down the NCAA to play in the Garden with his star guard, Dean "The Dream" Meminger, and three other New York teammates.

ITALY VS. HAWAII

In the summers, I would return to Five-Star, which was blossoming into a major institution. What had started as an academy with two dozen campers now attracted hundreds of the best players in the country and hundreds of coaches who made the journey to watch the sessions.

When I was finishing up at UMass, I got an offer to play in Italy. My last college game was a triple overtime loss to Jacksonville in the NIT's late game at the Garden. Afterward, that evening's teams met up at the Statler Hilton, including the University of Hawaii, who had beaten Fairfield. Garf stopped by to commiserate over the tough loss and congratulate me on finishing a great run at UMass. Then he asked if I was still planning on playing overseas. I told him I was.

"Kid, you're going to go there and you'll make pretty good money for five or six years, but when you come back, all your connections from Five-Star are going to have moved on. You're the youngest lecturer and coach ever at Five-Star. But if you go over there, you'll be out of sight and out of mind. Why don't you become a graduate assistant, work on your masters and get into coaching?"

"I've got my heart set on playing," I said. But I looked in the back room and saw the guys from Hawaii celebrating, and images of beaches, surfing, hula girls, and scenes from *Hawaii Five-O* popped into my head, and I joked, "Now Garf, if there's one place I'll be a graduate assistant and give up playing, it's Hawaii. If you can get me there, I'll go."

Garf introduced me to Bruce O'Neill, the coach at Hawaii, who was also a subscriber to Garf's *High School Basketball Illustrated*. I asked Bruce if he had any openings for a graduate assistant.

Bruce told me the G.A. position was tentatively filled, but he'd love to develop a connection with Five-Star. Keeping my options open, I said, "Well, maybe next year."

He said, "Sure. Write me a letter and I'll keep you in mind."

So I wrote him a letter, and I asked Hubie Brown and Chuck Daly to write recommendations for me. And in July, about two weeks before I was set to head off to Italy, I got a phone call from Bruce. His G.A., Artie Wilson, had decided to go to law school and the position was open, but he needed me there in forty-eight hours. The team was about to go play a preseason exhibition game in Japan, and my first job was going to be a babysitting gig—I had to make sure Bruce's 6'11" prize recruit, Tom Barker, was going to classes in Honolulu and didn't get poached by North Carolina State's Norm Sloan, who was passing through after his team's trip to Japan.

I talked to my parents and had dinner with Garf. In the end, I turned down my $19,000 offer from Italy and headed to Hawaii for free room and board.

The laid-back lifestyle of Hawaii was a little wasted on me. I would get to work at 6:45 in the morning and nobody would show up until maybe 9:00 a.m. So I'd have all my recruiting letters written and be ready for more work. Bruce promoted me to assistant coach after two months. I coached the JV team, but Bruce wanted me to spend most of the time recruiting. I was like a traveling salesman. I'd hit the road to recruit for a week, come back and coach a game, and then leave again. The trips paid off; I signed three players from the New York area, including George Lett and Edwin Torres of the Bronx, and a hot-shooting All-American guard, Reggie Carter, who played at Long Island Lutheran even though he was from Harlem. I would stay at my parents' house in Long Island for about ten days at a time and watch him play two or three games. I must have seen eighteen of Reggie's games during his senior year. It's been said that just showing up is half the battle when it comes to success, and it's true: being a persistent presence was definitely a factor in successfully landing a recruit. In fact, University of Maryland coach Lefty Driesell had an assistant coach named Dave Pritchett, a madman of a recruiter, who would actually rent an apartment to be near a great player.

With Reggie, I did even more than go to games and chat with his family. I got to know the coach at his AAU team at Riverside Church. I spent time with the head coach and director of Lutheran, Rev. Ed Visscher. Bottom line: if Reggie had a friend, I was going to become his friend, too.

That kind of dogged focus was a key to being a successful recruiter. DAMN Back then, there were no NCAA limitations on how many phone calls or visits you could make. So I would call players every evening. I wanted to let them know that I was a fan and someone they could talk to. If you are going to be a coach and a mentor, establishing open channels of communication—being approachable—is an important selling point.

10

While I made staying in contact and seeing games a major priority, I had one more advantage that very few assistants or head coaches had: Five-Star.

Because I was a counselor and lecturer at the premier basketball camp in the world, I was able to drill with players on the court. I was able to beat them one-on-one. I was able to show and share my knowledge of the game and my passion for coaching. It was a tremendous advantage over so many other coaches. I got to work out players. I got to bond with them. And I got to showcase my talents.

All these factors came into play recruiting Reggie, who came to Hawaii and averaged 16 points his freshman year (the NCAA started allowing freshmen to play varsity in 1972). He then transferred to St. Johns and wound up playing two years for the Knicks.

My second year at Hawaii, Bruce had staffing openings and asked if I knew any candidates. I recommended two guys from back East: one I had worked with at Five-Star, Peter Gillen, and the other was a super high school evaluator of talent named Al Menendez. Both added a great deal to the program. A lot of people thought recruiting was easy at the University of Hawaii. But the exact opposite was true. It was a twelve-hour flight from the East Coast, which is a long way to travel for a forty-eight-hour visit. And when recruits got back on that plane at the end of their visit, they would realize they were a very long way from home. So far, in fact, that it would be difficult for their friends and family to come see them.

While I was on the road recruiting, Bruce O'Neil and his other assistant coach were fired before the end of the 1975–76 season for making a TV commercial for Cutter Ford, a local car dealership, along with four players on the team. The ad was found to be against NCAA regulations and opened a Pandora's Box of NCAA violations from past years.

Bruce recommended Pete become the head coach. When I got off the road, though, Pete, who was older than I was, went to the A.D. and said, "Rick brought both me and Al here. He may be younger than us, but he has seniority. He should get the job."

I'm not sure that kind of decency exists much anymore. But I really appreciated what Pete did back then. It meant a lot to me. Of course, Pete did okay for himself—he's been the head coach of the Xavier Musketeers, Providence Friars, and Virginia Cavaliers, and worked as an analyst for CBS. And Al had a terrific run scouting for many years with the Indiana Pacers.

So I stepped in as the temporary head coach for six games. We only had seven eligible players on my roster for some of those games—which included one against Jerry Tarkanian's highly ranked UNLV team. So my 2–4 record wasn't as bad as it looks.

AN ORANGE INTERLUDE

When the season ended in Hawaii, newly appointed Syracuse University coach Jim Boeheim reached out to me. Jim had seen me in previous summers at Five-Star leading practice sessions and lecturing about one-on-one moves and man-to-man defense. Apparently he liked my work, because he offered me a job as an assistant coach. I became his first hire. Without question, my exposure at Five-Star was a major reason I got the job. Although Boeheim's Syracuse teams are famous for playing an airtight 2-3 zone defense, back then, Jim wanted to go man-to-man at times, and he wanted me to run that defense.

My new job came with a price—and I'm not talking about my $19,000 salary (with a car!). Jim hired me on my wedding night. I had to cancel my honeymoon to go recruit Louis Orr, a slinky forward from Cincinnati. It was a tough price to pay, but I like to think my bride, Joanne, and I made up for lost time later.

After my time in Hawaii, I was thrilled to be back East. I was twenty-two and I had a real job in a big-time basketball program—a job I had earned not only because of my coaching skills and my commitment to working with players but because of my early unbridled passion for the game. That desire led me to Five-Star, and Five-Star—and Garf—had helped shape me and showcase me, setting my whole career in motion.

We signed Louis Orr and I went on to have two great years with Jim at Syracuse. I got my first taste of NCAA excitement in 1977 with the team. Back then, the NCAA championship tournament was a thirty-two-team affair (it expanded to sixty-four teams in 1985). We won our ECAC division championship and I was very pleased with our defense; we played man-to-man about 50 percent of the time. We had two terrific freshmen, Orr, who later played for the Pacers and Knicks, and big man Roosevelt Bouie, who went on to a long career in Italy. We traveled to Rupp Arena in Lexington where we won our first NCAA Tournament game in a shootout with Tennessee, featuring the Ernie and Bernie show—Ernie Grunfeld scored 26 points and Bernard King went for 23, but we won the game in overtime 93–88. In the Round of 16, we faced North Carolina–Charlotte, a team featuring powerhouse big man—and future Boston Celtic great—Cedric Maxwell. UNC–Charlotte trounced us and very nearly won the tournament—losing in the Final Four by two points to Marquette, the eventual tournament champs.

I stayed after the game to watch the nightcap because one of my pals from Five-Star was the head coach of Detroit University, which was battling the mighty Michigan Wolverines. My pal walked out in a plaid jacket screaming at the Michigan fans, "We're coming after you to-night!"

It was none other than Dick Vitale.

Dick lost a really close game, but he put his school and himself on the map with that game. I was really proud of him.

Losing, of course, is part of the game. As a coach, I've gradually come to realize that how you react to losses is often an extension of expectations. By this I mean if you are coaching Manhattan College, a small school in the Metro Atlantic Division, and you end your season by losing the first game of the NCAA Tournament, you've defied expectations by just being there. So you and your team should feel terrific about all you've accomplished. But for the bigger programs—the UCLAs and Kentuckys of the world—anything short of an Elite Eight appearance will probably feel like a huge letdown. Syracuse finished the year with an amazing 26-4 record, and naturally we were disappointed to have Jim's fairy-tale first season come to an end. But the feeling was we had lost to a great team, we had a lot of returning players, and we would build on what had been a tremendous season. That was our message to our players.

ON THE ROAD WITH BOEHEIM

I had the utmost respect for Jim Boeheim. During his playing days at Syracuse, he had shared the backcourt with college superstar Dave Bing and then logged in years playing in the Eastern League, the closest thing pro basketball had to a minor league operation and the forerunner of the Continental Basketball Association. He had an intensity, drive, and focus that I could relate to.

We would go recruiting together. Jim liked to drive and didn't trust anybody else behind the wheel. We'd go visit a recruit or watch a game and then check into some dingy motel or if we were lucky, a Holiday Inn. Sharing a room is unheard of these days, but back then, it was what you did.

Unlike today, where there are restrictions on when you can and can't go on recruiting trips, assistant coaches lived on the road as traveling salesmen and this was not conducive to family life. In fact,

I don't know who tracked this information, but I remember being told assistant coaches had a very high divorce rate. As I said earlier, if I wanted a recruit I would see 80 percent of his high school games, call him every night, and do everything but tuck him into bed. So think about it: You are living on the road. You are working five weeks of the summer at Five-Star Basketball Camp. Life as an assistant coach was anything but glamorous. I would always turn in early. But Jim was usually reading something. He was a considerate roommate. Sometimes I'd wake up and he'd be watching an old movie on TV, his face a foot from the screen, so he could hear the whisper-level volume.

I'll never forget his wedding night to his first wife, Elaine, at a beautiful spot on Skaneateles Lake in central New York. My wife came up to me and said, "Where's Jim? It's time to cut the cake." Nobody had seen him, so I walked through the house and found him watching a Mets game on TV.

I said, "Jim, you are wanted. It's time to cut the cake."

"I'll be right there," he said. "The bases are loaded."

There's one recruiting story with Jim that sticks out in my mind. Probably because it involves me sticking my foot in my mouth.

As Boeheim's assistant, I did a lot of the recruiting legwork. I'd go watch high school games, and stay in touch with the recruit and the family. One of the players we were pursuing was named Rich Shrigley, who lived in Nashua, New Hampshire.

As declaration time approached, I realized it was time to make a final push, so Jim and I headed to Nashua. On our way, I said, "Jim, when we go in the home, I've got a great relationship with the mom and the young man, so let me do most of the talking with this one."

We knew Rich was also considering a few other schools, including NC State, which was coached by Norm Sloan. As a policy, we tried not to knock other schools while wooing potential players. Instead, we focused on our school's strengths. But in making my pitch, I decided to underscore one difference between the Orangemen and Sloan's NC State Wolfpack. I told Rich and his mom the one great thing about playing at Syracuse was that Coach Boeheim plays only eight players and doesn't even give out a full allotment of scholarships.

"Take NC State. Norm Sloan is an outstanding coach and they certainly have a great program. But they have fifteen guys who can play," I said, adding that the Wolfpack hand out all twelve scholarships and take transfers. "With Syracuse, you know you are going to get time on the floor."

Right then, Rich's mother interrupted me.

"You know, I've told Norman about that," she said.

I found that extremely strange that she would call Sloan by his first name—not even "Norm," but "Norman." So did Jim. We looked at each other.

"Mrs. Shrigley," I said, "you're talking as if you really know Coach Sloan."

"Yes, well, the reason I talk to him so personally is he's my brother."

My mouth dropped. Jim Boeheim almost fell off the couch with laughter and, as I've said many times, I was ready to crawl under it from embarrassment. He's never let me forget that moment—and that I had failed to learn our targeted player was related to college hoops royalty! I can laugh it about now, too. Who would have imagined that a young man from Nashua, New Hampshire, would be Norm Sloan's nephew? Rich decided to attend Boston College and that's the last time I mentioned another school's roster while recruiting.

The other recruiting story I laugh about with Jim involves a young, Panama-born player who was tearing up the court in Brooklyn. I kept close tabs on him, watching almost every game and talking to his mother every night.

Fred Moskowitz, who coached this budding star at William Grady

High School in Brighton Beach, would tell me in no uncertain terms that his player was "better than Albert King," another dominant Brooklyn legend and brother of Bernard King.

I finally got Jim to watch my prized recruit for the first time at the Wheelchair Classic, a New York charity event that pits top players from Brooklyn, Queens, the Bronx, and Manhattan against each other. And my star recruit had the worst game I'd ever seen him play. He was nervous. He dropped the ball, he shanked shots.

After the game, Jim said, "You went to see that guy play twelve times?"

"Everyone can have an off night," I said. "He'll come back in tomorrow's game."

Of course, the next night my star was even worse.

"He's not Albert King, he's not even King Albert," Jim scoffed.

I said, "Jim, trust me. We want him."

Jim said, "Sorry. No. We can't take him."

I was crushed. My dream player ended up playing for Kansas State University, where he became an All-American. His name, by the way, was Rolando Blackman. And he had a tremendous career with the Dallas Mavericks. And whenever Jim laughs about Rich Shrigley, I say, "Yeah, but I never said no to Rolando."

Pitino / Boeheim = Strong relationship
(1976-78)

2

YOUTH IS SERVED

To be successful, young coaches must be the first into

the gym and the last to leave. They must show the players and

staff that nothing is more important than

a strong work ethic.

▼

THE NEXT SEASON at 'Cuse was also impressive. We went 22-6, but suffered an early NCAA exit with a heartbreaking overtime loss to Western Kentucky. I was crushed for Jim and our players. I was also upset for myself—I had a hunch I wasn't going to be around next year—and wanted to go out with a bang.

My premonition soon proved correct. The athletic director of Boston University, John Simpson, called me. (1978-83)

"You come highly recommended by a coach who was a great player for us here named Jack Leaman," he said.

Jack, or Coach Leaman, as I knew him, had been my coach at the University of Massachusetts. He trusted me with the ball as his point guard, and now he was trusting me with the team he starred for back in the '50s—and led to the 1959 NCAA East Regional final. I was honored.

But I was a little less honored when Simpson offered me the head coaching position for $17,500, which was less than my salary at Syracuse. When I explained this to him, and noted that the Orangemen also provided me with a car, Simpson said, "We'll give you an automobile and we'll give you a basketball camp and you can make another $1,500."

I took the job because I thought it was a break to become a head coach. It proved to be the perfect move, kicking off what I consider to be the golden years of my career. What I learned, what I achieved, and the bonds I made resulted in some of the happiest years of my life. I didn't even mind that the new vehicle Simpson got me was a humiliating Renault Le Car, a low-cost mini that I will forever think of as a windup toy.

As the twenty-four-year-old rookie head coach at Boston University, I took over a losing program that had won only seventeen games over the previous two seasons and hadn't had a winning season in five years. I was absolutely thrilled. The program was the exact opposite of the outfits I would go on to coach. We averaged about five hundred to seven hundred spectators a game, and we didn't have band—so we rented local high school ensembles to play. We played on the third floor of the gym. We drove to every game in a Peter Pan bus.

It was a low-pressure situation. Boston University was widely known as a hockey school—and a very good one. The years I was there, the hockey team had four tremendous players—Jim Craig, Mike Eruzione, Dave Silk, and Jack O'Callahan—who went on to star for the Miracle on Ice team that won the gold medal in the 1980 Olympics. So it was an exciting time to be at the school.

The basketball team, though, was an afterthought in the university community—except when we played our greatest rival, Northeastern. I'm not sure what the situation is between the two teams now—and I'm well aware the hockey rivalry between BU and Boston College is almost

19

a matter of life and death for some—but back then, our basketball games against Northeastern were all-out wars. The teams despised each other and so did the fans. At some point during every single game we played against each other during the five years I was there, a fight erupted on the court. Every single one! Back then you didn't get ejected for fighting, and players on both teams took their best shots.

Northeastern's coach at this time was Jim Calhoun, and the animosity between the teams spilled over to the two of us. I used to go running around the Charles River and sometimes Jim would be jogging the other way. I saw him and he saw me, but we'd both put our heads down and run right by each other. Years later, when I became the Providence coach and he was the Connecticut coach, our rivalry cooled off and we became friendly.

The most interesting thing about my time at Boston University was that I was learning how to be a head coach while my players were only two or three years younger than I was. This is an extremely rare dynamic in coaching. I was learning on the job and, fortunately, I had a veteran team stocked with players who were twenty-one and twenty-two years old. Having older players helped me turn things around pretty quickly. I think my own relative youth helped a lot, too. Being so close in age allowed me to connect with them. At the end of each day, I would play one-on-one against anyone on the team. It was a fun daily ritual and I think it helped build a true sense of camaraderie between us. Decades have gone by and I'm still close with a lot of the players from that team. One of my forwards in the early '80s was Jay Twyman, the son of early NBA great Jack Twyman. We still play golf together. And of course I'm in touch with Brett Brown, a guard on the team, who is the current coach of the Philadelphia 76s.

Recruiting Brett turned out to be a two-for-one deal. Let me explain that. One of the nice things about old-school recruiting was that you would connect with the players' families. Back then, you could visit a

Brett:
BU Player   1979-83
BU Grad.Ass.   1983-84
Melbourne   1988-1998

family any number of times, whereas today you have limits on your contacts. While recruiting Brett, I became very friendly with his father, Bob, a high school coach from South Portland, Maine. I actually spotted both of them at the same time when I went to speak at a basketball camp in Maine. To be perfectly honest, I was much more impressed with the coach than I was with Brett. I liked Brett as a player, but I loved the intensity of the practices Bob ran. A few years later, I hired Bob as an assistant at BU.

So we weren't playing on TV. The stands were empty. Boosters weren't flooding the program with cash. There was really only one local writer who bothered to give us ink—a dynamo cub reporter named Lesley Visser, who I'm proud to say has gone on to become one of America's greatest sportscasters and remains a close friend. But the team bonded and improved, working together, sweating together, and improving together. I loved every minute of it.

We had a 91-51 record during my five-year run. In my final year there, we made the NCAA Tournament—the school's first appearance since my old coach Leaman led the school to the tourney twenty-four years earlier. The victories and the tournament appearance were both satisfying accomplishments—winning rarely gets old. And I cherish my friendships with the guys.

There were two other reasons that my first head-coaching job remains one of the best periods of my professional life. The first was that I was able to get my hands dirty, working and playing with the team. The one-on-one games in the evening were great fun, but it didn't end there. I would get out on the court and demonstrate. I would even join in scrimmages. It was fun for me, and often a learning experience for everyone on the court. And I'll admit it, I was young and competitive. I loved coaching, but I still loved playing and I enjoyed winning my battles on the court.

The second reason it was so joyful was that *time*—at least *time* as the

NCAA now defines it—simply didn't exist. There was no such thing as the "20-hour rule," which is the NCAA law limiting the amount of time student-athletes can train to twenty hours a week during the season. There was nobody constantly telling you to keep track of every minute of every day with your team, which is what programs have to do now.

LOL

With no restrictions on time beyond getting to class and hitting the books, a coach could improve players' skills just by working closely with them.

On a typical day we would have an early morning practice. Then, in between classes, I would take four guys and work with them on their skills. They'd go back to class. In the afternoon, the team would practice for three hours. Then at night, we'd play one-on-one. For a guy who had played hoops ten hours a day at Five-Star, it was bliss.

LESSONS & LECTURES

After five years at BU, I was ready for a new challenge. I had a family to take care of, and making more money was a concern. Ironically, my first attempt to leave Boston University ended in failure. But I was lucky to fail, strange as that sounds.

PATERNO LIKE PITINO?

Football coach Joe Paterno called to tell me he wanted to bring me to Penn State. Joe's star may have fallen in recent years due to the horrifying revelations that his defensive coordinator Jerry Sandusky was a child abuser. But in 1983, Joe had been head coach of the Nittany Lions for eighteen years and was pretty much the king at Penn State. Naturally, I thought I had a lock on the job. But then Paterno called me with a change of plans.

"Look," he said, "I really want the athletic director to offer you the job because something's come up."

"What's that?" I asked.

"Well, with the Italian thing of Paterno-Pitino, it could come off sounding too much like a fraternity."

I was shocked. "What does being Italian have to do with it, Joe?"

"I'd rather have the A.D. make the decision."

"Joe, you offered me the job. Are you taking it back?"

"No, you're going to get the job," he promised. "One hundred percent you are going to get the job."

So then the A.D. called me. "Look," he says. "We have to take a look at another guy named Bruce Parkhill. He's a local hero who played high school basketball here. But, listen, don't worry about this. Joe says you're the guy to hire."

Forty-eight hours later, the A.D. called again. He gave the job to Parkhill.

I was devastated. But I didn't have time to dwell on it too much because summer was coming and I had recruiting and Five-Star camp to prepare for. By 1983, Garf's camp had hit the big time. There were hundreds of college coaches packing the main court to evaluate the nation's best players.

After lunch, the campers and all the coaches gathered in an old gymnasium for the afternoon lecture, a daily ritual that was attended over the years by the likes of Michael Jordan, Patrick Ewing, Dominique Wilkins, Isiah Thomas, and Moses Malone, to name a few. Garf would kick things off. That gym was his Carnegie Hall, and for few minutes every day he morphed into a flamboyant basketball showman. He would deliver the most grandiose, impassioned, high-volume introductions for the guest speakers. He loved his moment in the spotlight and he deserved every second of it, too.

The pressure on the lecturers was intense. You had to follow Bob Knight, Dean Smith, Chuck Daly, and many other of the game's great coaches. I was the youngest lecturer to ever give a talk at Five-Star. But I knew from my days as a camper that you had to be a showman.

23

I would bring out some of the best players attending the camp and challenge them to stop me. Considering I'm just a shade under six feet and many of these players dwarfed me by as much as a foot, I'm sure people thought the odds were against me. But I was a much better basketball player from the ages of twenty-three to thirty than I was in college—thanks to all my scrimmaging as a coach and the fact that I traveled to dozens and dozens of basketball camps up and down the East Coast during the summer, delivering lectures and demonstrations about one-on-one moves. So when I issued my challenge to the campers, I would use a variety of jab steps and ball fakes to get to the rim. And no matter how big the players were, they could not block my shot. In the end, I announced during my lectures, I would "put them in jail," my phrase for finishing the play and scoring.

The lectures weren't just about demonstrating moves. These were also motivational talks. We wanted our campers to embrace what they were learning and to build confidence in their skills. We wanted them to know that with hard work and discipline they controlled their destiny. Keeping the attention of 250 campers and coaches sitting on benches and cement for a full hour required showmanship, storytelling skills, and the ability to connect with the audience. Try that today with instant-gratification-loving millennials and watch their fingers start to twitch.

At the end of the lectures, speakers would usually be rewarded with a standing ovation. If the campers weren't on their feet clapping at the end, God save you. That was like being booed off the stage. And Garf would let you know.

High school scout Tom Konchalski, who took over Garf's *High School Basketball Illustrated*, used to spend a lot of time at Five-Star. Here's what he had to say about my camp sessions:

It was sort of a setup because Rick Pitino was a good one-on-one player in college, but then, with his coach's analytical mind, he had the ability to break anyone down one-on-one. He would always use the term 'put 'em in jail'—and show how to reverse the ball and keep the rim between the ball and the defender. I remember Jumping Joe Ward, kid from Georgia who was about 6'5" who jumped out of the building. Rick would play him one-on-one and challenge him to block his shot. But he'd always put him in jail. He'd play all the campers and beat them.

HUBIE WANTS YOU TO CALL

One day in the summer of '83, Garf interrupted one of my sessions. He pulled me aside and said, "Hey, come to my office. Hubie Brown wants you to call him."

"What's he want to speak about?" I asked.

"I think you're going to like it," was all Howie would say.

I went to Garf's office—remember, this was 1983 and cell phones were still the stuff of science fiction stories and Dick Tracy cartoons—and called Hubie.

"Rick," he said. "Mike Fratello just got the head job with the Atlanta Hawks. I'd like you to come in for an interview. We'd like to talk about possibly hiring you to replace him."

One week later, I was the assistant coach of the New York Knicks.

The fascinating thing about this story is what it says about the strange breaks in life. If I had gotten the Penn State job, the Knicks opportunity would never have happened. And for whatever reason, nobody had been able to win at Penn State during that era, so I'd have been fired and would probably have scrambled for another assistant coaching job. Sometimes I joke that if I'd wound up at Penn State, there's a good chance I would be an equities broker on Wall Street right now, like many of my friends. And it's true: Who knows what would have happened?

GARDEN PARTIES

W'z GM?

The 1983–84 Knicks were, to me, a kind of personal dream team. As the assistant coach, I was working with Bernard King, Ernie Grunfeld, Ray Williams—players I had long admired. Dave DeBusschere, who played on those two amazing 1970 and 1973 championship Knicks teams, was the general manager. I had watched him play and rooted for him when he shared the floor with my idols: Walt Frazier and Earl "The Pearl" Monroe. So every moment was a special treat for me. I was rubbing shoulders with basketball deities.

But the greatest aspect of the job was working with Hubie. I had thought of him as Mr. Five-Star, because he was the head coach of the camp. But he became so much more than that: a leader, a friend, a coach, a mentor, a genius. There was no better person to learn the pro game from than Hubie Brown. He taught me so much about analytics and about game preparation. Spending two years with Hubie Brown was like spending ten years in a basketball library. Those two years had a tremendous impact on my career. Without him, I don't think I'd ever have achieved the level of success I've had as a coach.

When people talk about my meticulous attention to detail, a lot of that was instilled by Hubie. I've told people this for years: Hubie Brown is more organized than crime. And what he did with the Knicks was way ahead of his time in terms of scouting and game preparation. In the modern era, pro teams have multiple assistant coaches. Sometimes you look over at a bench and it seems like there are more guys in suits than there are guys in uniform. With the Knicks, Hubie had two assistants, me and Richie Adubato, who was our advance scout and would watch the most recent game of the team we were scheduled to play. He would fax over diagrams of the plays that were run, substitution patterns, and any observations about matchups and vulnerabilities. Then Hubie would have me enter the faxed information into a primitive computer system. I would spend three or four hours breaking down the tapes and the faxes, just hitting buttons and typing to get the scouting reports in shape. Today that process probably takes thirty minutes, thanks to advanced computer programs.

I would also chart the games while they were unfolding. The list of stats I kept was daunting. I tracked five categories of deflections during the game: blocked shots, loose ball recoveries, steals, tips from behind, and ball pressure deflections. I charted this because while I was coaching at BU I made an analytical breakthrough of my own: if we got thirty-five deflections per game, we would win 90 percent of games. Hubie loved this chart. But those were only five of about thirty different things I had to chart. I tracked every offensive possession—who scored on what play, who missed, who rebounded. And I tracked every defensive possession. Hubie actually wanted real-time analytics—and remember this was a pre-digital age—so he could refer to them during time-outs. I had to be ready to tell him the percentage of offensive efficiency for each of our offensive sets. Hubie would take these and use them to create his own statistical analysis after the game. He would also watch the game on video and analyze who ran plays correctly, who was out of position, who took shots out of their range, who passed out of double teams.

I remember one game we came in at halftime and we were losing. Some of our starters had played terrible defense and had zero deflections in the first half. I went to the blackboard and listed the three guys with the most deflections—Darrell Walker, 5; Rory Sparrow, 4; Trent Tucker, 3—and left off the guys who had none, which included our big scorers, Bernard King, Pat Cummings, and Louis Orr. Hubie looked at the board and erupted: "Those are the only guys with deflections! Where the hell is Bernard? Where the hell is Louis!" He was furious.

But Hubie didn't just accentuate the negative—he loved pointing out when plays were executed with precision. For Hubie, analytics could be teaching tools. If a player shot at a much higher percentage within ten feet of the basket, well, that fact, that data might motivate them to take smarter, more efficient shots and eliminate mid-range jumpers from their game. Hubie was one of the first coaches I encountered to really focus on using numbers in teachable, actionable ways.

Conducting these post-game autopsies were vital for two reasons. They helped gauge our most recent performance and told us what was and what wasn't working, which helped us focus our practices. They also provided us with a blueprint for the next time we faced the team. Now we had a record of what matchups worked, what defensive sets gave us trouble, and what offensive plays might need new adjustments.

My first year went by in a blur. One of the highlights was charting two road games in January 1984 when Bernard King scored 50 points in two consecutive games—something that hadn't been done in over twenty years. In the first game, against the San Antonio Spurs, Bernard hit 20 out of 30 shots. In the second game, against the Dallas Mavericks, he was even better, hitting eight shots in a row during the third quarter and finishing 20 for 28. That means he shot 69 percent over the two games, which stands as a truly mesmerizing shooting performance. Incredibly, Wilt Chamberlain had been the last guy to go for 50 two games in a row—back in 1962.

After the second game, Hubie praised Bernard for scoring his points in the flow of the game—and got a laugh at my expense. "He does it so quietly," he told reporters. "I wouldn't have known it except that Pitino was yelling it in my ear."

Hubie would have had to be deaf not to hear Bernard's teammates going nuts on the bench, yelling "Get it to B!"

Bernard hit 50 with seven seconds left in the game on a sweet twenty-two-foot jumper with Jay Vincent covering him like a blanket. That wasn't his last extraordinary game of '84. His performance in our first-round playoff series against Detroit was as heroic as any performance I've ever seen. He had two dislocated fingers and came down with the flu in the middle of the series—and he averaged 42 points a game, breaking Elgin Baylor's record for most points scored in a five-game series with 212 points and a 60 percent shooting percentage. And he did it against a gritty defensive team, an early version of Detroit's infamous Bad Boys. The only thing I regretted about that series was beating Chuck Daly, another Five-Star veteran. But Bernard's 44 points in our fierce 127-123 game-five overtime victory helped me get over it.

We lost the Eastern Conference Semifinals to the Boston Celtics—the eventual league champions—in seven games, unable to break their home-court advantage. The Celtics incredible front line of Robert Parish, Kevin McHale, and Larry Bird created some matchup problems for us. We were really proud of our effort and how far the team had come. With Bernard approaching the peak of his career, the future looked bright.

GETTING NICKED

Sometimes, no matter how hard you dig in, no matter how well you motivate your team, no matter how thoroughly you prepare, fate screws up your plans. Bernard King started the following year hell-bent on proving his series against the Pistons wasn't a fluke. He made it a mission to light up the scoreboard every night. He scored 34 points the first game of the season, and kept going, averaging a fraction under 33 points a game. Madison Square Garden was sold out every night because everyone wanted to see the league's leading scorer—a local hero from Brooklyn—work his magic.

But despite our success the previous year and Bernard's ascendance, our team struggled. We missed Bill Cartwright's and Ray Williams's presence.

In early March, Lou Lamoriello, the new athletic director of Providence College, reached out to me. Lou had inherited the position from Dave Gavitt, who was the first commissioner of the Big East Conference. According to Lou, Gavitt had recommended me as a future head coach of the Friars. I was flattered by Lou's interest, but I was very loyal to Hubie. Plus, I knew that the struggling Knicks had a shot at drafting Patrick Ewing, and the idea of coaching Ewing and King was very enticing. I told him I wasn't interested.

But Lou called back and asked if we could get together when the Big East Tournament came into town. The night before we met, I was at Madison Square Garden sitting with legendary Knick talent scouts Fuzzy Levane and Dick McGuire, watching Providence play St. John's in the tournament. Providence, whose three best players were graduating seniors, got thumped by twenty-eight points.

During the game, I told Dick and Fuzzy about the Providence opportunity. As the game went on and Providence got pounded, Dick turned to me: "You're not going to take this job, are you?"

"Why do you say that?"

"They're losing their three best players. They have nobody else," said Fuzzy.

"It'll take you four years to even get a competitive team," said Dick.

I nodded. They were absolutely right. Taking the job would be a suicide mission. I prepared myself. I was going to reject the offer and stay with the Knicks.

That night, I met Lou at the Abbey Tavern after the game. The Abbey was on the corner of Twenty-sixth and Third Avenue, just down the street from the old brownstone I called home as a kid. My aunt and uncle lived on the top floor, grandparents from Sicily had the middle floor, and we were on the ground floor. I believe they sold that brownstone for $28,000—a small fraction of what it would sell for today. I found Lou looking glum with his head down at the table. I said, "Lou, sorry about the game."

"No, it happens every year," he said. "All the Providence fans buy tickets to the whole tourney, because that's the only way they sell the tickets. They come in. We lose. We get killed. Now they have to return home and some feel it's a waste of money. But we have to make massive changes to the program and I'd like you to be our head coach. I will give you everything you need to build a winner."

I immediately forgot about what Fuzzy and Dick said. The words "head coach" instantly swayed me, and I told Lou I was very, very interested.

Over the next few weeks, we continued the discussions. It was not an easy time. I absolutely loved working with Hubie. It was like Five-Star with an expense account and all my heroes surrounding me.

And then on March 23, Bernard was hustling back to defend against a Kansas City Kings fast break and went up to stop Reggie Theus from hitting an easy layup. It was the kind of play Bernard had executed hundreds of times in his career. This time, though, Bernard landed and immediately crumbled to the floor in devastating pain. Hubie and our trainer rushed to his side. He had torn the anterior cruciate ligament in his right knee. The Knicks had been having a disappointing year as a team, and Bernard's success was one of the things that kept us going. I was devastated for Bernard. It was entirely possible his career was over—back then an ACL injury was usually impossible to fully recover from. I also felt awful for Hubie. We were in a jam. It was going to be hard to win without Bernard on the court.

I got on the team bus and Hubie sat down next to me. "Kid," he said—like Garf, he always called me Kid—"is that job at Providence still open?"

I was feeling so worried and rattled, I said, "Hubie, I told you. I'm not going to take that Providence job. I'm going to stay with you."

I'll never forget what happened next: He grabbed my shoulders and gave me a kiss on the forehead. "Kid," he said, "if you get that job offered to you, you need to take it."

"But we're going to be fine, Hubie."

"No. Bernard King was our team. We have no chance of winning and moving forward without him. Kid, you got my blessing to take that job and take care of your family."

I called Lou the next day and said I was ready to sign a contract. But Lou insisted I come see the campus before we sealed the deal. "When are you free?"

"Tomorrow evening."

"Drive up and I'll show you around."

"How can I see the campus at night?"

"I'll arrange it."

So I drove up and met Lou. He had a flashlight with him. It turns out he was worried about word leaking out that I was a candidate for the job and he actually wanted me there in the cover of darkness. So at ten at night, I got a flashlight tour of the campus. He showed me the gym, he showed me the offices, showed me the hockey arena. It was bizarre, but I really loved Lou's spirit and sincerity.

As it turned out, Hubie survived another season—although the Knicks finished 23-59. The next year, though, he got fired sixteen games into the season. He had seen it coming. He knew there was no replacing the leading scorer in the league. And he was right about me taking the Providence job.

Thinking back on the chain of events—except Bernard's devastating injury, of course—makes me laugh. I had been 100 percent set on refusing the Providence job. Logic and caution and two of the best basketball minds in the business—Dick and Fuzzy—had told me it would be a total disaster. There was no way in hell I was going to take the job. But all it took were the words "head coach" and I was interested. Still, it did take Bernard's knee horror and Hubie's blessing before I threw all caution to the wind.

I'm glad I did.

3

I spent two years coaching the Friars and it taught me

to never stop dreaming. When I woke up, the team

and I had taught each other that hard work

makes anything possible.

▼

WHEN I LOOK back on my two years at Providence College, I have two immediate thoughts. First, my tenure was way too short for such a magical time. Second, the Friars team taught me anything was possible through hard work and dedication.

When I arrived at the school, I thought it would take quite a few years of recruiting to turn the program around and compete in the Big East, a league with some of the best teams in the country. My first order of business was to meet the players who remained after the Friars' previous 11-win, 20-loss season. I had to evaluate our talent level and figure out what positions we would need to fill while we were recruiting. I met with each player privately and then had a short individual workout. The players were what I expected, polite young men with a great love for their school.

The first guy to come to my office was the team's big man, Jacek

Duda. He was grossly overweight. I knew from studying our roster that he had barely played last year. I wondered how he had ever landed on the team because he really didn't look like an athlete. I asked him how he got to Providence and learned he had defected from the Polish national team and came to Providence after his family settled in Central Falls, Rhode Island, a city with a large Polish community. He told me my predecessor, Joe Mullaney, spotted him on the street and offered him a scholarship.

I decided to be direct.

"Look, Jacek," I said. "If you want to play here, you have to lose sixty pounds."

The next guy that came in was a student manager named Ryan Ford, and I told him I planned to meet the managers the following day. But the young man had other ideas. "I was a manager last year and I think I can contribute to the team."

I couldn't believe it! The last thing you want is for your manager to think they are good enough to make the team. The irony was, in this case, the manager *was* good enough—and Ryan wound up on the Friars bench for the next three seasons as a guard.

The last guy to come for a meeting was a chunky, sweet-looking kid. He stood about my height and had played his high school ball at St. Agnes of Rockville Center, Long Island. He introduced himself as Billy Donovan and told me he was thinking about transferring. "I know you're going to bring in better players, so I think this would be a better move for me," he said, adding he was thinking of going to Fairfield or Northeastern. I thought that was smart, a step down in competition. I didn't bother working him out. I told him to come back the next day and I would find out which program had interest in him. I was actually relieved to get a scholarship back to put to good use.

I called Terry O'Connor, head coach of Fairfield, and asked if he could use a Big East backcourt player named Billy Donovan. He said he was all set in the backcourt for next season. I then called Jim Calhoun at Northeastern and asked if he needed Billy. He said his guards were much quicker and more talented. When Billy came by the next day, I didn't have the heart to tell him neither school was interested. I asked if he enjoyed being at Providence. He said he loved the school but was unhappy with his lack of playing time. We went to the gym to work out. He had a push shot and was also way out of shape. We played a few games of one-on-one and he asked me if I thought he could play next season.

"You would have to lose at least thirty pounds and religiously work out on the drills that I'm going to give you," I said. "With a lot of dedication, I think you could be my fourth guard." He was really focused on the drills I showed him, and I sensed he might share my passion for the game. I wished him luck and told him to call once a week with his progress.

After that, I really didn't give him much thought. My next move was hiring a staff, creating a weight program, and recruiting players who could get us out of the cellar. I decided to keep Bill Donlon on the staff for continuity and hired Gordie Chiesa as my other assistant. Herb Sendek was my graduate assistant the first year. Herb, of course, has gone on to be head coach at North Carolina State, Arizona State, and, most recently, Santa Clara.

We signed one great transfer, Delray Brooks, who had flamed out at Indiana under coach Bob Knight. Delray, who shared Indiana Mr. Basketball honors in 1984, had completely lost his confidence during his freshman year playing for Coach Knight. He arrived at Providence not knowing if he could ever regain the luster that he once had in high school. But I had seen him play at Five-Star camp, and I believed the talent was still there. He had to sit out his first year with us, but that was okay with me. My main objective with Delray was to get his confidence back, and so I concentrated more on the mental aspects of his development rather than the physical.

BILLY THE KID

All summer long, Billy Donovan worked on the drills I gave him. He came back in September after Labor Day, weighing 161 pounds, down 30 pounds. I was impressed by his work ethic. And I became more impressed when we played one-on-one. We battled hard on the court and he beat me in four out of five games. As I predicted, he was now a much quicker player and his game had improved dramatically.

Then, just as I had done at BU, I ran Billy and the rest of the team through the ringer. Monday through Friday, we'd practice from six thirty to seven thirty, have a team breakfast, and then break for classes. But since not everyone had a full morning of classes, I'd run three hour-long player development sessions in between players' classes. I'd take four players from nine to ten, four from ten to eleven, and four more from eleven to twelve. During these sessions we'd work on individual skills, including ball-handling, outside shooting, shot-blocking, low post moves, and one-on-one play. When Billy showed up for his hour, we worked on his jump shot, we worked on his ball fake, we worked on his moves. We worked on everything. And I told him, "Billy, all you have to do is become my fourth guard and you'll play twelve to fifteen minutes a game."

Typically, from three to six in the afternoon we'd hold team practices. So right there, Billy and the rest of the Friars practiced five hours a day. But Billy didn't stop there. Most nights we would meet back at the gym at 9:00 p.m. I'd join my three "bomb squad" Friars—Billy, Delray Brooks, and Pop Lewis—and we'd face off two-on-two, usually me and Pop versus Billy and Delray. The losing twosome bought the milkshakes at the cafeteria downstairs. We did that four nights a week. A far cry from where we are today.

I have never seen anybody in my life work as hard as Billy Donovan did on his game. And it paid off. By the end of our first year together, he was the Friars' third guard and helped the team win seventeen games and go to the NIT.

As I've written elsewhere, I believe success is a choice. For some people, achieving it can breed complacency. For others, it can breed a hunger for more success. Fortunately, Billy Donovan belonged to the second group. At the end of the season, I told him, "I want you to be captain next year. But you have to go from a good player to a great player. Let's plot that strategy. We have to get you stronger, quicker, and even better than you are now."

"Coach, I'm willing to do anything."

3-PTs

We went back to the gym and I showed him all I wanted him to work on again. This was 1986, and the new season would mark the formal implementation of the three-point shot across all of NCAA basketball. I said, "Billy, the three-point shot is going to come in, so you have to improve your range. And we're going to lead the nation in three-point shooting. I'm positive of that."

I was so sure he would rise to the occasion that I arranged a photo shoot for him, which he didn't want to do. I had him dress up in a cowboy outfit—a Stetson hat, a handkerchief, guns, spurs, and boots. Billy was very shy, introverted and humble, and when he looked in the mirror, he grimaced. "Coach, this is embarrassing."

I thought it was great. Midway through the season, I put his picture on the Friars' game program with a caption that read: *Billy the Kid, the fastest gun in the East.* I wanted him to believe that. Actually, I *needed* him to believe that, because having an outside game was a key part of my strategy.

ZERO
↓
HERO

The rest is history. He was the league's dominant outside shooter. He averaged 20.6 points, 3 rebounds, and 7.1 assists per game. He was the star on a team that made it to the Final Four. He was drafted into the NBA.

Billy Donovan's story is the most dramatic individual athletic transformation I have ever witnessed in my forty-plus years of coaching. His work ethic and dedication were second to none. His growth as a player in a two-year period was astounding. The results of his unmatched efforts led him to the NBA. It earned him a shot at becoming an assistant coach with me. From there he continued to pour himself into his work, coaching Florida to two consecutive NCAA championships.

But none of those things would have happened if the current NCAA training rules for college athletes were in place back then. There is no question in my mind that if Billy Donovan had to adhere to a twenty-hour limit back then, there was no way he would have achieved his astounding, life-changing level of performance.

Let me be clear: I'm not against NCAA rules limiting practice time. But the current blanket, across-the-board rules—installed to protect all student-athletes—are detrimental and punitive to those who want to and can manage an increased workload.

The rule really hurts student-athletes who are geared toward competing in the Olympics. Athletes from other countries don't have a 20-hour rule. They often train full-time, seven days a week. How can a collegiate high jumper, wrestler, or sprinter compete against that?

They can't. And that is unfair.

You would think there could be a waiver for the twelve months leading up to the Olympics, or some other way to let these kids shine. But don't count on it. The NCAA's track record when it comes to creativity and proactive problem solving hasn't been exactly stellar.

But it's not just future Olympians who deserve flexibility when it comes to training. Best-selling author Malcolm Gladwell has written about the 10,000-hour rule—how logging in ten thousand hours of dedicated practice is one of the requirements for success in any field. I'm not entirely sure about that—there are some athletes out there who were born with incredible physiques; you can't teach or train someone to have a seven-foot wingspan like Milwaukee Bucks 6'11" point forward Giannis Antetokounmpo or the agility, grace, and size of Houston Rockets Hall of Famer Hakeem Olajuwon, who grew up playing soccer and didn't touch a basketball until he was in his mid teens. I'm pretty sure there was no way Hakeem logged ten thousand hours before he hit the NBA, but he had unique athleticism. There are late bloomers out there, who, if they had the guidance and time, might blossom like Billy. But we will never know about them because the 20-hour rule is holding them back. As with any generation of athletes, some of today's Millennials feel entitled, and they want to start any endeavor at the middle instead of the beginning. They need to start at the bottom and work tirelessly to get to the top.

PRACTICING COMMUNICATION

Billy did a lot of the work. But my staff deserves credit, too. My second year at Providence, we brought in a new assistant coach, Stu Jackson, who would go on to coach the Knicks. He joined Gordy Chiesa, who had a long career as an NBA assistant coach, and Herb Sendek, who I promoted from G.A. Our new graduate assistant was a young man named Jeff Van Gundy, who had been a high school coach in Rochester and was the son of a coach. Jeff epitomizes an incredible work ethic. I would get into the office at 6:15 a.m., and Jeff would beat me to work every day. Eventually we found out his secret—some nights, he would sleep on a couch in our office. *That* was dedication. Years later, he coached some of the best Knicks teams this side of Red Holtzman. But all my assistants were instrumental in helping transform the players we had, and I'm forever grateful to them.

I've always said there are two key goals to team practice sessions. First, make sure the intensity level is high every minute of every practice. To do that, you need to keep things moving fast. Second, make sure your players are communicating on the floor. When you get your players to talk more in practice, when they communicate, talking on defense, talking on offense—you are going to have a lively practice with very few dead spots. I hate dead spots. This builds continuity and leads to all-out intensity in games.

Getting players to talk and communicate on defense is probably the toughest aspect in all of coaching. Calling out picks, calling out switches, what defense you're in. It is fundamental, basic stuff. But it is one of the most difficult things to instill in players. Why? Well, some players are just not that verbal. They aren't necessarily big talkers. But the other factor is that they are exhausted.

Picture it this way. If you're a long-distance runner and you're on your eighth mile, the last thing you feel like having is a conversation with somebody next to you. It's the same out on the court.

So at Providence, and everywhere else I've coached, I've preached maximum physical fitness so my players are able to master fundamental skills and maintain communication. We drilled shot blocking every day. Blocking shots with your left hand, with your right hand. If someone is going for a block, what has to happen elsewhere on the court? Where are the guards? Who's moving to fill the lane? We practice boxing out on free throws and calling out our assignments. All those things, I believe, must be drilled with a communications component. So you tell your players, "Hey! Why didn't we talk after that whistle? Why didn't we talk on that play? How come we didn't hear any voices? Let's do it again!"

Listen, chatter on the floor is good for morale, too. Communication is a key part of teamwork. Everything must be drilled—including talking—in order for you to be efficient, fundamentally sound, and united.

With the Friars, we drilled a lot. And it paid off.

A HEAVENLY RUN

Billy Donovan may have been one of the greatest transformation stories I've ever witnessed in my lifetime. But the whole Friars team transformed. Not a single player averaged double figures in scoring the year before I took over. Two years later, we had four guys in double figures and we were in the running for the national title. So allow me to share a few highlights of that journey.

Putting Billy the Kid on the Providence basketball program wasn't my only brazen move. I was so confident about my team shedding our reputation as a Big East punching bag, I told reporters that investing in Friars season tickets would provide a better return than putting your money in the stock market.

One of the things that helped prove me right was a game we lost. Just before the season started, we played an exhibition game against the Soviet Union national team. We took about twenty three-pointers, but they took thirty and beat us. So that was an eye-opener. Initially, I had thought taking fifteen to twenty three-point shots would put us over the top in most games. Now I realized we had to launch at least twenty-plus shots from downtown to get the most out of the new rule and to lead the nation in three-point shooting.

3-PTs

But I was confident we could do that. By now, when I played two-on-two with my star guards, Billy wasn't just every bit as good as me, he had started to dominate me. And Delray and Pop also had outstanding strokes. In fact, they both had higher three-point percentages than Billy at season's end.

We got off to a great start. By January we were 4-2 in the Big East when Georgetown, a perennial powerhouse in the conference, came to play us in Providence. Big John Thompson's mighty Hoyas were ranked high in the national polls at the time. And John was a former Providence star who played on the school's 1963 NIT championship team. So this game was a sold-out affair for us, something that rarely happened since the mid and late '70s when Dave Gavitt was on the sidelines and Ernie DiGregorio and Marvin Barnes were on the court.

Our arena was absolutely buzzing at game time. My guys rose to the occasion, and we played Georgetown hard, fighting tooth and nail. At one point, Georgetown's Perry McDonald went in for a layup, and Jacek Duda blocked his shot. Unfortunately, Perry's hand slammed against the backboard and he hurt his finger.

John Thompson came running toward half court and swearing a blue streak. I asked Gordie Chiesa, "Who do you think he's yelling at?" and Gordie said, "He's talking to you, Coach."

So I walked to half court. "What's up, Big John?"

"You guys are the dirtiest motherfuckers I've ever coached against in my life," he yelled. *LOL*

My Friars were the basketball equivalent of choir boys! So I started laughing and that made John go ballistic. He started swearing even more. The crowd, of course, could hear him and they started going berserk. I stood my ground—even though it felt like I was staring at John's navel—and cursed back at him.

Eventually we went back to our benches. And Georgetown, as you might expect, played every possession as if it were their last. We also worked on a high pick-and-roll, which today is used every other play in the NBA. Back then, however, it was a rarity. We would create a little *PNR* false movement and get Billy the ball about ten feet from half court. Our center would run out and set a flat screen—which means he stood behind the defender guarding Billy. Then Billy would go right or left and drive down the lane. He had the option to take the ball to the basket for a layup or pass to his teammates in the corners for a three-point shot.

With less than five seconds to go, the score was tied when Billy the Kid found Pop Lewis, who hit a three-point shot and we won the game, 82–79.

We used the high screen to beat a number of other teams that year. One of the most memorable victories came against St. John's. After we pulled off the play and the whistle sounded, Lou Carnesecca successfully protested and we were actually called back from the locker room to give the Redmen another shot at winning the game.

That Georgetown victory was my favorite regular-season win of that year, putting us at 5-2 in the Big East. But I wasn't too happy about going and shaking hands with the man who just cursed at me. Unfortunately, there was no getting around this end-of-game ritual of good sportsmanship. So I walked toward him and we shook hands.

Then Big John put his arm around me. "Hey, Rick, I'm really, really proud of what you're doing with my alma mater," he said. "I had to put on that show because my team was flat and they took you guys lightly. And I was trying to rally them."

LOL

I was shocked. I thought he was going to curse me out, and here he was, praising the job I was doing. "Thanks, John."

His arm was still around me. "One last thing, before I let you go," he said. "You're going to play us last game of the season at Georgetown, and we are going to kick your fucking ass in big-time."

LOL

That's a verbatim quote.

Sure enough, we went to Georgetown and they destroyed us. We lost by eleven points. But it didn't bother me too much because our season record was still really strong. We had gone 11-6 in the Big East and 20-7 for all our games. When the Big East tournament started, we blitzed the St. John's University team led by Mark Jackson, winning by thirty points. Unfortunately, that second game was against Georgetown, and they really had our number this time, beating us by eighteen points, our worst loss of the season.

On the way back to Providence, we stopped at Lenox Hill Hospital to pick up our point guard Carlton Screen, who had torn up his knee during the St. John's game. It was sobering to see Paco—that was my name for Carlton—on crutches. But as soon as he sat down, I addressed the team.

"Look, guys, don't be down about Georgetown," I said. "They have our number; we're never going to see them again. Let's celebrate. We're going to go home and watch March Madness on TV, and find out where we're going in the tournament. We had a highly successful season, so don't get down. We're going to win, Paco Screen will get his knee healthy again, and he'll get back on the court. So let's be upbeat, play your music, let's have some fun."

I spent the ride with my wife, Joanne, by my side. For the last five months, Joanne had made the ninety-minute drive to a hospital in Boston. There she would spend twelve hours a day feeding and caring for our baby, Daniel, who was born prematurely and arrived weighing only four pounds. When he hit eight pounds, he finally came home. Doctors said Joanne need to take a break. They were worried she would become totally exhausted. I took their suggestion, hired a nurse, and we headed to the tournament.

Just before the bus crossed the state line between Connecticut and Rhode Island, a state trooper pulled the bus over. At the time, I thought, "Hmm, maybe somebody got advance word about the March Madness seedings."

I could not have been more wrong.

"You need to come with me," the trooper said.

I was taken to a phone booth and put in touch with Dr. Joe Flynn at a Providence hospital. Dr. Flynn was crying as he told me that Daniel had died. He said it was crib death, or Sudden Infant Death Syndrome, SAD also known as SIDS.

I hung up the phone, my heart broken in a million pieces. I whispered to Joanne that Daniel had died. She passed out in my arms right there, overcome by grief. We were rushed to the hospital. Seeing our tiny, lifeless baby on the ER bed was the most painful sight of my life.

Joanne was completely shattered, blaming herself for leaving him. Of course, it wasn't her fault at all. SIDS could have happened at any time. It was the saddest, most tragic moment of our lives.

The trauma lasted for months, and you can never truly heal from losing a child. But one of the things that got me through the agony of Daniel's death was my team. The players showed me so much love on a daily basis. They turned practice and our games into a meaningful distraction. And for anyone consumed by grief, meaningful distractions are a blessing.

The selection committee didn't do us any favors. We had to go play Alabama Birmingham on their home court, which meant we had about forty fans in the crowd—just the families of our players, basically. Amazingly, after falling behind in the game, we rallied and pulled out the win. Next up was Austin Peay, an underdog from Tennessee. I didn't know too much about this team, except that in the '70s a legendary Brooklyn player, Fly Williams, played for them and inspired a cheer that matched his audacious game: "The Fly is open, let's go Peay!"

Fly, of course, was long gone, but fast-break-loving Austin Peay gave us a serious game. They were up by two when we sent one of their big men, Bob Thomas, to the foul line with thirty-six seconds left. He missed the front end of a one-and-one. We got the rebound and went to our bread and butter—the high screen. But instead of driving to the hoop, Billy pulled back, exchanged passes with Jacek, and started backing in. When the man guarding him fell down, Billy the Kid turned to hit a jumper from just beyond the elbow. The game was tied now, but Austin Peay had the ball. They put up a shot and Delray Brooks fouled Bob Thomas again—with two seconds left! I called two time-outs in a row to give Thomas time to get nervous about his upcoming foul shot. Sure enough, he missed. We headed into overtime and finally put the game away. Hello, Sweet 16!

Now we had to play Alabama, who went 16-2 in the SEC, and was stocked with four future NBA draft picks on their team—Derrick McKey, Jim Farmer, Michael Ainsley, and Terry Coner. As you would expect, we were heavy underdogs, but for the first time in the tournament, we made it look easy. My guys blew them out, shooting an incredible 67 percent for the game. It was a dream come true; we were one game away from going to the Final Four—and as fate would have it, we played the game at Freedom Hall in Louisville, Kentucky, a place I would come to know well.

But the thing about dreams is you eventually wake up, and in our case, we awoke to find out we had to play Georgetown again—the one team we were intimidated by. And I had one day to prepare them for the game.

I got my team together and I could see they were dejected and nervous. I decided to accentuate the positive.

"In every great achievement, you need some luck. And you guys are the luckiest bunch I've ever seen," I said, ignoring the fact that some of the players were looking at me like I was nuts. "The one thing you want is to play a team that will take you lightly, and that's Georgetown. You have the biggest psychological advantage of all time. We are on fire right now offensively. But Georgetown will take us lightly because they've blown us out twice!"

I could see some of the players were paying attention and nodding. They were buying it.

"What is it that Georgetown does to us?" I ask.

"They pressure our guards and take away the three-point shot," Delray said.

"That's right. So here's what we're going to do: We're going to let Darryl Wright"—our small forward—"and others bring the ball up to keep the pressure off Billy and Delray. Then we're going to go inside to the low post. And we're going to score with Jacek, Dave Kipfer, and Steve Wright early in the game. Everybody got it?"

My players immediately went from dejection to euphoria. In just a few minutes, I'd sold them a bill of goods they could believe in.

Actually, there was one doubter.

"Coach?" My big man had raised his hand.

"Yes, Jacek, what is it?"

"Bad idea."

"What do you mean 'bad idea'?"

"Don't go to me. I can't score against Georgetown. Don't throw me the ball. Go to Steve Wright, start Steve Wright if you want, go to Dave Kipfer, don't go to me."

"Jacek, let me ask you a question. Who's the most famous Polish person?"

"The pope."

"Right. Who's the second most popular famous person in Poland?"

"Lech Walesa, the Solidarity leader."

"Okay. Jacek. You'll never catch the pope. But if we go inside and you score, you're going after Lech Walesa tomorrow."

The whole team cracked up over this. I was just trying to loosen them up and get them to believe in themselves.

It worked. We went inside after the opening whistle and Duda scored. I immediately pulled him out of the game because he was right: he was primarily a defensive rebounder and screener with a nice jump hook. Steve Wright, his very athletic backup, held down the middle. And we had a great game. By halftime, we were up by seventeen, and the game was never close. Billy Donovan got to the line a ton and wound up hitting 16 out of 18 free throws, and our small forward Darryl Wright went 4 for 4 from the three-point line and was named the MVP of the game and the region.

Wow

Two years earlier, Providence had been languishing in the cellar of the Big East. Now we were on our way to the Final Four! I'm sad to say Syracuse had our number in the semifinal. But nothing can take away the joy of that amazing run. Nothing. Providence College molded my beliefs that anything could be accomplished, and I don't care who you're coaching or what type of player you're coaching. With hard work, with dedication, with focus and guidance, and, yes, some luck, anything is possible.

BEST-MADE PLANS

I was thirty-three years of age when I showed up at Providence, and my two years there were the best time of my life from a work perspective. I loved teaching. But I was still young enough to play ball and hold my own on the court with my players. I think the fact that I could walk the walk helped me talk the talk and relate to my players.

Looking back on my career, I consider leaving Providence as my greatest professional regret. It's where I enjoyed the purity of the game the most. It's a town my wife loved. I had real bonds with the guys on the team and my assistants. Billy Donovan became a colleague and lifelong friend. And so did my A.D., Lou Lamoriello. It had everything I always wanted in a basketball program.

After we got to the Final Four, Lou asked what kind of raise I wanted. I was making $90K and I said, "I don't know, Lou. It's a Catholic school. How about $100,000 and ten years?"

He laughed and said, "You just made it to the Final Four and you're only asking for a $10,000 raise! How about you let me take care of it?"

He ended up giving me a seven-year deal that started at $135,000 with incremental raises. But not long after the ink was dry, the Knicks came calling, offering me the head coaching job. It was the second time they'd called. The first time I rejected them for a number of reasons— Joanne and I loved Providence, we had just been to the Final Four, and the contract the Knicks were offering was very incentive-based, which

I didn't like. When the Knicks called again, I told them I was honored and flattered, but there was no way the school would let me go.

Knicks president Jack Diller said, "No. I talked to Lou Lamoriello. He got permission for me to speak to you."

I was shocked. I got Lou on the phone. "Lou, did you give permission to Jack Diller to speak to me?"

"Yes."

"Why'd you do that?" I was totally confused. I figured Lou wanted me to stay.

"I really think if you want to go, you should listen to them and you should hear them out."

"Lou, we've already been through that, and I turned down the job."

He said, "I think there are circumstances now that you should listen to them and then make up your mind. I'll support you either way."

None of this made any sense to me. Why would my boss, who just signed me, agree to let me go? Not only that, he knew how happy I was at Providence College.

But I really liked and trusted Lou. And the thought of coaching the team I had worshipped as a kid was enticing. So I met with the Knicks and struck a deal to become their next head coach. Not long after, I found out why Lou allowed me to speak to the Knicks: he'd signed a deal of his own to become the general manager of the New Jersey Devils, a job he kept for twenty-eight years. He didn't want me to pass over the Knicks out of loyalty to him—and then be stuck with an A.D. who might want to bring in his own coach.

It wouldn't have been the same without Lou there. But in hindsight, I wish that magical run could have lasted a few more years.

4

CAMELOT

From famine to feast: Kentucky's "Shame" to the greatest Final

Four run in Wildcats history.

▼

THE LATE C.M. Newton was known in coaching circles as a country gentleman who played on Kentucky's 1951 national championship team and went on to integrate the SEC as the head coach of the University of Alabama. In early 1989 when I was in the middle of my second season as the Knicks head coach, C.M., then the athletic director at the University of Kentucky, called me up. He said he was looking for a new Wildcats head coach and that Big East commissioner David Gavitt had once again recommended me.

I told him things were going great in New York and I wasn't sure I'd be interested. At the time, that was an understatement. I was in the middle of my second year as Knicks head coach and having a great time. We had won thirty-eight games my first year, an improvement of fourteen wins over the prior year. Now, thanks in part to the addition of workhorse power forward Charles Oakley taking some of the pressure off Patrick Ewing, we were leading the Atlantic Division. And Joanne loved our life in Bedford, New York, and was thrilled to live near her family.

But C.M. was gracefully persistent and asked if he could come see me and Joanne at our home. I said sure.

Before he arrived, I told Joanne that we were going to get the greatest sales pitch in history. "C.M is going to blow you away with the tradition of Kentucky basketball. The prominence of the team in that state is hard to describe. Basketball is practically a religion there, so prepare to be blown out of the house when he starts talking about it."

Instead of presenting an upbeat version of the school, C.M. was so brutally honest, I couldn't fathom why he had come. He told us the program had hit its lowest point since the 1950s when Ralph Beard, the star of Kentucky's Fabulous Five, and teammates Alex Groza and Dale Barnstable admitted to point shaving during Kentucky games. The school had just been hit with NCAA sanctions. He listed the challenges the school was facing. The Wildcats were banned from appearing on TV and banned from playing in the NCAA Tournament for two years. Top recruits were transferring out of the program. The school was going to lose important revenue streams because of the tournament bans, and the NCAA had even cut its scholarships. "The morale on campus and in the community is the lowest I've ever seen it."

Joanne, who did not want to move from New York, listened for about fifteen minutes and then excused herself, telling C.M. she needed to speak to me for a second about running some errands for the kids at school. I walked her out of the room and she gave me a major dose of New York sarcasm: "I have to leave now because I just got blown out of my house with all the great things I'm hearing about Kentucky basketball."

Of course, I started laughing. And I went and told C.M. how his vision of Kentucky hoops had defied any possible expectation. "You've painted such a disturbing picture, I'm not sure who would want to coach there."

He laughed, too, and said he just wanted me to be fully aware of the trials of the job.

I thanked him and said I didn't think I was interested.

"I can see how, being in first place with the Knicks, this isn't the job for you. But is there anyone you would recommend?"

"P.J. Carlesimo at Seton Hall. He would be great for the job."

C.M. approached P.J. and offered him the position. They had some serious discussions, but P.J. opted not to take it.

A short time after P.J. turned down the job, Joanne and I went out to dinner with him at Bravo Gianni in Manhattan. I asked him why he turned it down. He was single at the time and didn't think it was a good town for someone without a family. He reiterated how much respect and admiration he had for C.M.

With P.J. out of the picture, though, C.M. called me a second time.

The Knicks had just won the division with a 52-30 record. To put that in perspective, the last time the Knicks had won a division title was the 1972–73 season, back when I was still a wide-eyed fan playing college ball. So I was truly proud to have helped elevate the team to approach the levels of the great Red Holzman.

C.M. said he knew we were just getting ready to start our playoff series against the Sixers and their star Charles Barkley. He said, "Look, I'm willing to wait until after the playoffs to continue our discussion." And I agreed. I was so focused on the Knicks, any talk of Kentucky would have to wait.

Going into the playoffs, I had high hopes for making a championship run. The hard-nosed Detroit Pistons were the favorites in the East. The Bad Boys were a deep team, with Isaiah Thomas, Dennis Rodman, Bill Laimbeer, and Rick Mahorn, but we had won all four of our games against them that season. If we had to play them in the conference finals, I really liked our chances.

We swept the Sixers in three games. The thing everyone remembers about that series was our postgame celebration. Mark Jackson and Patrick Ewing and a couple of other players grabbed a broom from a custodian and just swept the floor as a joke. They were excited and celebrating their victory—an upset on Philly's home court. They were in the moment, and I don't think they meant anything mean-spirited at all. But the move definitely wasn't the most gracious victory celebration, and it generated a lot of bad ink.

Then we played Chicago. We lost our home-court advantage when the Bulls upset us in overtime in the first game. Down three games to two in the series, we played the sixth game in Chicago. We were losing by four points when Trent Tucker hit a three-pointer with six seconds on the clock—and got fouled. He hit the foul shot to tie the game.

At this point, Chicago called time-out to advance the ball to half court. I huddled with my guys. Jordan had scored 38 points at this point. I said: "There is one guy who is not going to beat us—Jordan. Do not let him catch the ball." I told Trent Tucker to lock him down, to face-guard him. I wanted our defense to help Trent sandwich him. "If Scottie Pippen or Horace Grant beat us, so be it. But don't let Jordan catch the ball."

The play starts and Michael runs Trent into a pick, then gives a slight push to Mark Jackson and gets the pass, which he takes into the lane. He launches a jumper and draws a foul. He hits both free throws to put the Bulls up by two, 113–111.

With no timeouts left, we got the ball, rushed it up court, and Johnny Newman had a wide-open look from about thirty-five feet out. Still, it was a tough shot and it went long. Our championship dreams instantly vanished.

Years later, I was at a dinner with Jordan. I was introduced at the dais, and I told the crowd, "I want everyone to know: Michael is responsible for me coaching college basketball. If he hadn't scored 40 points and gotten open when I'd ordered up a double-team back in 1989, I'd still be coaching the Knicks today."

I was joking. But only a bit.

With the season over and Kentucky's offer still in the air, I went to the GM, Al Bianchi, to get a read on what he thought about my longevity at the Garden. We had a strange relationship, Al and me. Off the court we were fine with each other. But our differences occurred *on* the court. He wanted the Knicks to play like the thuggish, plodding, physical defensive-focused Detroit Pistons. That was never my game.

"Al, Kentucky's come after me for the second time," I said.

"You know, kid, you should keep all your options open in this business and just listen," he said.

Remember, we'd been averaging 116.7 points per game. Madison Square Garden was sold out every night. We were playing exciting ball—pressing, running, shooting threes. If not for that damn Michael Jordan, we probably would have made a run to the finals!

But Al's answer telegraphed a lot. I knew then and there he wasn't a fan of my style of coaching. His response was anything but a commitment to me.

Still, there was one person who told me in no uncertain terms to stay with the Knicks: Hollywood producer Stanley Jaffe, who made *The Accused, Kramer vs. Kramer,* and *Bad News Bears,* to name a few of his hits. Stanley was my neighbor at the time in Bedford, a small town about an hour's drive from Manhattan. His wife, Melinda, and my wife were friendly, but I never expected him to give me career advice.

One day I was out playing baseball with three of my kids at a local park. You may have seen this park, because Stanley filmed a scene there in his Academy Award–nominated movie *Fatal Attraction*. There's a moment when Glenn Close watches kids playing, and we were in that exact spot when Stanley pulled up in his Mercedes. He got out of the car and said, "Coach, can I interrupt your game?"

I called time-out with the kids and walked over to him. "What's up?"

"I don't want you to take the Kentucky job," he said.

I was surprised. Stanley was a Knicks season ticket holder. But other than that, there was no context for this intervention.

"What's the deal, Stanley? You going to make a movie about me?" I was kidding, but Stanley wasn't.

"No, you have to trust me. I can't tell you why," he said. "But you have to trust me. Don't take the job. I'll take care of you, and make sure everything goes great with the Knicks."

I said, "Stanley, how am I going to do that? You're not giving me any concrete reasons to stay. You're a producer. You make movies."

"You just have to believe in me and trust me," he said.

I went back to playing ball with my kids. I knew Stanley was very well connected with Martin Davis, the CEO of Paramount Communications, which owned the Knicks. But I couldn't figure out how he would have any inside information about the team.

That night I called him up. "Stanley, look. I do trust you, but I'm set on taking the Kentucky job."

"I wish you believed in me. You can do great things for the Knicks," he said.

I interviewed with Kentucky and I took the job, leaving my assistant coach, Stu Jackson, to assume the Knicks' hot seat. About nine months later, on March 1, I was in Kentucky and Stanley called me from London. He said, "I want you to pick up the *Post* or the *Times* tomorrow."

The Internet wasn't really around in 1991, so I tracked down the *Post*. Splashed on the back page was a headline about the Madison Square Garden Massacre—Bianchi had gotten the ax and Jack Diller, president of the Knicks and Rangers, was relieved of his Knick duties. As for my pal Stanley Jaffe, about two weeks later, he was named president and chief operating officer of Paramount Communications! He knew he had the deal but obviously couldn't tell me about it. If he could have just given me a hint, I wouldn't have taken the Kentucky job. I would have stayed. Under Stanley's watch, Pat Riley was eventually brought in to coach the Knicks in the 1991–92 season, and a new era at the Garden began.

FALSE START

But even signing my new deal came with a hitch. Thinking about it now, maybe I should have taken it as foreshadowing, or at least an example of how the entire state of Kentucky puts its basketball teams under a microscope. Joanne and I flew to Lexington, ready to sign the contract. But while I was there, a local paper ran a story about the violations that took place in Hawaii.

Obviously feeling the pressure from the media, C.M. called. "We're going to have to move in a different direction," he told us.

I understood the university's position and was okay with it. Joanne wanted to stay in New York, because that's where her family was. We were both content with the idea of me staying with the Knicks.

The next morning, C.M. came by to take us to the airport. "The president wants you to stop by the office. He wants to apologize for what happened," he said

"That's okay, C. M. He doesn't have to apologize."

"No, he wants to speak with you."

So we went to meet with the university president, David Roselle. He sat us down and said, "Look, I've called the NCAA. I've done my due diligence with a lot of different people about you. You're the right guy to clean up this mess. And it's a big mess, Rick. I don't want to mislead you. We have two years of probation. We have all these sanctions. But

I know you're the right guy to clean it up. Please accept our apologies for what happened yesterday. We want you to be our coach."

Now, suddenly, the emotions swung back the other way. For the third time in a twenty-four-hour span, Joanne and I changed our minds. Soon, the university held a press conference and announced my appointment as the first step in the process of rebuilding the Kentucky basketball program.

Leaving such a great team in New York was hard. I always wonder, could we have won a championship? I'll never know for sure.

MY FIRST KENTUCKY WALTZ

One thing I do know for sure is that recruiting Jamal Mashburn made my mission at the University of Kentucky a lot easier.

You might think recruiting for Kentucky is a walk in the park. Normally, it's a coveted program. I like to compare the Wildcats to the Dallas Cowboys. The teams have a legacy and the swagger that comes with being a dominant force for a long period of time. And everywhere you go, those teams are either hated or loved. I think Duke has ascended to a similar level today. College hoops fans either love them or hate them. There's no in between.

Kentucky, as I'll discuss in greater detail soon, was a true basketball empire. I call it the Roman Empire of college hoops. But when I arrived, the empire had almost burned to the ground. And top recruits were not interested in joining a team with zero TV exposure and a March Madness ban.

The sanctions were so tough that *Sports Illustrated* came up with an unforgettable magazine cover: a kid in a Wildcats uniform slumping with his back to the camera beneath a telling headline: "Kentucky's Shame."

The accompanying cover copy provided the basic detail.

After finding that the Wildcats sent one player cash and that another Kentucky player cheated on his entrance exam, the NCAA placed the 'Cats on probation for three years. Did they get off easy?

If the sanctions weren't humiliating enough, I still had to go on what I call the traveling salesman tour—stopping in at local stores, taverns, and restaurants and pleading with owners not to give Wildcat players any freebies. Not a drink, not a meal, not a T-shirt, not a pair of shoe-laces. Any gift to one of our players from a commercial enterprise could be considered an "extra benefit." That's the term the NCAA uses for free gifts or services given to matriculating student-athletes. So although handing out no-strings-attached gifts to my players might have seemed like a generous act, it risked hurting our team.

Most venues understood all this. Only one store owner said, "Look, we're going to give discounts to whoever we want. You can't tell us what to do."

I said, "Well, I will publicly say that you are endangering Kentucky basketball and I don't think that would be too good for your business." They got the message.

So we got the culture around the team cleaned up, but the team's most highly rated players transferred out as soon as the NCAA sanctions hit—it was a no-brainer for them. Because of the penalties, the NCAA let them transfer to new teams without having to sit out for a year. The only players that stayed were the local products. John Pelphrey, Deron Feldhaus, Richie Falmer, and Reggie Hanson—all played high school ball in Kentucky. They did not want to leave because most of them had already spent a lifetime bleeding University of Kentucky blue. They didn't care if they played one minute or thirty minutes. When they put on that uniform, it was like putting on priestly vestments. It was everything in their life.

Most of my native Kentucky players hadn't played much the previous year, when the team finished with a losing record. But with conditioning and rigorous drilling, we started to have success. We actually beat an LSU team 100–95 with three future NBA first-round draft picks: Stanley Roberts, Chris Jackson—who later changed his name to Mahmoud Abdul-Rauf—and a guy named Shaquille O'Neal.

We finished the season with a .500 winning percentage, and fans loved our dogged style of play. By the end of the season, I was feeling pretty hopeful about the future. Initially, I had thought it might take five years to return Kentucky to its expected place as a basketball powerhouse. Now I thought it might take a little less time. Recruiting was still a problem, as we had one more year away from March Madness. So signing a game-changing new recruit seemed unlikely—until Jamal Mashburn showed up for his campus visit.

THE MONSTER MASH

The first time Jamal Mashburn ever stepped on the University of Kentucky campus he had a Syracuse cap on his head. I said, "Mash, I wouldn't wear a Syracuse hat around the University of Kentucky."

"It doesn't matter, Coach," he replied. "I'm coming."

That was it. It took about thirty seconds to get him on board. I couldn't believe it. I said, "Well, don't you want to see the arena? You have to see the school before you decide."

"No, my family and I decided long ago. I am coming to play for the Knicks coach."

Jamal, of course, was a New York hoops standout. He played for Cardinal Hayes High School and was a member of the city's legendary

Gauchos travel team. He wasn't a McDonald's All-American because he hadn't been a dominant force in his early high school career. I first witnessed Jamal play at the Five-Star basketball camp and used him in some of the drills I ran during my guest lectures. He was out of shape and probably thirty pounds heavier than he should have been, with a body fat content that was way too high. (During those first years at Kentucky, I instituted a rule: every frontcourt player on our team had to be below 10 percent body fat content, and guards had to be below 8 percent—and I've kept that rule ever since.)

But Mash had great hands and a terrific feel for the game. Although he wasn't highly ranked at that time, I thought he had a strong future. Herb Sendek and I followed Mash throughout the summer and were very bullish on him. He was so young for his class—he was only sixteen years old when he started his senior year in high school—it was no wonder he was outranked by other, older players. But by the end of his senior year, when he scored 18 points and nabbed 7 rebounds to lead his school to its first New York Catholic High School championship since 1944, it was clear the 6'8" forward was going to be something special.

I really admire Mash for what he did. Just think of it today. There probably isn't a young man alive who would choose a school that was banned from television or the NCAA Tournament for his first year. But Mash came anyway, and I am tremendously grateful that he did.

Jamal was a model student-athlete, but I did face my first dilemma involving strippers and players during his freshman year. Someone tipped me off that Jamal and Gimel Martinez traveled ten miles out of town to visit a strip club called Pure Gold. I immediately blew a gasket. The Wildcats were still under sanctions. The last thing we needed was to have underage players caught in a strip club.

I knew Jamal and Gimel were not familiar with Lexington or its surroundings and that given the fact neither one of them had their driver's license, someone had to have taken them to the club. I called both players into my office and they confirmed the visit. Concerned a booster might have led them astray, I asked who brought them there. They said it was a team member, but wouldn't name names.

After all the players on the team denied accompanying the M&M boys to Pure Gold, I realized it had to be one of our eight team managers.

I went to talk to Bill Keightley, our equipment manager, and asked him to find out which team manager took the M&M boys to Pure Gold.

He came back and said no one would talk, so I told him to let it be known we were going to pull all the managers' grades and would fire anyone who had a GPA below 2.5.

That threat loosened some tongues and Bill reported back to me quickly.

"Coach, I found out who it was. But there are some problems."

"Who did it?"

Mr. Bill told me the strip club enabler was the younger brother of the team's head manager Spencer Tatum. His name was Vincent Tatum.

"What's his story?"

"That leads us to the second problem, Coach."

"What's that, Mr. Bill?"

"Young Vincent is not enrolled at our school."

"How can he be a manager?"

"He's enrolled at Lexington Community College, which is affiliated with UK."

"How did that get by us, Mr. Bill?"

"We have a third problem."

"What's that?"

"Young Vincent has three Fs and two Incompletes."

I called Vinnie to my office and told him in no uncertain terms that his future as a basketball manager was over.

I went ballistic over two players visiting a strip club, but the public never found out about the sequence of events or my vigilance once I learned what had happened. Years later, as we'll see, I was falsely accused of knowing that strippers were visiting my players in a dormitory and not doing anything about it. Oh, the irony.

One last thing about this story: I did give Vinnie a second chance. He became the Louisville Cardinals equipment manager for over fifteen years, not to mention one of my closest friends.

We went 22-6 during Mash's first year at Kentucky. Reggie Hanson and John Pelphrey led the team in scoring, each averaging 14.4 points a game, but Jamal was right behind them knocking down 12.9 and grabbing more than 7 rebounds a game. We won the SEC division, but of course, we were still under NCAA sanctions, so we couldn't be acknowledged as champs. Still, we celebrated locally. The Lexington fire department came by and we rode the fire engines around town in an impromptu parade.

Jamal wasn't the only notable newcomer that year. In 1990, we hired the first female assistant coach in Division 1 Men's Basketball history. Her name was Bernadette Locke, and she was a driven young woman who we hired away from the University of Georgia. What drove that decision? Bernadette was highly recommended. Period. She had a reputation as a stellar recruiter, a hard worker, and a sharp coach. But I also wanted to change the culture and shake things up. Having a woman on staff sent a message that Kentucky was changing, evolving, shedding any suspect old ways while forging ahead and being a leader in college basketball. Normally, hiring an assistant coach is a one-day story. But as the season unfolded, Bernadette generated media interest for the entire year, and that really helped the Kentucky image.

While Bernadette's mix of class and grace was exactly what I'd hoped for, nobody made more of an impact on the court than Jamal.

As a sophomore he cracked the senior-heavy starting five, his scoring climbed to 21 points a game, and he became one of the dominant sophomores in the nation. We went 23-6. The NCAA's two-year ban on postseason play was over, and we won the SEC tournament. We also won our first three March Madness games, before facing off against Duke in what would become one of the great Elite Eight games in history.

Duke was the number 1 seed when we met at the Spectrum in Philadelphia. This was a team stocked with talent—Grant Hill, Christian Laettner, Bobby Hurley, Cherokee Parks—that had only lost two games all season. But we gave them a battle. At one point, Laettner intentionally stomped on one of our bench players, Aminu Timberlake, literally stepping on his chest. From my perspective, it was such a dirty move, the referees should have thrown Laettner out of the game immediately. To this day, I wonder how the referees ever let him stay in. But at no point did we get intimidated. We came back from five points down at halftime to send the game into overtime.

You know the ending. You've probably seen "The Shot." But here's what happened. We were up by one point, 103–102, with 2.1 seconds left. Jamal and our big man, Gimel Martinez, had both fouled out, and Sean Woods, John Pelphrey, and Dale Brown all had four fouls when Grant Hill launched a Hail Mary bomb to Laettner at the foul line. The odds of going down court and scoring in 2.1 seconds were pretty slim, so I had given my guys strict instructions not to foul—that would have been a gift to Duke. So Laettner—who hadn't missed shot the entire game—leaped and caught the ball, brought it down, took a dribble, and then hit a turnaround jumper from the foul line. Game over.

In hindsight, the mistake I made was telling my players not to foul. I told my guys that the ball would be going to Laettner, and predicted he'd either pass it to the wing or shoot it himself. I should have said, "That ball is going to Laettner. Knock it down, steal it, do whatever you can." Except for Laettner's bush-league tactic—it was a game that deserves its place in history. Duke shot the lights out that night, with an incredible .654 shooting percentage. So I have no regrets.

In fact, I was incredibly proud of my guys. They had played their hearts out on the national stage and had gone *mano a mano* against more highly touted players. Jamal went 11 for 16, scoring 28 points with 10 boards before fouling out in regulation, and Sean Woods and Dale Brown played the games of their lives. I was heartbroken for my team, especially my graduating seniors. But I was grateful, too. We had shown the world Kentucky basketball was back.

Our fans felt the same way I did. When we arrived home from the Duke game, Wildcats faithful lined the roads to cheer us as we drove to Rupp Arena. And when we got there, the fans were filling the arena. My four seniors, the guys who never fled the team when the NCAA sanctions came down and were dubbed the Unforgettables, watched as a banner was raised with their names on it: Deron Feldhaus, John Pelphrey, Richie Farmer, and Sean Woods. It was a spine-tingling moment.

The next year we had a 23-3 regular-season record, finishing second in the SEC. One of the games I'll never forget was our NCAA Tournament Sweet 16 face-off against Wake Forest that pitted Jamal against highly touted power forward Rodney Rogers.

Jamal dominated the first half, scoring 21 points. But what I remember most about that game was that, at the start of the second half, Jamal had four open looks at the basket and passed the ball each time. During the first mandatory time-out, I said, "Mash, why are you passing up easy baskets?"

His response tells you about Jamal's character: "I have enough points. Let the other guys get some confidence going." I sat Mash for the last ten minutes and he went 8-for-13 for 23 points. Rodney went 4-for-9 for 14 points, and we won 103–69.

The next game we faced Florida State for the Final Four birth. They had an incredible team, with four future NBA players in the starting five: Heisman Trophy winner Charlie Ward, Sam Cassell, Bob Sura, and Douglas Edwards. We won 106–81 and marched all the way to the

NCAA semifinals against Michigan and its Fab Five—Chris Webber, Jalen Rose, Juwan Howard, Jimmy King, and Ray Jackson. Unfortunately, Mash fouled out in regulation and we lost in overtime, 81–78.

Not long after that game, I received a call from Jamal's mother, Helen. At this point, Mash was weighing going pro. He'd averaged 21 points and 8 rebounds a game for two years running, led the team to Elite Eight and Final Four tournament appearances, and was clearly one of the most dominant players in college basketball.

"Rick, you've got to give me some insight into how Jamal should manage his money."

"Helen, I know nothing about money," I said. "But I'll try and get some answers about who Jamal should work with."

I met with a few brokers in New York—Goldman Sachs, Merrill Lynch, Lehman Brothers, JP Morgan. Then I met with Mario Gabelli of Gabelli Assets in Rye, New York.

I was doing my homework. "Mario, where do you get your talent from?" I asked, trying to understand his operation. "University of Chicago? Wharton School? Yale? Harvard?"

"No. I like my people to have PhDs."

"Really? PhDs for trading bonds and equities?"

"I want them to be poor, hungry, and driven. I don't give a damn where they go to school."

That sold me right away, of course, because I want my players to have PHDs, too—passion, hunger, and drive. So I recommended him to Jamal. Then I found a bright young accountant in Lexington named Rick Avare. I wanted him to make sure Jamal paid his taxes correctly and be a low-key, on-the-ball business manager and CPA.

I got back on the phone with Jamal's mom and I made my debut as a financial planner. We made a pie chart—a circle with a slice each for investments, living expenses, savings, taxes, taking care of mom, and other business opportunities—and then we told Rick to make it happen.

Around this time, the sneaker companies started approaching Jamal. Nike offered him $250,000, and Adidas offered him $200,000 to wear their shoes. But I'd just read Grant Hill had signed a major sneaker endorsement deal with Fila, an Italian-based athletic gear company that was trying to transfer its success in the tennis market to the basketball shoe business. I sent Rick Avare to Baltimore to meet with the Fila team, and he instantly justified my faith in him by putting together a $7.5 million, five-year deal. Fila announced the deal with a press conference in Harlem, giving out two thousand shoes to underprivileged kids, and presented Mash with a brand-new Ferrari—courtesy of Fila's partnership with the Italian car manufacturer.

The Dallas Mavericks made Jamal the fourth pick in the NBA draft. So he wore Fila gear during his first years there. But then Mash started complaining about the sneakers. "Coach, these shoes are killing me."

Later I told Rick Avare, "I don't care if he has the worst blisters in the world, you make sure he keeps wearing them."

But eventually Jamal broke the contract.

Three years after Jamal turned pro, he decided to form a company with Rick and me, called MAP, as in Mashburn, Avare, and Pitino. Today, MAP owns three Lexus dealerships, a Toyota dealership, and a number of other interests. And Jamal and Rick are heavily invested in other ventures without me.

We've been in business together for twenty-five years. We have never had a business argument. We have total faith in each other to do the best for our company. Jamal still calls me Coach—and so, in fact, does our partner, Rick—but we are friends, partners, equals. The relationships I've made through basketball have frequently transcended basic player-coach dynamics. Part of that has to do with the intimacy of our work—I'm in the business of helping players improve their basketball skills, but I'm also committed to building their classroom skills and their life skills—and when you spend hours and hours together doing that, real bonds develop. The result of this work is that I have a large basketball family. But my relationship with Jamal remains one of the best, closest, and most gratifying I've ever had with one of my players.

THE UNTOUCHABLES

My Wildcats teams continued to perform at the highest level. Thanks to the reputation of our program and my crack assistant coaches—Tubby Smith, Bernadette, Herb, and bench newcomer Billy Donovan—our recruiting classes allowed us to stockpile tremendous talent.

At one point, Billy and I went down to Memphis for a home visit with Deuce Ford, a highly touted 6'5" swingman whose style fit perfectly into our system. I talked nonstop for forty-five minutes about the virtues of the Roman Empire. Twenty-four thousand people will watch you play every night. Great TV exposure. A legacy of fifty-six All-Americans and the best facilities in college basketball. When I was done, I noticed that everyone had questions on their paper. I said, "I've talked a lot. I see you have questions."

But Deuce's mom said I'd answered all her questions. The dad said the same thing. As for his coach, he had no questions either. He said, "No, Coach, you've talked about style of play and how you would use Deuce with your offense."

There was dead silence after that. It did not feel right. There was no real connection in the room.

Billy and I left. I said, "How long have we been recruiting Deuce?"

"Two years."

"Well, that was a lot of wasted effort."

"Why do you say that, Coach? It went really well."

"That did not go well at all. I never allowed for interaction. All I did was talk and never listen. I didn't build any trust."

His response to me: "Coach, you've been reading too many of those motivational books. We're going to be fine."

The next day we learned Deuce had whittled his list from his top ten schools to his top five. We did not make the cut.

I asked Billy what our next move was.

"We have another appointment in Brownsville, Tennessee, to go visit Tony Delk," he said. Tony was a combo guard that was on our list, but we hadn't shown him as much attention as we had on Deuce. "But I think we should cancel it. It might be a waste of time."

"Why is that?"

"There are three front-runners—Arkansas, Memphis, and Tennessee."

"Let's give it a shot."

We walked into the Delk home and met his parents; Tony's brothers David and Richard, who played Division 2 basketball; a girlfriend; and his high school coach. I wasn't going to blow this opportunity as I had with Deuce. I immediately started asking our hosts questions. What did Tony's mom want him to study?

"Business," she said. And she gave me a five-minute dissertation on the value of studying business as opposed to communications.

I turned to the two brothers. I said, "I feel like Tony will have the ball in his hands in our system and may run a lot of pick and rolls."

They got excited and said he needed to learn to play point if he wanted to make it to the NBA.

"Well, that's not going to happen unless he learns to make other players better," I said.

Then I took a whiteboard out of my bag. I told the coach I'd watched him run three-point plays for Tony. Could he diagram one for me?

I asked more questions, I got more feedback. I spoke about 20 percent of the time. And listened the other 80. Listening four times the amount you speak builds great trust in the room. Ninety minutes later,

Billy pointed to his watch to let me know we had a flight to catch. The mom turned to us and apologized for not offering us any food or drink. She asked if we wanted to stay for some barbeque.

I said, "Yes, ma'am, that would be great."

We stayed another two hours, missed our flight, and wound up driving the car all the way back to Lexington.

During the ride, Billy turned to me and said, "What was that all about, asking all those questions?"

"What do you mean?"

"You didn't cover our schedule, our dorm, our tutoring. You didn't cover anything about Kentucky basketball."

"No. All I did was listen, ask questions, laugh, and socialize. In other words, all I did was try to form a bond."

The next day, we called Tony to see if we made his top five. We not only made the cut, but he told us the whole family was coming to visit the next weekend.

He finished his visit on Sunday morning and called that night to say he was committing to us.

Deuce Ford signed with Memphis and transferred to LSU after blowing out his knee. Tony spent four years at Kentucky, was the MVP of the 1996 NCAA Championship team, and went on to an eleven-year career in the NBA.

By 1996, my team was called The Untouchables. They were that good. With Tony, Antoine Walker, and Walter McCarty all averaging double figures, we romped through our SEC games with an average margin of victory of more than twenty points. Our only blemish was a game against the University of Massachusetts—and that was my fault because I played Tony at point guard. We had a rematch in the Final Four and beat UMass 81–74, setting up the finale against Syracuse and my old pal Jim Boeheim on a cold rainy night at the Meadowlands in New Jersey.

We had tremendous pressure on us that year. I have never felt more urgency to win. Every game, every round, we were the big favorite. Everyone expected us to cut down the nets at the end of the tournament. Hell, I expected us to win, too. I firmly believe that my second string that year could have been a Final Four team. But I had been in the game long enough to know that being totally prepared, having more raw talent, and being more experienced doesn't guarantee victory. On any given night, miracles can happen and so can disasters. You try to prepare and motivate your team to execute to their potential. But basketball, despite what statistics junkies may tell you, is never an exact science.

When the final buzzer sounded, we had won 76–67 and I felt a mixture of elation and relief. Six years after I took over a broken program, we had finally done it. We had just won the sixth NCAA Tournament in Wildcat history.

The following year, we'd lost the nucleus of our team—three great seniors, Mark Pope, Walter McCarty, and Tony Delk, and underclassman Antoine Walker. But as I said earlier, our second team was pretty awesome, too, and now they got their time in the spotlight. And even though our best basketball player, Derek Anderson, blew out his knee with an ACL tear early in the season, we still sailed through the tournament. Amazingly, Derek was medically cleared to play in the Final Four Championship game against an Arizona team that had three high-scoring guards, Mike Bibby, Jason Terry, and Miles Simon. After our semifinal victory over Minnesota, Derek had a full practice with us. He was dominant. After practice, I asked our medical team what they thought, and they gave me the thumbs-up. "He's ready to play."

Then I went to see Derek in the trainer's room and asked how he felt.

"I feel great, Coach."

"Are you ready to go tomorrow?"

"It's your decision, Coach. Whatever you think."

That answer really bothered me. If he would have turned to me and said, "Coach, I'm ready to go out there and destroy Arizona," I wouldn't have had any trepidation at all. The fact that he deferred to me meant I had a decision to make. I had to weigh a number of factors. First, I felt in my bones that we were going to beat Arizona, with or without Derek. Second, Derek was on track to be a first-round draft pick and he hadn't played competitive basketball in over six months. I knew that if he got hurt playing in the final, I would never forgive myself.

While I did insert Derek into the game to shoot two foul shots when a technical was assessed, I kept him on the bench for the rest of the time—and I would do it again if the same circumstances arose. I cannot take risks with a young man's future.

We lost the final in overtime, 85–79. That was my final game at Kentucky, although I didn't know it at the time. The next year, my former assistant Tubby Smith took over and did an incredible coaching job, leading the team to its seventh NCAA title. So for three years in a row, three teams I helped put together made it to the series final and won twice. That stands as the most successful three-year run in Wildcat history. I'm proud to have been part of that.

OTHER UNTOUCHABLES

My players weren't the only people I considered untouchable. I made many great friends during my years in Lexington. Being a New Yorker and speaking a much different dialect than what you hear in Eastern Kentucky, I always felt a bit like an outsider. But over time I became close with lifelong members of the Wildcat nation. I really enjoyed my time with Cawood Ledford, Kentucky's legendary play-by-play radio announcer from Harlan, Kentucky. He was revered by the Kentucky faithful and might be the most popular non-player in Wildcat nation.

On the air and off it, he was a masterful speaker, full of great expressions such as, "He shot that one from Paducah," and of course, "Bullseye!" The last game he broadcast was the Duke game in 1992 with "The Shot." But he remained part of the scene even after he retired.

Bill Keightley, the equipment manager for at least thirty years, was another remarkable friend. He started out as a postal worker who worked part-time for the Wildcats and sat one seat behind the end of the bench. I become so fond of Mr. Bill that I made sure he got a hefty raise and added to his workload. "Mr. Bill," I said, "you are no longer at the end of the bench. You are now sitting in the first seat, to the right of me."

"Nah, Coach, I can't do that."

"Yes, you can," I said. "And you have one assignment: make sure I don't go out of the coaching box and get a technical foul. That's it."

I made a thousand managerial moves at Kentucky. But moving Mr. Bill beside me as my right-hand man was one of the best. He kept me out of trouble.

Of course, I also relished my time with C.M., who was such a polished human being and ally to me. Equally cherished, of course, was the woman who was the power behind the throne, my assistant, Marta McMackin. She is a wonderful woman and has remained near and dear to me—even when I eventually left the Big Blue nation.

Because of my players, the staff, and the community, I absolutely loved my time in Lexington. I always remember our standard operating procedure for visiting recruits and their families. We'd take them to historic Claiborne Farm. First Danzig would trot out. Then Mr. Prospector, and at last here came Big Red—the mighty Secretariat.

I called it Camelot. Every day was a wonder. We met and worked with wonderful people. We learned about horse racing. The kids loved being there. My work was both challenging and gratifying. I'm not kidding when I say that for seven years I didn't have a bad day.

FROM BLUEGRASS TO CELTIC GREEN

I was now a high-profile coach whose teams were making deep runs into the NCAA Tournament. Nike offered me a major endorsement deal. Not Kentucky. Just me. And if you are wondering about the logic of this—or how and why coaches were getting big money, don't worry. I will delve into the history of sneaker sponsorships later in the book.

That wasn't the only money coming my way. That spring, Paul Gaston, the owner of the Boston Celtics, came calling, offering me what felt like the keys to a whole new kingdom. We spent weeks and weeks negotiating back and forth because I was very conflicted about leaving. I was the coach of college basketball's greatest empire. But I was being offered a job with the NBA's greatest empire.

I had my business partner Rick negotiate the deal with Gaston and eventually they reached a six-year agreement for $32 million.

Rick called me up. "Paul says he's not going to give you a penny more. He'll fly to Lexington tomorrow to sign you."

This was the Boston Celtics. I'd be going back to the place where I'd started as a head coach. I knew the town well. I had many friends there and I felt my mission was complete at Kentucky. I'd helped lift the program from its nadir to its zenith. But I still had trepidation about leaving college basketball's greatest empire—even if it was to join the NBA's greatest empire. It was a tough call.

I slept on it, woke up, and called Rick. "Call Paul and tell him to cancel his trip. I'm not going."

Joanne was relieved. And so was I.

Rick tried to call Paul, but he couldn't reach him before his plane lifted off. When Rick called me to explain that Paul was en route, I said, "Rick, you have to meet him at the airport and apologize. I'm 100 percent positive we want to stay here."

The next phone call I got was from Rick again. "Coach," he said. "We are driving up the street."

"What do you mean 'we'?"

"Paul is with me. I'll explain when I get there."

When Rick and Paul walked into my house, Rick said, "Hey, Joanne, would you show Paul your memorabilia room downstairs? I need a couple minutes to talk to Coach."

When we were alone, I said, "Rick, I told you to tell him I wasn't interested."

"Coach, when he got off the plane, I didn't want to embarrass ourselves. I remembered he said he wouldn't give us a penny more than $32 million. So I told him we wanted $50 million and three extra years as just president, thinking he'd just turn around and go home."

"So what happened?"

"He went for it! He threw up his hands and said, 'I've had enough. Let's just get this deal done.'"

At that point I felt this just must be fate. It was the right thing to do, given the circumstances. It's not like I was joining the Washington Generals, the team that the Harlem Globetrotters humiliate every game. I was going to the greatest franchise in NBA history.

That is the true story of how I negotiated myself into a corner, went against my own instincts, and left Kentucky. Looking back on it today, I wish that plane never flew into Lexington.

And that's why every time Dick Vitale calls me and says that I'd actually have more collegiate coaching victories than Coach K if I had stayed in Kentucky for four years instead of going to Boston, I say: "Dick, will you please stop talking about that?"

He may be right.

5

Embracing new challenges is an admirable trait.

So is sticking to what you do best. Warning: balancing

those two things can be tricky.

▼

WHEN I ARRIVED in Boston, I felt I had truly arrived at the pinnacle of my profession. Coaching the Boston Celtics was a dream job. The organization was unmatched in the history of the NBA, having won sixteen championships at that time. It was an honor to be part of the team, and work with one of the sport's true legends, Red Auerbach, who became chairman of the Celtics' board when I arrived.

Unfortunately, I wasn't just the head coach. I was also the team president.

That's my biggest regret about the move—taking on those dual roles. My longtime friend and supporter David Gavitt had been the Celtics CEO. As I started negotiating with the Celtics, he had advised me to push to be appointed president of the team. Based on his experiences there, he believed that having both titles would ensure my ability to carry out my vision for the team.

What I didn't realize was that there is just too much going on in the NBA to have two jobs. If I would have only been the basketball coach and concentrated on teaching the game, the Boston Celtics would have been fine.

But as team president, I was trying to save the owner money when it came to management and personnel decisions. I also thought about trades every day. Things that used to concern me in very tangential ways when I was just a coach—budgets, payrolls, ticket sales, marketing promotions—took up more of my time, and I was consumed by trying to make deals. As the Celtics coach, however, I really should have just been thinking about offense and defense. It was a big mistake on my part and it cost me one of the truly great jobs in professional basketball.

I realize now, too, that I was blinded by the potential of the upcoming 1997 draft. We had two lottery picks. And for some harebrained reason—like the fact that I'm more of an optimist than a pessimist—I started to think the odds were in our favor to draft Tim Duncan and Keith Van Horn. And of course, the odds *were* in our favor—but only compared to the other lottery teams. We had a 27.5 percent chance of getting the first pick, while San Antonio had a 21.6 percent chance, and Denver had a 16.6 percent chance. Of course the prudent thing would have been to realize that *there was a 72.5 percent chance we wouldn't get the first pick.*

As someone who has based so much of his career on analytics, I can't believe I talked myself into missing that point. The statistics were definitely not in my favor, but I got caught up in a dream. That was my second big mistake. And not to beat a dead horse, but even if the Celtics had had a 72.5 percent chance of getting Tim Duncan, it's important to remember good odds never matter when reality has other plans. In our case, the worst possible scenario unfolded. Instead of getting the first and second picks, we got the third and sixth. We drafted two great players—Chauncey Billups and one of my Kentucky stars, Ron

Mercer—but neither of them was the immediate game changer Duncan was.

Midway through the season, I wound up trading Chauncey, which I really regret. I pulled the trigger on a deal to send him to Toronto for Kenny Anderson. At the time there was a debate about whether Chauncey was a better shooting guard than a point guard. Kenny, of course, was clearly a point guard. And most of Kenny's salary was covered in the trade, so we saved $11 or $12 million on the deal. But as a coach, I shouldn't have even thought about that. Coaches shouldn't care about saving owners money. My number-one priority should have been to help develop Chauncey into a point guard, not coming in under budget. I should have stuck with Chauncey—who later blossomed in Detroit—and not looked for a trade. It was a major mistake on my part.

THE PICK THAT ALMOST WAS

The year before I arrived, the Celtics had won fifteen games. My first year there we won thirty-six games so things were moving in the right direction. That spring I finished my workouts and scouting for the draft, and I told Chris Wallace, who I'd hired as the Celtics GM, that I was going on a one-week vacation to Italy with my brother-in-law Billy Minardi and our wives. While I was over there, Chris called me and asked if I would mind working out a player.

I said, "Chris, I'm in Rome. How am I supposed to do that?"

"I can get this prospect to fly in from Germany with his trainer. I've arranged for a court to be set up in a tennis bubble with full security, so nobody will see you working with him."

"Okay, Chris. Joanne and Stephanie can go sightseeing, and Billy and I will go work him out."

We showed up at this tennis bubble outside Rome. And I met this tall, blond German fellow, about 6'11", and his trainer. We worked out for forty-five minutes, and I ran Billy ragged as he helped us with drills. We did full-court ball-handling drills, full-court shooting drills, three-point shooting, one-on-one moves. Basically every offensive drill I could think of. After twenty-five minutes, we took a break and I turned to Billy.

"I'm looking at an athletic version of Larry Bird."

We were both stunned. He was executing 360 dunks, windmill dunks, and jump shots from another zip code. I couldn't believe this player's skill set. After another twenty minutes, I said, "Go shower and let's meet for lunch."

The player, as you may have already guessed, was Dirk Nowitzki. I called Chris Wallace and raved about him, thanking him for arranging the workout. Then I called Red Auerbach. "I just found the next Larry Bird. Incredible athlete. Incredible length, quickness, and shooting ability."

"He's that good?"

"Red, he's that good."

At lunch I told Dirk, "We will draft you with our first pick at number 10."

"How can we be sure you will do it?" asked his trainer.

"I'll put Red Auerbach on the phone, and if he gives you his word, that's as good as gold." So that's what happened. I was super pumped. I didn't breathe a word of our plans to anyone beyond the Celtics inner circle. Red, Chris, and my assistant coach, Jim O'Brien.

Dirk turned down an invitation to the 1998 draft and put out the word he was considering playing another year in Europe, and planned to come to the NBA the following year. We hoped this stance would turn off other teams.

Going into the draft, the Dallas Mavericks were the only team we were worried about. Back in March, Dirk, nineteen at the time, had played at the Nike Hoops Summit in San Antonio. His pickup team of international players faced off against a USA Basketball's Junior Team that featured future NBA stars Rashard Lewis and Al Harrington. Dirk dominated the game, scoring 33 points and hauling down 14 rebounds, as his team won 104–99. That performance put him on the radar of a few NBA teams. We'd heard that Dallas liked him.

But when the sixth pick was announced, the Dallas Mavericks picked Robert Traylor. I breathed a huge sigh of relief. We felt like we were home free to get Dirk. I started high-fiving people and telling my staff we were about to draft the next Larry Bird. In our mock draft, we thought Sacramento would take a guard with the seventh pick and Philly would follow suit with the eighth pick. The only real mystery to us was who the Bucks would pick before we could announce Dirk.

I should have known Dallas's Don Nelson had hatched a shrewd master plan. I have to give him credit, as much as it pains me. He approached this draft like a visionary grandmaster and outplayed the entire league.

Nellie, who had coached Milwaukee for eleven years, knew the Bucks wanted Traylor. So he got the Bucks to use their ninth pick—the pick right before us—to take Nowitzki and use their nineteenth pick for Pat Garrity. Then he traded Traylor for Nowitzki and Garrity.

But he still wasn't done. He traded Martin Müürsepp, Bubba Wells, and Pat Garrity and a 1999 first-round draft selection to Phoenix for Steve Nash. His vision was to pair Dirk with Nash—two future NBA MVPs. And he did it.

We were devastated. Absolutely crushed. And I was furious. But I didn't have any time to be angry. We had five minutes to get our act together and make our pick—and we were so confident about landing Dirk, we didn't have a plan B. Thankfully, Paul Pierce, who we had projected as the second or third pick of the first round, was still up on the board.

We loved Pierce. How and why he was still available remains one of the great mysteries in the history of the draft. One theory is that negative rumors started swirling about Paul. Just before the draft, according to a *Sports Illustrated* report, Denver Nuggets general manager Dan Issel called Paul a great scorer who "might be a little soft." There was also chatter that Paul didn't have great workouts. Finally, the second-round loss of Paul's top-seeded Kansas team to eighth-seeded Rhode Island in the NCAA Tourney might have impacted Paul's reputation in some people's eyes, although that would mean ignoring "The Truth" still scored 23 points.

We placed a call to Kansas coach Roy Williams right away and he told us Paul had no health problems whatsoever. That's all I needed to hear. We took him.

But I still wanted to know how Dirk slipped past us. I thought we had been so careful plotting to take Nowitzki. But not careful enough, I guess. I later was told that, somehow, Don Nelson Jr., the Mavericks overseas scout, got tipped off that I had worked out Dirk in Rome.

The amazing thing about this whole drama is that, years later, whenever I ask people who they would rather have drafted—Dirk Nowitzki or Paul Pierce—I get a split decision. They both won a championship, they were both perennial all-stars. Even now, I'm not sure who the better pick would be.

One last thing about that 1998 draft. It is a fascinating case study of the inexact science of making draft picks. So many of the first ten picks seem completely bizarre. But they must have all seemed like good ideas at the time—to someone!

1. LA Clippers—Michael Olowokandi
2. Vancouver—Mike Bibby
3. Denver—Raef LaFrentz
4. Toronto—Antawn Jamison

5. Golden State—Vince Carter

6. Dallas—Robert Traylor

7. Sacramento—Jason Williams

8. Philadelphia—Larry Hughes

9. Milwaukee—Dirk Nowitzki

10. Boston—Paul Pierce

Amazing, right? None of the first four picks came close to making the impact of high-flying Vince Carter. The same goes for the three other players selected before Dirk and Paul. I'm sure every GM had good reasons to make the picks they did. Believe me, millions of dollars are spent analyzing talent and potential at both the college recruiting level and the NBA draft, and yet the only sure thing is that there is no such thing as a sure thing.

BAD BOUNCES

As excited as we were to land Paul, any chance at creating a cohesive unit for my young Celtics team was shattered when the NBA owners voted to reopen the collective bargaining agreement with the Players Union in 1998, and then, when no deal was struck, decided to lock out the players and suspend all league business.

As team president, I sided with management. As a coach, however, this was a disaster. A lockout meant I couldn't make any trades or transactions of any kind. It also meant there were no team practices or supervised workouts. From a developmental standpoint, this was the worst possible scenario. I knew we were behind the eight ball in terms of talent. So player development for the young guys was crucial. Without that we would remain stagnant. We couldn't focus on improving our fitness, on drilling more, on honing skills and teamwork.

The lockout prevented any of this from happening for six months. For top-tier athletes, that is a daunting amount of time to go without supervision. It's rare for these guys to go a month without training in some way.

When the lockout finally ended, we had less than a month to get ready for a short fifty-game season. The abbreviated preseason was really detrimental to our young team. We started out playing .500 ball for the first fourteen games, but the competition improved at a faster rate than we did. Our inability to land a dominant center didn't help our cause, either.

The next year was rough, too. On September 25, 2000, Paul Pierce got stabbed eleven times. This was not a good way to start what was supposed to be our breakout year in Boston.

It happened in a nightspot called the Buzz Club in Boston's Theatre District. As Paul later testified in court, he had been talking to a few young women, which apparently bothered some men in attendance. Later that evening, in a pool room at the back of the club, he was stabbed in the face, neck, and back. One knife wound missed his heart by a centimeter. He could have died. Fortunately, Tony Battie was there with his brother and they rushed Paul to the hospital.

I visited him after he came out of surgery to repair a damaged lung. It was very scary.

After the attack, I got called in to try and keep the peace. There were concerns that a gang in town still had a hit on Paul, and I met with a community leader who had contact with the suspects. I said, "Look, let's put this to rest. Paul meant nothing by it. He's sorry it happened this way." I was just trying to make sure Paul was okay. That was my only thought process: keep him safe. In the end, Paul testified at the trial of two of his attackers. One assailant was convicted of the stabbing and sentenced to eight years in prison while a second got a year sentence for hitting and kicking Paul.

Unfortunately, the incident really hurt the team, too. Paul has always been a warrior, and he was in the lineup for the start of the season, but he really wasn't at the top of his game that year.

The next year was more of the same. We did not have a dominant center—and the team faltered from the start. Our fans were furious. I was exhausted and frustrated. For the first time in my head coaching career, I had failed to bring about a significant turnaround for my team. I was to blame for taking on too much responsibility and diluting my focus. I knew I needed to do something, to press reset for the team and myself. I stepped down and left the team in the capable hands of my assistant, Jim O'Brien, who did an incredible job getting the Celtics to the Eastern Conference Finals the following year.

THE SILVER LINING

It didn't turn out like I wanted on the basketball court, but I certainly cherish the memories of the people I met in the Celtic organization.

I loved having two basketball legends, Bob Cousy and Tom Heinsohn, around. As the Celtics' TV and radio personalities—along with Mike Gorman—they would travel with the team, as did another great guy, PR director Jeff Twiss. On the air or off it, Cooz and Tom would banter back and forth. It was good-natured even if some discussions got heated. When we were weighing trading Chauncey Billups, because we were frustrated by his lack of pure point guard skills, I asked Cooz if he thought Chauncey could grow into the job. The short answer was no. He didn't think Chauncey had a great feel for the position but thought he would still be a very good player down the road.

Heinsohn chimed in: "Be patient, Rick. I think he'll be an excellent point guard."

"Oh, you're going to take over my position?" Cooz fired back. "You don't trust my judgement?"

"Of course I trust your judgement. But the game is changing. I think he can do it."

They kept going at each other. I ended up just walking away laughing.

The interesting thing is they both were right. I should have had more patience and worked harder with Chauncey. He bounced from Toronto to Denver to Minnesota to Orlando before settling in with the Detroit Pistons and leading them to an NBA Championship over the Lakers in 2004.

Chauncey was traded multiple times because people couldn't figure out his ideal position. In today's NBA that wouldn't even come up for discussion. What is Russell Westbrook's position? What is Steph Curry's? They are combo players, capable of playing point guard or shooting guard. When Chauncey came into the league, everyone was still hung up on rigidly defined positions. The point guard was primarily the setup man, devoted to delivering the ball to shooters. Power forwards had to be big, strong Charles Oakley or Rick Mahorn types. Centers—"true centers" they are called these days—played near the basket and rarely shot from more than fifteen feet from the hoop. The small forward was the slasher. Today those roles are not as fixed; players aren't as pigeon-holed. Centers now shoot three-pointers, combo guards dominate the traditional point guard position, and power forwards—see the Knicks' Kristaps Porzingis—are versatile enough to slash to the hoop and shoot from the outside.

The other lesson I draw from Chauncey is that coaches need to have patience with players. Let's remember the pros have a twenty-four-second clock, which basically means you are running an eighteen-second offense. That's a significant time crunch compared to college ball, where you have more time to reverse the ball back and forth as you search for a high percentage shot. And don't forget, a college coach has more time—ideally four years—for player development.

Working with Red Auerbach was also a privilege. One night I

called Red and vented about my players not buying into the team aspect of the game. Red told me he'd noticed that during time-outs I spent a lot of time diagramming plays and giving instruction. He told me: "I liked to get my players involved. I would have them stand around me. I would say, 'Hey, Russ, what do you think we should run? Hey, Cooz, what do you think we should run?' to get their input and opinion."

The next game we were playing the Lakers and I decided to give Red's advice a shot. When my guys Walter McCarty, Antoine Walker, and the rest came to the bench, I said, "Hey guys, we need a basket. What do you think we should run?"

Dead silence.

I tried again: "What do you think is going to work here?"

Dead silence.

Finally, Antoine had enough. "How the fuck do we know? You're the coach. You get paid to make the plays. We get paid to execute!"

To his credit, Red roared when I told him this story. "Keep asking them," he said. "When they mature, they won't shut up!"

I was also privileged to get to know Bill Russell. Once, over lunch with Russ, I told him about my frustrations with the team—that my players were too focused on their personal statistics and thought about offense instead of defense. I believe this is a common problem in the NBA. When you are losing, players may focus on personal stats because they don't see their effort translating into wins and getting into the playoffs. So I asked Russ if he'd come in and talk about teamwork and Celtic pride.

He said he'd be happy to do it.

Russ can be a very shy, introverted person. So the fact he was coming in meant a lot to me, and I was really very interested in what he would say. Russ bleeds Celtic green like no one else, and nobody—not Michael Jordan, not LeBron James—has ever achieved more success on the court in the history of the game. Red once told me he would sometimes have to sit Russ during practice because he was so talented he would actually ruin practice. He'd block too many shots, score too many baskets, and keep the team from executing drills.

I was really hoping he'd bring that kind of intensity to inspire my guys.

I never dreamed he'd give a speech worthy of a Shakespeare soliloquy.

He started off straight from the heart: "I watch you guys all the time. The Celtics are my family. Win, I'm happy. Lose, I'm not. So I'm in your corner."

Then he began addressing the players in the locker room. But he never called them by their name. He just called each player by his uniform number.

He turned to Kenny Anderson. "Number Seven, I remember you from Seattle. Seven is not like Cousy. I used to outlet the ball to Cousy and the first thing he did was look up the court and try to advance the ball for an easy basket. Seven holds onto the ball all the way up the court and then tries to make a great pass. I think Seven holds onto the ball so long because he wants that assist. If he passes the ball early, he won't get that stat."

He turned to our center, Tony Battie. "Number Four, you are a lot like me. You like to block shots, but you always knock it out of bounds when you make your block. You need to know, it's still the other team's ball when that happens. Number Four, I would suggest you keep the ball in bounds so you can get possession of the basketball."

Then he turned to Paul Pierce. "Number Thirty-four, you are an amazing rookie. You remind me of Havlicek when he came in the league. But you have some skills over Havlicek. Because when you make a great steal or a great shot, you seem to know exactly where the cameras are located. Havlicek never had the ability to know where the cameras were. That is an amazing ability!"

"Number Fifty-two"—he was talking to Vitaly Potapenko now—"Where are you from?"

"I'm from the Ukraine."

"Do you think American statisticians are not going to record your rebound? Because you hold onto the ball so long, flailing your arms, you don't outlet the ball quickly enough to start a fast break."

Finally he turned to Antoine Walker. "Number Eight likes to shoot all the time. I know people like that. Number Eight is not changing. It's on you guys to make sure you get him to take good shots."

At this point it was pretty obvious he was poking at the players for focusing on stats instead of winning.

"I always looked at how I could help my teammates be better. That's the difference between team ego and individual ego. My ego was centered around my team's accomplishments, not my accomplishments. That's the difference. Right now, you all have individual ego and that is a problem to a team. You are just about numbers and stats. Seven, Four, Fifty-two, assists, points, rebounds, blocks. The only number I cared about was the final score.

"I won eleven world championships. I let my team down for the twelfth one because I got hurt. In college I won fifty-six straight games and two national championships. And in between, I won an Olympic gold medal.

"But then, I was never interested in stats.

"But I'm all about team and you're not."

It was a powerful speech that I will never forget. It crystallized the importance of reducing individual ego and developing a team ego. Bill's words made an immediate impact on our players—but only for a handful of games. Soon we reverted back to our old bad habits.

So I left the Celtics disappointed I had not gotten the team further along, but immensely grateful I got to work with so many people I truly admired. Today I look at the team and I'm thrilled to watch them orchestrate for an incredible young coach, Brad Stevens. I believe he is going to take them back to the promised land of Red Auerbach. No question.

6

MY NEW KENTUCKY HOME

Louisville bliss. Tremendous sorrow. A second national

championship. None of it can be stripped away. Ever.

▼

THE RETURN

I was still coaching at Boston when C.M. Newton called to tell me that
the new A.D. at Louisville, Tom Jurich, wanted to grab a cup of coffee
with me during my annual trip to the Kentucky Derby. We met at the
home of Louisville booster Harry Jones. My coaching pal Ralph
Willard, my guest at the Derby, was with me.

Tom said, "Denny Crum is probably going to step down and retire
in the next few years. And when that time arises, I'd like to sit down and
talk with you about coming to Louisville."

I said, "Tom, it's great to meet you. C.M. says you are going to do
great things. But since you are just getting to know this state, I want to
tell you one thing you can take to the bank: the Kentucky coach can
never coach at Louisville. It's not a workable situation."

Tom immediately told me I was wrong and that years had elapsed since I had gone to the Celtics. "You can come back. They still love you here."

"Tom, once you get to know this place, you'll understand."

At that point, a bird—a cardinal—landed on the back of a chair and Ralph and I exchanged looks. When we left, I said, "Ralph, did you see what I saw?"

"The cardinal that landed just as you were telling Tom you could never be a Louisville Cardinal? How could I miss it?"

We both laughed, not just at the appearance of the bird, but at the thought this A.D. could possibly think I would coach the University of Louisville, a team that I absolutely despised while I was at Kentucky.

A year later, Joanne and I were sitting in our Miami home and watching Denny Crum announce his resignation. The cameras went to Tom Jurich and he was asked, "Do you have a coach in mind?"

The normal response in this situation is, "I have a list of candidates and we'll be conducting interviews in the near future." But Tom said, "Yes, I have some people in mind, and the first person I'm going to contact is the ex-Kentucky coach, Rick Pitino."

Joanne and I almost fell off the couch.

A few days later, Tom came to town and spent a day with me. We went golfing, we had dinner. The next morning, he offered me the job.

Tom was obviously an energetic go-getter. He had made a name for himself running Colorado State University's athletic program. The fact that he was coming after me showed an audacious, creative streak that impressed the hell out of me. But I still felt Louisville landing Kentucky's former coach was an unthinkable move.

Joanne and I went back to our home in Boston. At this time, I was also in discussions to become the head coach of the University of Michigan. I just could not fathom the Louisville job. There are about 1.2 million people in and around the Louisville metropolitan area. It's safe to assume at least 300,000 of those people are University of Kentucky fans. I didn't want to deal with that.

After a number of conversations with Michigan A.D. William Martin, I began to lean toward the idea of becoming a Wolverine. But Joanne was not enamored with the idea of moving to Michigan. She'd never been to Ann Arbor, and it didn't help my cause that I had never been there, either. But I asked Michigan to send me a contract.

"I think you are making a big mistake," Joanne said.

"Why is that?"

"You don't know anyone there. You barely know the A.D. Meanwhile, we spent a lot of time with Tom, and C.M. loves him. Just because Kentucky plays Louisville for one game every two years doesn't me you shouldn't take the job. That's one day! You have so many friends there. Why wouldn't you go back to the place you called Camelot?!"

"There's just no way a Kentucky coach can go to Louisville! It's a big deal. We don't want to do that. We'll be miserable. You don't want to put yourself in that situation."

I used to use the phrase "I'd rather live one day a lion than a thousand as a lamb" a lot. I find it inspiring. But at that moment, it inspired my furious wife.

"I didn't know I'd married such a lamb," Joanne fumed. Then she hit me one more time with her logic: "So, you're not going to go back to a place where you have so many fond memories?"

I sat there in our living room and I thought about it, going over my concerns, weighing advantages and disadvantages. I had great trepidation about going to Louisville. Later on, I discovered many of my reservations about taking the job—many of them rooted in the rabid fanaticism of the fans and the intensity of the rivalry between the two schools—were entirely correct. But I decided going there was better for my family. The devil you know is better than the devil you don't know.

At around noon I called Martin, the Michigan A.D. But between noon and 1:30 p.m. he would play either squash or racquetball. So his assistant said, "Is it a matter of life or death?"

I said no and she transferred me to his voice mail. I left him a message thanking him for his efforts but saying I had had a change of heart and would be taking the Louisville job. It was months before we actually reconnected and I could apologize in person.

Not long after that, I called Tom Jurich and told him I was in.

He said, "Great. I want to have a press conference at 4:00 p.m. to make this announcement. I'll have a plane there to pick you up at 2:00 p.m."

"How are you going to do that? It's twelve thirty now."

Tom had already arranged for a Citation 10, an extremely fast plane, to pick me up in Boston.

I later found out Joanne had been talking to Tom that morning, and had been plotting to win me over. She told him, "You get the plane here, and I'll change his mind." Neither of them wanted to give me time to reconsider.

I found out the plane was owned by the CEO of Papa John's Pizza, John Schnatter, whose company was based in Louisville.

In the years to come, I would find out a lot more about John Schnatter, and I'll share some of that information in an upcoming chapter. For now, though, let me just say that knowing what I know today about him, including the fact that he would be instrumental in getting me fired, I would have jumped on a bus, taken a train, or walked rather than step on his plane.

The press conference at Louisville was a fanfare-filled event with bands playing and cheerleaders cheering. But as you might expect, the rest of the basketball-loving commonwealth of Kentucky was in a state of shock. For the Wildcat faithful—about 80 percent of the state—I had gone from a much-honored hero to an absolute villain. A Judas! I was now leading the 'Cats' most hated rival.

GETTING WITH THE PROGRAM

Louisville's once-great program was a wreck when I arrived. Talent was in short supply and the players' conditioning was awful. The team was coming off a 12-19 season. I knew I would need some players. So my first order of business was to meet the team.

Tom had warned me about my players. They were out of shape, lazy, underachievers. And even worse, they had taken to ripping their coach, Hall of Famer Denny Crum, with anonymous quotes. That had me extremely upset. Crum was an innovator and legend who deserved the utmost respect.

I realized from talking to Tom that the culture of the team was going to have to change big-time. The first thing I did was introduce myself and shake each player's hand. As I got to the fourth player, I said, "Hey, guys, are you going to tell me your names? Or do you think I actually know who your sorry asses are after you won only twelve games last year? Because if you do, you're mistaken. Why would I bother learning about a group of players that would knock a Hall of Fame coach, not stick together, and play under .500 ball?"

I wanted to shake up the team and put them on notice that things were about to change. I think I achieved that.

Then I set about evaluating each and every one of them. I learned very quickly that what Tom had told me was only partly true. They were much worse than he described. I couldn't believe Denny had managed to win twelve games with this group of athletes who were so out of shape.

They were surly, fundamentally poor, and physically unfit. There was really only one talented player on the team—Reece Gaines, a 6'6" guard who would later turn out to be a lottery pick.

One player, Ellis Myles from Compton, California, was forty pounds overweight. He was dogging it in the drills, so I stopped the workout and said, "Ellis, let me tell you, if you don't start putting out in these drills, you are either going to quit or you are going to be back on a plane to Compton very soon. So I would suggest that you get after it and show me what you have." We exchanged more words. But after that player-development meeting, Ellis worked for months to get his body in shape and became, pound for pound, one of the toughest players I've ever coached. He eventually led us to a Final Four.

Another player had major knee problems, and a shot like a corkscrew. A third couldn't understand English, as he was from another country, and didn't even really understand the game. I found out he had been recruited because the assistant coaches hoped his future draft pick brother would come to Louisville! There was a major problem with every single player. So I needed new ones. Fast.

NEW RECRUITS

Fortunately, the annual rite of summer for all college basketball coaches was coming up—the ABCD camp run by Sonny Vaccaro. As you will see later in the book, Sonny has had tremendous influence on both college and pro basketball. But for right now, just think of him as the charismatic ringmaster of basketball's biggest recruiting event. At this time, ABCD was the dominant basketball camp, having supplanted Garf's Five-Star Camp in terms of luring top talent. So a hundred or so of the best high school athletes were on hand, and so were hundreds of coaches looking to land their next star.

Sonny always had a sense of drama and theater. It didn't matter whether he was running a charity game, signing a major player to an endorsement contract, or running a clinic—he liked to make a big deal out of whatever he was doing. At ABCD he would find out what college a player was planning on attending and, around lunchtime, he'd announce the verbal commitment. He'd say something like, "Tommy Slamdunk, from Crossover, New Jersey, has just decided he will attend the University of North Carolina!"

When I arrived at his camp in Princeton, New Jersey, Sonny came over to talk to me. "This kid Francisco Garcia and his family remember you from the Knicks and he wants to play for you at Louisville."

I said, "Well, I've heard of him. Let me watch him play."

Francisco was really, really thin. He was 6'6" and weighed maybe 150 pounds soaking wet. But there was no question he had outstanding basketball skills.

After the game, Sonny asked what I thought about Francisco.

"Sonny, it's going to take a while to get some bulk on him. But I'm interested. Let me watch him one more time."

I was even more impressed after Francisco's afternoon performance. I thought we could build his body up and that he had the skills to become a great wing. I said, "Okay, Sonny. I like him a lot. If he wants to come, I'll take him."

Remember, my team back home not only had a poor attitude, but had bad skills, as well. So I was very excited to get someone other than Reece Gaines with a terrific skill set.

"Okay," Sonny said. "We'll announce he's coming."

I said, "Come on, Sonny, what are you talking about? He's never visited the campus. Nobody declares until they have a campus visit."

"He is."

The next day at lunch, Sonny made the announcement. "Francisco Garcia attends University of Louisville."

The whole thing happened again with Taquan Dean from Neptune, New Jersey. Taquan never visited campus. I did go to visit Taquan's guardians. But in one year, I got two players to commit without a campus visit—and I tried to convince both of them to come on Louisville's dime, but they had already made up their minds. That is unheard of these days. Of course, it helped that neither player was highly ranked at the time.

I'm sure the fact that I had been the Knicks coach was one reason both players wanted to work with me. But I think Sonny and other coaches may have tipped them off about my track record with player development. Taquan knew he had to learn to handle a basketball better. And Francisco knew he needed to build strength and that his game would benefit from our running, pressing style.

All my life I've been a dogged recruiter. In the old days back at Hawaii, Syracuse, and even during my Kentucky days, I would start by visiting the high school, meeting the coach, meeting the principal. And then I'd go on home visits and try to sell family members—parents, aunts and uncles, even grandparents—on my program. From there, I'd go watch the athlete play and arrange for him to visit our campus. And somewhere in April, he would decide on what school he was going to attend.

Fast-forward to today's recruiting. It's totally different. Now when you go recruiting, you probably only go into the home 5 percent of the time. You generally meet at the school, which is often where you'll first see the recruit's family members. Ironically, the high school coach will be there about 50 percent of time, but the player's AAU coach is almost always on hand.

It was really a relief to sign Francisco and Taquan without a lot of wear and tear. They were a year away from joining us in Louisville, but thanks to them, I felt my future at the school was in good shape. Looking back, I realize that in all my years recruiting, there have been very few times great players fell into my lap with minimal effort. Francisco and Taquan were pretty much the only two, until a kid named Brian Bowen popped up. We'll get to him in a few chapters.

That first year at Louisville proved to be the most difficult of the four times I took over a collegiate program. Turning around Boston

University, Providence, and Kentucky were cakewalks in comparison. At Louisville, transforming attitudes, instilling discipline, and developing skills were real challenges. And an unexpected tragedy made things that much harder.

THE BIGGEST LOSS

On September 11, 2001, I was walking down the steps at our practice facility in Louisville, on my way to begin a Detroit recruiting trip. My secretary called me. I could hear the urgency in her voice. "Come back. You have to see this."

"What is it?"

"Something happened to the Twin Towers."

I ran back into the building. My heart was racing as I watched TV reports. My brother-in-law Billy Minardi worked at the World Trade Center as a trader for Cantor Fitzgerald. I had no idea if he was in the building or if by some miracle he had gotten out.

Billy was my best friend and brother-in-law. He was killed in the Twin Towers attack. His death shattered the lives of his wife, Stephanie, and their three children, Willie, Robert, and Christine. It left me, my wife, and my kids reeling. No words can convey the devastation, emptiness, and anger we all felt over this senseless act. The attack had roiled America, shocked the world, created geopolitical tensions around the globe. People everywhere were traumatized by the sickening image of the Towers falling. But it is impossible to make an accounting of the heartbreak and damage suffered by Billy's immediate and extended family. As I've said many times, it has changed the way we think and the way we view the past and the future.

Joanne and I rushed to New York. We spent the first seven or eight days looking for answers, hoping to just have an iota of hope. There were false claims printed on the Internet saying Billy was alive. We were all waiting, just looking for answers to this horrifying event.

I was also trying to help my sister-in-law cope and plan for the future of her children. It was a difficult job. Eventually, Joanne and I convinced her to relocate to Louisville, to be a family near us and with us.

Once they were nearby, I started to think about what I could do that would keep my connection to Billy alive. I wanted to build a tribute to this man who had given me and my family so much love and joy. I wanted to do something that would honor his memory. It would be something that his greatest legacy—his kids—could see and be proud of.

I came up with the idea of building Billy Minardi Hall, a state-of-the-art dorm for the Louisville basketball team. I approached University of Louisville president James Ramsey to discuss the idea. He said he would look at the project, but there was one problem. "I can't do it, because then I'd have to do it for football, women's basketball, and baseball," he told me.

I made a counter proposal. "How about I raise the money, give you a $5 million building, and turn the keys over to you. You just give me a plot of land."

We had a deal. I went out and raised $5 million, about half from private donors I knew in the business community and half from Billy's friends back East. And in 2003, Minardi Hall was completed. The red-brick residential facility housed thirty-eight two-bedroom suites tailor-made for basketball players with queen-size beds and high showers. There was also a game room, theater room, and a kitchen for an on-site chef.

When it was done, I felt a great sense of accomplishment. I had helped build something that would last and that contributed to the community and the university I called home. And that would keep Billy's name and memory alive.

Billy Minardi Hall wasn't my first building project. Ten years earlier in Lexington, I met Father Ed Bradley. He was a huge UK fan who ran a soup kitchen out of his church basement at St. Stephen Cathedral in Owensboro, Kentucky. I invited him to say a pregame prayer for the team, and soon we became good friends. Father Bradley told me of his dream to establish a shelter for abused and neglected women and children. When he found an ideal space for the shelter, I helped him raise $125,000 by establishing a fund-raising golf tournament. He bought the building and honored Joanne and me by calling it the Daniel Pitino Shelter.

Inspired by Father Bradley, Joanne and I decided we would enhance the Daniel Pitino Foundation, which we had founded years earlier, and made a major donation to the shelter. When I'm asked to give speeches locally, I ask for donations to be made to the shelter and we still donate about $60,000 to it annually. We set up a foundation office in Lexington and have given over $8 million in Kentucky and elsewhere to children's charities and others in need.

Projects like Billy Minardi Hall, the shelter, and Daniel's foundation have helped cement Joanne and me to our communities. These buildings connected us to Kentucky, creating bonds that drew us closer to a place we had come to cherish—a place we called home.

A NEW EMPIRE

Somehow, we got through that first year.

The Louisville team began to right itself. We finished 19-13. The following season we made it to the NCAA Tournament. In my fourth year at Louisville, history repeated itself. We made it to the Final Four, just as my Kentucky team had done during my fourth year at Lexington. Juniors Francisco Garcia and Taquan Dean teamed up with my senior star, Larry O'Bannon, to lead us to the top spot in Conference USA.

Speaking of Larry O'Bannon, he was one of my favorite early U of L players. A local hero, Larry played for Louisville's Male High School and joined the team as a walk-on—although we found a scholarship for him pretty quickly. Over the next four years, he became a major force as an undersized forward. I will never forget his Senior-Night performance against nineteenth-ranked North Carolina–Charlotte. He lit up the opposition with 33 points. You can probably guess by now how much I like working with players individually. It's the key, in my opinion, to basketball success. Larry was another case of a player who really benefited from specially tailored drills to improve his game. It was gratifying and fulfilling to watch as he went from a walk-on freshman to having his name chanted by 19,000 adoring fans on Senior Night.

We got far deeper into the tournament than anyone expected—all the way to the Final Four. Unfortunately, in the semifinal, our big three scorers shot horrendously against Illinois and we got crushed on the boards. Credit Illinois, who lost the championship game to North Carolina. They defended well.

That year, Tom Jurich walked into my office and asked me to place a call to Michael Tranghese, the commissioner of the Big East. "I think we are going to have a shot at getting in the Big East," he said, clearly excited. "They have to get better football programs to survive. The whole country is going to divide up into major football networks, so the Big East needs better teams." Since I knew Mike from my days at Providence, when he was the assistant commissioner to Dave Gavitt, I picked up the phone and asked him what Louisville's chances were for joining the league and what we could do to improve our chances.

Mike downplayed any expansion, but said he would certainly be back in touch if things changed. Of course, Tom—who was very plugged into the college football universe—urged me to stay in contact with Mike. He was positive the Big East would be expanding, so I put in a call to Mike once every ten days.

At the time, Louisville was in Conference USA. The school had never been in a major athletic conference. Why is this important? Being part of a conference with better teams translates directly into more revenue for a school. Bigger conferences get more TV exposure and money. That exposure is also very valuable in and of itself. It is pure marketing that builds awareness and name recognition for a school.

In 2005, Tom's hunch came true. He was absolutely right about reaching out to Mike. We officially joined one of college basketball's most famous and lucrative conferences, along with the University of Cincinnati, Depaul, Loyola, Marquette, and South Florida. From a pure basketball standpoint, this was the first time in Louisville history that we were in a major conference with strong TV exposure, but the deal put all our school athletic programs in the limelight. In our immediate location, the biggest rival schools, Kentucky and Indiana, had always been in bigger conferences. Kentucky in the SEC and Indiana in the Big 10. Now we would be on more equal footing.

Cardinals basketball settled into a good rhythm. We honed our team's personality, building an identity that consisted of relentless pressing defense and fast-moving offenses that relied on penetration and three-point shooting.

We won the Big East in 2009, going 16-2. We also made annual March Madness appearances, but never advanced past the Elite Eight. It was frustrating. On one hand, we were a dominant force, always in the mix, and playing great, competitive hoops. On the other, we were always falling just a bit short.

Then, in 2011, things began to change. We had a great team, filled with unique players and people. Our 6'11" center was from Senegal— Gorgui Dieng. Chane Behanan was our burly freshman forward. We had two blue-chip McDonald's All-Americans in junior Peyton Siva and freshman Wayne Blackshear. Also at guard, we had New Jersey's Chris Smith, a transfer whose brother was NBA wingman J.R. Smith, and underrated New Yorker Russ Smith, who was starting to come into his own.

Russ was a major beneficiary of the lesson I learned from drafting Chauncey Billups while I was coaching the Celtics—be patient with player development. There were a number of cynics who wondered why we gave a scholarship to Russ, a high-scoring but wildly undisciplined New York City guard—so wild not one other Big East school actively recruited him. And I agreed. All evidence showed he would not rise to the U of L level, but there was something about him we loved. He played little as a freshman and wanted to transfer. Russ's dad called me and asked if his son would play the following year. I said, "He's going to have to change his game."

After that, Russ's dad told his son: "You are not transferring. You are going to listen to Rick."

I'm glad he did. When Russ arrived at U of L, there was no such thing as a bad shot in his mind. I didn't want to take away his confidence or creativity, but to echo what Bill Russell told the Celtics about Antoine Walker, we just had to make him take better shots. He needed to learn when to pass, when to stop dribbling and keep other players involved, and when, really, to shoot.

As a sophomore, Russ started getting some minutes. As a junior, he was an integral part of the team that won the Big East Tournament and made it to the Final Four. As a senior, he was a first-team college All-American, and helped us repeat in the Big East and win the National Championship. If I didn't learn my lesson with Chauncey Billups, Russ Smith would have been gone from my life as a freshman. Instead, he went from an unwanted gunner to an All-American to a huge star in China's professional league, where he once averaged 61 points a game.

THE CHAMPS

In the 2011–12 season we reeled off six Big East victories in a row at one point and then started losing with annoying frequency, finishing seventh in the league. But, just like that, we went on a tournament run, ultimately beating Cincinnati in a defensive battle to win the Big East tournament. And when March Madness started, the streak continued, as we beat Davidson, New Mexico, highly ranked Michigan State, and Florida.

That set us up for the Final Four semifinal against—who else?—the University of Kentucky. This was an incredible team with a trio of one-and-done recruits led by Anthony Davis, Michael Kidd-Gilchrist, and Marquis Teague. We lost 69–61 to a team with superior athleticism.

When we got home the next day, I addressed the team. "Guys, you just got a great taste of something very special. Now you should be hungry to get back to the Final Four and win the whole thing. The way to do that is to improve your skills over the summer. This is going to be a summer of patience, focus, and hard work, so that next year we cut the nets down."

And that was it. From day one, our focus was the championship. We lost Chris Smith, but added sixth man Luke Hancock, who was now eligible after transferring from George Mason the previous year—a move he made after Mason coach Jim Larranaga decided to go to the University of Miami.

I called Jim to get his take on Luke. He said, "If you want somebody to take the shot with five seconds left in the game, Luke's your man. If you want someone to make the right pass, Luke's your man. He's not going to guard for you, but offensively, he can do those things."

I was excited to have his firepower, and I wasn't worried about his defense. Louisville played total team D. We didn't rely on one person stopping another person. It was all about rotations, about knowing where the best places on the court are to trap. And that was perfect for Luke, because he was an ideal player for our complicated match-up zone and our team-based strategy meant we could disguise any weaknesses.

When the season started, Luke was coming off a torn labrum injury. It took him some time to work his shoulder back up to full strength. On his return, he shot atrociously—so badly that people starting razzing me about his shooting ability. But I knew he had a great stroke.

All our work paid off. We lost only five games the entire season, and four of those losses—to Duke, Georgetown, Syracuse, and Notre Dame—were by five points or fewer. Villanova was the only outlier; they beat us by nine.

The most painful loss was a truly epic five-overtime game to Notre Dame in South Bend. That was the game that Russ Smith frustrated the hell out of me. It was as if he went completely deaf. He didn't listen to me in regulation. And things got much worse after that.

In the first overtime, the score was tied with about fifteen seconds left and we had the ball. "Okay, Russ," I said during our timeout, "I'm going to make this easy for you. We are going to inbound the ball to you. The rest of the team is going to set up with all four guys on either the baseline or the perimeter. All you have to do is dribble back and forth at half court, stay away from your guy, and I'm going to count down with the clock. You are not to shoot until there are six seconds left on the clock. Not seven seconds, not eight seconds. At six seconds you go one-on-one, score, get fouled, and we win the game. Drive to the basket and get fouled. Got it?"

"Six seconds. I drive to the basket."

We inbounded the ball. Four guys went to the baseline. I counted down, shouting so Russ could hear me "...nine...eight...seven...." But Russ was oblivious. He barely got the ball over the half court line with 6 seconds left. With five seconds left, I start waving and screaming for him to get going, but he's still wasting time. Then finally, standing about ten feet beyond the college three-point line he picked up his dribble with three seconds left and jacked up a crazy shot.

I went ballistic. He came to the sideline and I asked if there was something wrong with him. I called the team doctor over to our huddle and pointed to Russ. "Doc, do you have any medicine for this young man? He needs help."

Everyone started laughing, but it wasn't funny. Russ had completely lost his mind. I was used to calling him "Russdiculous" because of his fantasy-based shot selection. But this was a whole new low. And when we finally lost in the fifth overtime, I was upset. The next day I made the team watch the film of the last part of regulation and the five overtimes. Russ was practically hiding under his chair. The team was still exhausted from the game, and watching all the mistakes was torture, so I wanted to end the meeting on a high note.

"Guys," I said, "we have to play sixteen games to win the Big East tournament and to win a championship. I want to go 16 and 0. We are going to win all our games for the rest of the season. Then we are going to win our second Big East Tournament. And when we win, we are not cutting down the nets. Leave 'em alone. We are not cutting down the nets until we win it all."

Sure enough, we went into the Garden and made it to the finals against Syracuse. We stunk up the court in the first half, letting Syracuse hit a bunch of long-range bombs and stifle us with their zone defense. We went into the break losing 35–22. Four minutes into the second half, we were down by sixteen and I changed our offensive alignment. We went to a 1-4 high, with two big men at the elbows and dunk artist Montrezl Harrell on the baseline. Gorgui would get the ball on the foul line and either look for the three-point shooters on the perimeter or pass to Montrezl for dunks on the baseline. Then our full-court press and conditioning kicked in. We forced a flurry of turnovers, and with

Peyton Siva orchestrating things, we scored an incredible 56 points in the second half to win 78–61. It was a tremendous team performance. But I was especially thrilled that Peyton won the tournament's most valuable player award, joining the great Patrick Ewing as the only players to win the honor twice.

President Clinton came into the locker room after the game and shook hands with everyone. He schmoozed with Gorgui about Senegal and seemed to know something about every single player. It was one of the most memorable postgames ever. Our PR guy, Kenny Klein, kept saying we had to go to the postgame press conference, but I said, "I'm not leaving until President Clinton leaves."

In the NCAA Tourney, we made it the Final Four. The semifinal game was against Wichita State, the best defensive team in the country, in my opinion. They were expertly coached and well prepared.

"If we are not the better defensive team tonight, we will not get to play for the championship," I warned my guys. "It's going to be very difficult to score against Wichita State. It's going to be a low-scoring game."

Sure enough, it was our lowest-scoring game of the tournament. We could not get Luke free for three-pointers the entire game. Gregg Marshall's players never left him alone, even when Peyton or Russ drove the lane. We were down twelve points with about twelve minutes left in the game when I decided to sub in Tim Henderson, a walk-on player. To put it politely, Tim did not have a great reputation as a shooter. So when Luke drove the lane, Wichita defenders left Tim open in the corner. Luke passed the rock and—boom—Tim drained a three-pointer. The next possession, Russ Smith went into the lane, passed to Tim in the same exact spot, and he knocked down another! Now the momentum had totally changed; the atmosphere was electrifying. We were back in the game. It was an amazing comeback; we won by four points and Tim earned a new nickname: Wichita.

Just days before the semifinal, I received two pieces of great news. I had been elected to the Naismith Memorial Basketball Hall of Fame and my eldest son, Richard—a former assistant for me at Louisville—had been hired by the University of Minnesota, becoming the youngest head coach in the Big Ten Conference. So going into our final against Michigan, it felt like I was on the greatest run of my life. People were telling me I was living the best week ever.

The Michigan team was impressive. They had five future NBA players—Tim Hardaway Jr., Trey Burke, Glenn Robinson, Nik Stauskas, and Mitch McGary. But they were a young team, and my Cardinals were veterans in comparison. I knew it would be the opposite of the Wichita State game—more of a high-flying shoot-out—and I felt we were up to the task.

We ended the first half a point down.

CBS TV reporter Jim Gray grabbed me for few words at the break. I have no idea what I said. But I remember he told me that Goldencents, a horse I owned a small percentage of, had just won the Santa Anita Derby and punched its ticket to the Kentucky Derby. This was more great news. But it certainly wasn't on my mind at the time.

We came back out, and Luke Hancock had a fairy-tale game, shooting five-for-five from three-point range. He scored 22 points, leading us to victory and winning Final Four Most Outstanding Player honors. I think the only person happier than Luke when he got his award was me—I remembered all the doubters who told me he couldn't shoot.

A reporter asked me if I had any celebrations planned, and I blabbed about how my tattoo-loving players used absolutely any event in the world as an excuse to get new ink. "If they say hello, they get a tattoo," I said. Then I recalled that the players had asked me: "If you win the national championship, Coach, are you getting a tattoo?" And I said, "Hell, yes, I'm getting a tattoo."

I did, too. On my left shoulder blade: a cardinal-red Louisville "L" with "2013 NCAA Champions" and our record: 35-5.

When we got back to Louisville, another reporter approached me. And instead of asking me a question, he presented me with a net. "Coach, this is from Madison Square Garden," he said. "You didn't cut down the net there, but I know how important the Big East and the Garden are to you, so I took it down as a present."

My second championship was totally different than the one with Kentucky. They were both incredibly gratifying. But we didn't face nearly as much pressure in Louisville as we did in Lexington. It certainly was a perfect week.

TWO NEW STARS

There are two Louisville players tearing up the NBA these days that everyone asks me about—Terry Rozier of the Boston Celtics and Donovan Mitchell of the Utah Jazz. How both of them landed with the Cardinals is an interesting story.

My son Richard spotted Terry. He told me there was a kid from Cleveland, Ohio, who fit our system perfectly. He was intense and athletic and quick, and he was ranked in the 70s among the top recruits in his class. I went to see Terry and was blown away. Richard was absolutely right.

There are a number of high school basketball ranking services—Scout, Rivals, and even ESPN has a recruiting database. They rank all the top high school players according to their own grading system. We read their lists, but obviously we make our own evaluations based on our needs and what we think of each player's potential. One of the key things is not just their skill level now, but their upside in the future. So a rating service might rank a player seventh in the nation, but we might rank him twenty-seventh if he doesn't fit into our needs. We also look for explosiveness in players, and although defense is a premium in our style, I'd rather recruit offense and teach defense.

According to our rankings, Terry was in the top thirty. And it just so happened that he was also a fan of a documentary about Sebastian Telfair called *Through the Fire*. Sebastian was a standout guard at Brooklyn's powerhouse Lincoln High, the same school where his cousin Stephon Marbury played. While there were rumblings Sebastian was going to go pro—something no point guards had done straight out of high school—he declared for Louisville in 2004.

One day I received a message to come see Sebastian at a high school playoff game. So I showed up and sat next to Jay-Z.

When I asked Jay why he was there, he said he came out to see one of Sebastian's last games.

So I said, "You can come to Louisville, too. You'll see him play a lot."

"I don't think so, Coach."

That's how I first found out Telfair decided to go straight to the NBA. But there's a little ironic touch involved in his decision. At the same time Telfair announced he would go pro, word broke that he had also signed an endorsement deal with Adidas that reportedly paid him a minimum of $1 million a year for six years. Coincidentally, Tiny Morton, who coached both Telfair's high school and AAU team, had also reportedly signed on as an Adidas consultant one year earlier. Obviously, this would not be the only Adidas recruiting headache I would experience.

At any rate, I was glad we had some connection to Sebastian, because Terry was impressed that Telfair was once Louisville-bound. That and the fact that we were probably the biggest school recruiting him helped close the deal. When he arrived, Terry had a new obsession. He worshipped Dwyane Wade. He walked like Dwyane. He talked like Dwyane, too. It's great to see him breaking out with the Celtics. He doesn't need to emulate anyone now.

One more thing about Sebastian. He had his struggles in the NBA. And I want to note that if a player has a deficiency in his game, going to college is good for really honing in on a weakness and improving. Sebastian didn't have a great jump shot, but he had everything else. Player development at the collegiate level could have helped that.

Donovan Mitchell is a case in point. He came to college with truly freakish athletic ability. He wasn't as highly ranked as Sebastian Telfair coming out of high school. Part of that had to do with the fact that he broke his wrist while playing high school baseball—shortstop Donovan crashed into his catcher while fielding a pop-up, and left his teammate with a broken jaw. Donovan's injury kept him out of AAU ball until his junior year. He was awesome his senior year, but his game needed some fine-tuning when it came to ball handling and getting more arc on his jump shot. Thanks to some very hard work to fulfill his potential, he left the University of Louisville a complete basketball player, with a great jumper and the ball on a leash.

My other son, Ryan, had initially tipped me off to Donovan. I'll always remember that moment.

"Dad," he said, "my friends are telling me there's a kid from Greenwich, Connecticut, who is a big-time player you need to check out."

"Ryan," I said. "I can assure you of one thing—there are no basketball players that live in Greenwich."

Ryan laughed. He knew Greenwich was an affluent suburb about an hour outside of New York City. It was a hotbed of future bankers, not ballers.

"Maybe if he plays lacrosse, we'll check him out," I joked.

"No, Dad. He goes to Brewster Academy. He's from Greenwich, but he doesn't play there. And his dad works for the New York Mets."

So I told my assistant, Kenny Johnson, to keep an eye on Donovan. And when we went to scout Under Armour games in South Carolina, we decided to watch him.

After five minutes, I turned to Kenny. "Who is recruiting this kid?"

"Indiana, Providence, and Villanova."

"We have to get on that list. I love his game."

I was completely blown away by Donovan's athleticism. I can remember an inbounds play with about two seconds before the end of the quarter. Donovan's teammate was inbounding the ball in front of the bench. He threw a high pass to the far side of the basket, and out of nowhere, two hands appeared at the top of the square. Donovan caught the ball and threw it down. The timing, the balance, and the leaping ability—the things that allowed him to execute this play—were just astounding.

During his campus visit, we took Donovan and his family out to dinner. During the meal, I could see Donovan and his mom having a conversation with their eyes, but I didn't know what it was about. Eventually, Donovan went to the restroom. A minute or two later, my cell phone started blowing up in my pocket. But I have a rule: I try to never take my phone out during a meal. Still, with Donovan gone from the table for a while and his secret signals with his mom, I started to get nervous.

Finally, I slipped my phone out and read my texts. All my kids were messaging me: "Congrats, Dad! You got Donovan."

"What are you talking about?" I texted back.

"He just announced on Twitter, he's coming to Louisville."

So now I knew what was going on. He had gone to the restroom to tweet his declaration.

When Donovan came back to the table, he said, "Coach, stand up."

"What's up?"

"I want to give you a hug. I'm a Louisville Cardinal."

Now he's a contender to become NBA rookie of the year.

I knew Donovan was going to be a great pro, but I did not know how quickly he would ascend. He was drafted by the perfect team—the

Jazz—and the perfect coach in Quin Snyder. Some coaches don't like playing rookies right away, and some teams have veterans who have more experience. It was a perfect fit—and that is what has to happen sometimes in order to become a rookie of the year candidate. If Utah had an established shooting guard like Jimmy Butler on the team, Donovan might have languished on the bench.

Fortunately for everyone—Donovan, Utah, fans, the NBA—that wasn't the case.

7

CARDINAL SINS

None of it makes any sense. Why would someone
who worked incredibly hard for me as a captain of our team,
dean's list student, and outstanding leader of men get involved
with something that would tear his life apart.

▼

FAST-FORWARD FROM THE 2013 championship to September 2015, and I was in Mexico City coaching the Puerto Rican national team at the International Basketball Federation's qualifying tournament for the Olympics. A number of people wondered if I had taken the job to land a future recruit. But that wasn't the case at all. The team was filled with older players. I had volunteered to coach because I've always loved Puerto Rico, I loved the idea of trying to get the team into the Olympics, and I was interested in learning about the international game. I had Louisville assistant coach Mike Balado with me, and while we were trying to regroup after an ugly first game against Brazil, my cell phone rang. Kenny Klein, the University of Louisville sports information director, was on the line.

I've had some tough phone calls in my life, agonizing and heartbreaking calls. But this was the strangest, most unlikely call I've ever received in my life. And one of the most disturbing.

Kenny told me a crisis was unfolding back in Kentucky. A woman named Katina Powell had written a book claiming Andre McGee—a former Cardinals guard who had spent four years with the team as a graduate assistant and director of basketball operations—had brought strippers onto campus to entertain and have sex with potential recruits.

I could not believe what I was hearing. Immediately, I called Kareem Richardson, who had been my assistant coach when Louisville won the NCAA Basketball Championship in 2013. Kareem had moved on to become the head coach of the University of Missouri at Kansas City, and he had hired Andre as an assistant.

"Kareem," I said, "get Andre on the phone. I think he's in big trouble."

"Why, what happened?" Kareem asked.

I told him that a woman had written a book accusing Andre of the sordid recruiting violations.

Kareem located Andre and conferenced him into our call.

I tried to maintain my cool. I said, "Andre, did you know a person named Katina Powell?"

"Yes, I fooled around with her a little bit."

"Where'd you meet her?"

"Well, she's a party planner, and I met her at a convention downtown."

"Did you bring girls to our dormitory?"

"Well, I brought girls in, but all they did was stay in the lobby and listen to music when the recruits came in."

"You sure? Because I just heard she's written a book. And apparently she's saying you arranged for stripper shows and paid for the girls to have sex with some of the recruits."

"No, Coach, I swear. I'm telling you: I did not do any of that."

I was beyond furious. I tore into Andre for even bringing girls on campus. Outsiders have no place in the dorms or in the recruitment process. But really, I was enraged just by the fact that Andre had admitted he knew the woman making these outrageous charges. To me, that suggested the stories this woman was spinning weren't fiction.

I finished ripping into him with a grim prediction: "If any of this turns out to be true, Andre, your career is over."

He hung up, but Kareem was still on the phone. "Do you believe Andre?" I asked.

"Yeah, Coach. I do. I don't know why he would lie."

With Kareem's endorsement haunting me, I started to feel guilty. I had blasted Andre because of some book I hadn't read, written by someone I'd never heard of. I wondered if I had been too harsh. Maybe this was a rush to judgment, something I would face firsthand in the near future, but I was also giving him an opportunity to possibly save himself.

I also thought about my relationship with Andre. I trusted him, believed in him. He had been the captain of the Cardinals team that went to the NCAA Elite Eight in 2008. When a pro career didn't work out, he earned a master's degree in physiology. I knew him to be a highly intelligent young man with two great parents, Jackie and Anthony, who I'd met years earlier while recruiting Andre at Canyon Springs High School outside Los Angeles.

Then I thought about his career path. He had seen other assistant coaches—Kevin Willard, who became head coach of Seton Hall, and Mick Cronin, who is now the head coach at Cincinnati—work for me and go on to prosper elsewhere. He knew he was moving up the ladder. I'd promoted him from a graduate assistant position to operations coach. He was aware that Jeff Van Gundy had held a similar graduate assistant position for me at Providence, and he must have known, when he was working at Louisville, that he was on the same path taken by thirty of my former assistants. My mantra to my staff was pretty simple: Listen, watch, learn, follow all compliance regulations, and work harder than anybody else. All he had to do was follow those rules, and he was on track to possibly become a head coach one day. He must have known that. Why would he do something so reckless as hiring strippers for recruits? When I looked at things that way, none of these allegations made any sense.

So I texted Andre the following:

I've had to endure much more difficult times in my life. If you are telling the truth, and money was not exchanged, it will pass. People are lying and the truth will come out. You made a mistake, tell the truth and your problems will become part of your past. I love you, son, and will stick by you if you tell the truth to the end.

The following day, I sent him another text.

'Dre, if you are telling the truth, you need to fight for your reputation. Not for Louisville, not for UMKC, but for the two most important people in your life, your parents.

When I returned from coaching in Mexico City, Kenny Klein took me through the highlights—or should I say lowlights—of the book.

The details were brutal. There were pictures. There were journal entries. Obviously, this was not what Andre told me on the phone.

According to the book and subsequent investigations, Katina Powell, the woman Andre McGee called a "party planner," was a self-described "escort queen" who provided prostitutes—including her own daughters—for McGee's on-campus parties. McGee was put in contact with her by a guy named Tink who ran a barbershop in downtown Louisville that was once called Cardinal Cutz. Powell's book claims that Tink contacted her and asked if she was interested in having her girls perform for some players on the Louisville campus. That first night, Andre met Katina and her girls at a side door at Minardi Hall, the team's residence, and led them into a two-bedroom suite. It was a routine that would be repeated numerous times.

Katina Powell's journals are excerpted in the book, and one entry reports that while women she brought to the campus stripped, Andre *"would find out which dancer each recruit and player wanted to have sex with. Then he would work a side-deal with me to negotiate the price. Usually $100–120 each... Andre paid me and I paid the girls on the spot. After the dancing, some of them went into other rooms with players."*

I called up Kareem again. "Tell Andre he better get a lawyer because he's got a major problem," I said. I even recommended a friend of mine, Scott Cox. That was my last semi-direct communication with Andre, who actually hired Cox. My only concern at this point was Andre McGee's welfare, as I could not believe what this woman was writing.

Although I haven't talked to Andre, I did reach out to Cox and ask him to have Andre release a statement. All I wanted was one sentence: *Nobody in the entire Louisville athletic department had anything to do with the events described in Katina Powell's book, nor did they have any knowledge of those events.* As far as I was concerned, Andre's silence— under the direction of his attorney—had hung the entire Louisville department out to dry. But Cox has refused to let Andre breathe a word about his activities to anyone, probably out of concern that the kinds of charges Andre might theoretically face—such as promoting prostitution, a Class D felony offense—have no statute of limitations.

If Cox's legal assessment is correct, and there is no statute of limitations for their actions, we will never know the truth of why any of this took place. I'm going to close my feelings with this statement: I know Andre McGee's parents very well. They taught him to do the right things, I taught him to do the right things. So there are many questions in my mind that definitely go unanswered regarding why this all took place.

Redemption for Andre seems a long way off. His actions were documented in Katina Powell's book and, if true, they were shocking and horrifying—not just on a recruiting-gone-wild level, but on a fundamental human level. As the guy who apparently paid and orchestrated all these parties, he showed contempt for his school, his team, his charges, and those women.

That said, the other central figure in *Breaking Cardinal Rules*, author Katina Powell, doesn't come off any better. Powell, who wrote the book with a journalist named Dick Cady, seems to want to portray herself as a shrewd survivor, proud she has figured out a way to get paid—by providing sex and strippers and pimping other women—and spend her days high on pot. There's never a moment of regret—not even when she writes that she brought her three daughters to campus to "entertain" prospects and players, or that her youngest daughters were fifteen and seventeen at the time of those first shows.

In one instance, she claims she arranged for her youngest daughter to sleep with highly recruited guard Antonio Blakeney—in town for an AAU tournament—while she slept with Blakeney's guardian at the Embassy Suites hotel in Louisville. (Blakeney, who ended up attending Louisiana State University before playing for the Chicago Bulls, issued a statement via his mother, according to the book, denying ever being at the hotel.)

In fact, this is what Powell had to say in defense of her tragic family business: "People may think that I expose my kids. But, shit, they enjoy themselves. They meet new people...for those who have a problem wit' this, kiss my ass."

In other words: don't judge.

But it's hard not to—although part of me thinks, on some level, those are the words of a person who has been victimized herself, and doesn't realize it.

At any rate, you can see why I was shocked and furious: Andre and Powell seemed to have endangered minors.

PARANOIA SETS IN

There was another reason I was horrified by what Andre and Powell had done, and it was completely personal.

119

The parties had been staged in Minardi Hall—the dorm I'd helped build to honor my best friend in the world. Anyone who knows me knows what Billy meant to me and how important it was to honor his name and his spirit.

So the very idea that Andre, who lived in Minardi Hall, would use this building for such vile, illegal activities turned my stomach. He had sullied the place I was most proud of in all of Louisville—and he knew, or should have known, how much it meant to me. It drove me out of my mind.

All day, every day, my head was flooded with thoughts about the scandal. That people must have known about Andre's actions, that Andre's recklessness was inexplicable. That dangerous, irresponsible parties could have destroyed young lives. That the strippers, the sex, and the money had contaminated Minardi Hall! I became overwhelmed and enraged as I tried to process what had happened and how it had happened.

And worse, I became totally paranoid.

I'm not exaggerating. I investigated every single detail, determined to find out the truth about how Andre McGee could have had so many wild parties and not have a single word leak out. Just like everyone else who heard about the situation, I was certain someone in our program must have known. There is absolutely no way he could have orchestrated this by himself with dead silence.

At Louisville, we monitored all our recruits' social media—it's a good way to learn what makes our recruits tick. That means my staff had seen the Facebook, Instagram, and Twitter accounts of everyone who had visited over the last four years. There was not one single mention of strippers or outrageous parties by any of the recruits that came in.

Think about that. Katina Powell claimed in her book that she had arranged about twenty-two shows on campus. While the NCAA later determined there were at least thirteen events, either way, that's still a considerable number of parties over four years. And not one word on social media. It seemed impossible.

I interviewed many of the managers that worked for us from 2010 to

2014. If they weren't in town, I got them on the phone. I would basically accuse them of a conspiracy of silence. "You lived in this dorm. You didn't come to me and tell me this was going on? You know how special that dorm is to me?" Not one single manager saw anything. No strippers. Nothing.

The next person to be grilled was Anthony Wright. Anthony is a terrific guy, a former All-American receiver for the University of Maine, who was in his third year as the team's director of academic services after spending seven years as our assistant director. He was responsible for making sure our players performed as well in the classroom as they did on court.

He was also Andre's best friend.

I called him into my office and asked what he knew about Andre's exploits. He looked me in the eye and said he was as shocked as I was.

"He never told me a thing," Anthony said.

I didn't believe him. "You guys were practically joined at the hip!" I railed. "He never mentioned anything?"

If I stopped to think about it, Anthony was about ten years older than Andre. And given his intense dedication to mentoring our players and making sure our team has a collective grade-point average of around 3.0—something he's excelled at—it was entirely possible that Andre knew Anthony would have busted him immediately for putting kids at risk.

Still, I asked Anthony every conceivable question about Andre's behavior that might have raised a red flag. Did Andre ever mention Katina? Did he ever mention strippers? Did he ever flash extra cash? Did he ever mention this barbershop guy, Tink? I asked Anthony where he was during *this* recruit's visit and *that* recruit's visit. I was trying to flush him out. It didn't seem possible Andre would keep this from his close friend. In the end, though, Anthony never waivered—not even when I got into his face, which is something I'll always regret.

When Anthony left, my level of distrust was peaking. I zeroed in on my assistant coaches, calling them into my office, one by one. Each of them swore up and down that they had no idea what Andre was up to. I couldn't imagine they didn't know anything about what was going on. They were in that dormitory constantly, spoke with Andre multiple times a day, and were around the recruits nonstop each visit. But all of them stuck to their story: They knew nothing of wrongdoing and would have stopped it immediately if they knew. I became so paranoid at one point that I wanted my assistant, Mike Balado, to take a lie detector test because I felt no one was telling the truth. And Mike was one of my favorite assistants. I was thrilled when he landed the head coaching job at Arkansas State.

I went to the head of security at Minardi Hall, a man who'd worked there for six years, and I grilled him. He said he hadn't seen a single thing.

"Come on! There were multiple parties," I said. "How could you *not* see anything?"

"Well, these women coming in, they probably looked like college students," he said. "They don't look any different from anyone else."

I couldn't challenge him there. Katina Powell wrote in her book that she instructed her girls not to dress up until it was time for them to dress down. But I had video cameras checked, looking for these women. We turned up nothing.

Then I talked to my nephews. One of Billy's kids and two other nephews had resided in the dorm while working as team managers. One of them had even lived on the same floor with Andre McGee.

They all said the same thing: "Uncle Rick, if we saw anything that was wrong, we would have come to you right away. The name on this dormitory means everything to us, and we would never allow anything like this to ever happen here."

Finally, here were people I had to believe. They were family. They were as invested in Louisville and Minardi Hall as I was. They lived on the premises and they still didn't see anything. For the first time, my paranoia began ease up.

So I started to accept that these late-night parties were done on the deep down-low. They appeared to be criminal enterprises. And criminals usually try not to call attention to themselves (except, apparently, when they want to sell some books). And even though there was still a big part of me that was skeptical that Andre could have done all this in secret and on his own, another part of me began to think it might be true.

The last people I called into my office were ex-players. Six members of that championship team swear they never saw anything that would raise their eyebrows. Even most-outsanding-player Luke Hancock said over and over to me that he lived in that dorm for his entire time as a Louisville Cardinal and never saw anything.

After a two-week period, Louisville's compliance officers advised me to stop interviewing people and stop trying to conduct my own investigation. They warned me that I might be interfering with the university's own investigation, or worse, the ensuing NCAA investigation.

I toned down my behavior and began to come to grips with the reality of the situation: The Louisville basketball program was in big trouble. We had all loved Andre and he'd never showed any signs of being reckless or shirking his responsibilities as a player. He was a model student and leader. Needless to say, everyone in the athletic department was shocked and disappointed.

THE ROAD NOT TAKEN

When the news broke about Katina Powell's forthcoming book, Louisville's athletic director, Tom Jurich, circled the administration's wagons. The school hired Chuck Smrt, a seventeen-year veteran of the NCAA's compliance enforcement division, as a consultant to guide us through the crisis. Smrt had previously coordinated the major infractions process at the NCAA, so the theory was that his relationships and experience would help us put a strategy in place to best navigate the approaching NCAA investigation and, it was hoped, mitigate any future penalties and sanctions.

Tom, Smrt, and Leslie Chambers Strohm, the university's general counsel, led a meeting to discuss our game plan with other top administrators. A highly regarded crisis management expert with a background in law and criminal investigations came to listen in as an unofficial advisor. This investigator sat quietly as the group talked about administrative issues and academic concerns and, mostly, what the school should do to telegraph to the NCAA that it was taking the charges extremely seriously.

After about thirty minutes, the investigator asked if he could interject.

"You are not talking about this the right way," he said. "This is criminal behavior that went on, folks."

"You don't understand," Smrt said. "The NCAA won't look lightly on this."

After the meeting, the investigator scoffed to me privately. "The NCAA is like a little-league operation. As far as law enforcement goes, they're no different than the Knights of Columbus." But to the room he said, "Guys, listen: we're talking about *breaking the law*."

"How do you know that?" Smrt asked.

"Based on the details in this book, these people are criminals. These people conspired to come on to your campus to make money. They criminally trespassed onto your campus to engage in prostitution and may have had underaged girls involved in sex acts, which gets you into human trafficking territory. And you guys are worrying about the NCAA?"

Everybody sat there stunned.

In just a few minutes, the investigator laid out a plan to stop the book from surfacing. He suggested going to court in Indianapolis, where the publisher of the book was located, and requesting a temporary restraining order to allow the university to read the book and corroborate whether the claims in the book were valid or were injurious.

"This book apparently talks about sex with minors—the author's own daughters and underage recruits," the investigator said. "You have to get this in front of a judge to protect these kids. Every judge in America would allow a motion or issue a restraining order. They'd say, 'Get these people in here. I want to know why they are writing a book admitting to endangering underage kids.'"

He added that a case involving minors would also automatically be sealed to protect the victims. "Stop the book, investigate it, silence it."

Smrt and the others kicked around his idea. It was very aggressive. But it made a lot of sense to me. The University of Louisville was the victim here—it appeared that a woman had come on campus, acted as a pimp, and was now about to profit from her enterprise by writing a book. By discussing how to appease the NCAA and possibly self-administer sanctions, it seemed as if we were taking responsibility for someone else's crime.

In 2010, the University of North Carolina at Chapel Hill became embroiled in an academic fraud scandal. The crisis involved athletes being advised to take no-show, no-work classes, including a reported 185 courses that never actually held classes and only required a final paper.

Although the initial charges were tied to the UNC football team, one report found that at least five players on Roy Williams's 2005 NCAA Championship winning basketball team took three no-stress classes each.

UNC fought the charges tooth and nail, wracking up millions of dollars in legal fees to defend the school. They challenged the NCAA evidence every step of the way, insisting the classes were offered to— and benefited—*all* students at the university, not just athletes. And guess what? In 2017, the NCAA finally agreed that there had been no violation of its academic rules.

UNC had launched an aggressive defense. But there was no smoking gun in their case. There was no book alleging sordid on-campus sexcapades. So the challenges facing Louisville were much more daunting.

Maybe that difference in severity was why president Ramsey, Smrt, Strohm—who had been general counsel at scandal-plagued UNC— were wary of the investigator's aggressive tactics. They seemed to think working with the NCAA, which was Smrt's stock-in-trade, would soften the blows in the future.

In the end, all parties took their options to the school president, and the decision was made to administer self-imposed sanctions. That decision ignored the unofficial investigator's suggestions. Looking back on it, his ideas were the right way to attack the problem.

It was a tough pill to swallow. We were the eleventh-ranked team in the country at the time, but we put ourselves on voluntary probation— meaning we pulled out of the 2016 ACC and March Madness tournaments. We also limited the number of scholarships we gave out and cut back on the number of days coaches would go out recruiting.

I went along with the sanctions. I considered myself a soldier in the Louisville army. Yes, we were guilty—of having a rogue employee on our staff. And I was guilty of making a bad hire, of trusting someone I had worked with for years. After three decades of instructing, delegating, managing, and, yes, trusting my staff, I got burned. Badly. Self-punishment seemed like the correct move at the time, but in the end, after the NCAA hit us even harder, it was a mistake to take those early sanctions. I would not advise any school to ever voluntarily penalize themselves because they hope the NCAA will be lenient in the future. In my view, this rarely, if ever, happens.

By now I knew that 99 percent of my team was innocent of willfully breaking any rules. And my feeling is that you should fight when you are innocent—and we were innocent of knowing anything about what was going on in that dormitory. In this regard, I think Jurich's investigator was 100 percent correct. He felt Louisville was the victim here, and a woman came on campus to commit crimes and enrich herself. With the clarity of twenty-twenty hindsight, that's the case we should have presented to the NCAA.

Instead, we ignored the investigator's suggestions and his final prediction: trying to cuddle up to the NCAA was going to get us hammered.

FOLLOWING THE MONEY

The investigations soon started in earnest. Chuck Smrt interviewed all our players.

Beforehand, I held a meeting and urged my players to stick to the truth. "If any of you know anything, make sure you tell the NCAA the gospel truth," I said. "Do not lie; do not deceive anyone."

While I made this speech, I was looking at my team captain, Mangok Mathiang. At this point I knew that a photo of Mangok—standing shirtless between Katina Powell and one of her daughters—appeared in the book with a caption saying he had stopped by one of their parties "but didn't have sex."

"Do any of you guys know anything about these stripper parties?" I asked. I didn't think any of the other players were at any of the parties, but I was hoping that Mangok would say something.

Instead, another player raised his hand, and said, "Yes, Coach. I know something."

I was shocked. "How do you know? You weren't here at this time."

"I was a recruit," he said. "I came in and Andre McGee had me go to a strip party and asked if I wanted to be with any of the girls."

I immediately let Tom Jurich, the school president and compliance, know we had a witness to Andre's crass parties. And I told the young man I was proud of him for telling the truth. Compliance reported the player to the NCAA and they suspended him for a week. He was soon reinstated after he did some community service.

While the NCAA began digging in earnest, the Louisville media was conducting its own probes. They reported, for instance, that Katina Powell denied her daughters were underage while working the on-campus stripper shows. The denial came after Commonwealth Attorney Thomas Wine, who serves as an elected prosecutor in the Louisville area, told reporters he was consulting with University of Louisville Police and the Metro Police Crimes Against Children Unit regarding the possible criminal violations revealed in the book, which he said caused "grave concern." No charges have been filed against Powell, but there does seem to be a contradiction somewhere. Was she lying in her book about her daughters' ages or lying to the press?

And was she lying about anything else? Some of the best reporting on this issue was done by a journalist named Eric Crawford. (Full disclosure: Eric co-wrote a book with me, a best seller about maximizing every minute of your life, *The One-Day Contract*. Unfortunately, this hasn't stopped Eric from maximizing his life by raking me over the coals at times.)

To his credit, Eric tried to do what the NCAA would do when it comes to investigating recruiting violations—those deadly sins the organization calls "impermissible inducements" for recruits and "extra benefits" when they involve matriculating student-athletes. Since the NCAA attempts to put dollar values on these benefits and inducements when handing out penalties, Eric decided to see how much money Andre actually spent on his stripper parties. (Speaking of benefits, the NCAA allows schools to pay for "reasonable entertainment expenses" while hosting recruits during official visits. Obviously, furnishing strippers and paying prostitutes don't qualify as reasonable. But if Andre McGee had bought a recruit a video game or a $500 front-row-seat ticket to a Kendrick Lamar concert or paid for a haircut—all those actions would likely have been deemed "inducements" by the NCAA.)

To determine Andre's actual expenditures, Eric investigated the claims Powell made in her book about the money she made.

Breaking Cardinal Rules claims "more than $10,000 cash changed hands to Katina for supplying the women"—not counting the single dollar bills McGee was said to have provided recruits to throw at the dancers as tip money or the "side-deal" money for sex.

But Eric added up the numbers listed on a page reprinted from Katina Powell's journal. The ledger listed nineteen on-campus events and added up to $5,820.

So instead of the $10,000 Powell claimed to have earned, she barely made half that—assuming Andre didn't suddenly start tripling his payouts for the final three shows.

A year later, when the NCAA issued its own violation report, Crawford's numbers were largely confirmed. NCAA investigators determined that at least thirteen events occurred on campus and concluded that McGee had spent at least $5,400 to make them happen. Based on the numbers in the NCAA findings, Eric estimated Andre had ponied up $2,760 for the strip shows, $1,700 for sex acts, and $940 in cash that was given to players and recruits.

The money issue is important. When the news of the scandal first broke, one of the story lines was: Where did Andre get the money for this? Who paid for it? The implication in those questions, of course, was that someone other than Andre was funding these X-rated affairs. And, maybe, just maybe, they were Cardinal boosters or even the coaching staff.

And in a world where some strippers do rake in thousands of dollars a night, it would be easy for casual observers to assume Andre's parties were big-money affairs. In fact, ESPN's *Outside the Lines* quoted a source close to the NCAA saying: "If this guy's spending $2,000 to $3,000 on a recruiting weekend, where's this money coming from?"

Actually, Andre McGee tells Katina Powell exactly where the money came from, according to her book. "McGee always liked to say that the ATM was his best friend," she writes. As for spending thousands of dollars a night, the NCAA's numbers suggest McGee's flesh fests cost, on average, about $400 a night. Which means that Andre, who Powell said sometimes needed extra time to pay her, could afford to cover the cost for the events himself. It might have been tough when he was a graduate assistant, but not when he started making $105,000 as the director of operations. Put me down as a doubting Thomas with everything she has to say about Andre in this regard.

THE MOTIVE MYSTERY

As far as I know, Andre McGee has still not breathed a word to anyone regarding his activities at Louisville. The last I heard, he was driving an Uber outside Kansas City. But I haven't stopped thinking about him or trying to understand what drove him to do what he did.

And I'm not alone. I can't begin to calculate the number of hours all the people tied to the case have wondered what compelled Andre to engage in this behavior. From his friends and assistant coaches to his former teammates, nobody can figure out why Andre did what he did.

Andre's job didn't really involve recruiting—and even if it did, a low-rent strip show or sexual favor wasn't going to win a recruit. It didn't help the visit—some players told investigators the shows embarrassed them. It could only get Andre into trouble, hurt his future, and bring down the program.

I got some insight, strangely enough, on election day 2015, when I went to vote. A woman who was working at the booths recognized me and pulled me aside to tell me she wanted to talk about Katina Powell. She told me she lived across the street from Powell and had known her for years. According to her, Katina lied about all the money she earned.

I listened and thanked her. She told me she had even shared her information with Chuck Smrt.

Then I asked, "Tell me, because it's been driving me crazy for months, why would Andre do any of this?"

"You don't know?" she said in disbelief.

"Absolutely not," I said.

"He came into the 'hood, and to all these girls, he was a really big deal. They treated him like he was LeBron James. He was a big man again. Not on campus but in the 'hood."

I think that's the key here. His ego was inflated. He wanted to live large. Like so many college basketball standouts, Andre wasn't able to make it as a pro in Europe. I guess he simply wasn't good enough. It is a difficult transition to go from collegiate big shot to a regular citizen. And when his fan, Tink the barber, suggested stripper shows, Andre probably felt he was back in the big time. A player.

Why do people make mistakes? Why do we hurt the people in our lives we love the most? It's a very simple answer. It's the word that ruins most leaders: ego. In a spiritual sense, it's edging God out of your life; from the standpoint of character, it's edging greatness out. You think you're bigger than you are and you do things that are wrong. And you know it's wrong, but you do it anyway.

Why would Andre McGee, who was moving up the college coaching ladder, risk it all for a few stupid, dangerous parties? Ego. That's the only answer I can come up with.

I asked John F. Murray, an expert on clinical and sports psychology, what he thought might have driven Andre to do the things described in Powell's book.

"Obviously, you have a significant level of narcissism," said Murray, the former team psychologist for Sydney Greene's squads at Florida Atlantic University. "There's a competitiveness and the recruiting advantage if you have available sex for the recruits. And I imagine the sex was a lure for him, too."

But Murray, who has not treated Andre, says the ring-leader attitude is "all part of the narcissistic constellation. He seems to have thought he was bulletproof and felt he was never going to get caught. He also didn't have any empathy for the women or the other people who were being affected by his actions.

"Combine sex with narcissism, competitiveness, and a kind of stupidity—that he thinks he's not going to face any consequences—and you have a perfect storm."

Unfortunately, Andre's perfect storm set off plenty of aftershocks. Over the next two years, the scandal he initiated haunted our program, our school, and our community.

I didn't realize it at the time, but Andre's narcissistic ego trip helped set in motion a flood of even more bizarre and sinister actions. And these events—like Louisville's strippergate—were totally unimaginable, too.

8

CLOSED COURT

How the NCAA's Committee on Infractions practices justice.

Or doesn't.

▼

ON APRIL 26, 2016, I met with four members of the NCAA Enforcement division on the University of Louisville campus in the company of my attorney, Scott Tompsett. The go-to lawyer for coaches facing NCAA infractions and/or compliance issues, Scott has handled dozens of cases involving the enforcement investigators. As a result of those cases, Scott was extremely cynical of the tactics used by the enforcement staff. He warned me not to get upset with them, and predicted they would be very antagonistic. So I was ready to do battle.

As it turned out, the enforcement officers were generally respectful and professional and I have a great deal of respect for them. They have an extremely difficult job.

But my inquisitors had no evidence I knew about Andre McGee's stripper events because none existed. As I just explained, I had no clue. No one they interviewed said I was complicit in any way. Additionally, they had no evidence that any other employee in my program knew about Andre's antics either. There are probably multiple reasons for that—starting with the fact that Andre knew I would have fired him the moment I learned of a single compliance infraction and ending with the fact that his "events" reportedly involved potentially criminal acts like prostitution and underage sex.

Given there was no evidence of any wrongdoing on my part anywhere—except for actually hiring him—the investigators began asking questions about my management of Andre. That seemed fair enough. Andre reported to me. I had recruited him, coached him, hired him, and managed him. It seemed fair to ask about our professional relationship, why I had hired him, how we interacted and communicated, and what his responsibilities were.

But then they started asking question after question after question about recruiting visits. I couldn't figure out what they were getting at. It seemed like a fishing expedition to find fault with my interactions with the visiting high school players—as if something I said during a Sunday breakfast with a recruit and his family might be construed as a violation. It was very strange. But I understand it now. They were prospecting to find a violation.

But let me back up a bit and talk about a typical recruiting weekend.

On what the NCAA calls an "official" visit, families generally arrive on campus sometime on Friday afternoon and spend the next 48 hours in and around campus. The assistant coach who has spent the most time recruiting the young athlete will escort the family to a team practice and tour the basketball facilities. Before they check into their hotel, we will meet briefly to discuss the practice they watched and how their son would fit into our program. I answer questions and try to get them to relax and get to know what I'm about as a person. After our guests freshen up, I'd meet them at their hotel with the assistant coach, and we'd head out to dinner.

Dinner will include the prospect, his family or guardians, a student host (generally a player from our team), an assistant coach, and me. After dessert, the prospect and the host will head out to join other team members for the rest of the evening while the parents will sit and talk with me and the assistant coach.

The next day will be jam-packed with a campus tour, meetings with professors, administrators, strength coaches, and academic advisors. Our guests will watch some form of a basketball workout and head to a football event or other activity on campus.

Student-athletes, by the way, can make up to five official visits starting on January 1 of their junior year. Schools foot the bill for all official trips, plus pay for transit, food, and lodging for two of the athlete's guardians, as well as reasonable entertainment costs. A recruit can make as many unofficial visits as he wants—but the school can't pay for related expenses for those trips. Things can get murky with unofficial visits. This is where you'll find that shoe companies, AAU teams, and even agents are providing perks for players and their families. Flights, hotels, and meals are quite expensive. Oftentimes AAU coaches will join the visit. Guess who pays their tab? Usually the team of the AAU coach. And guess who pays the AAU team? The shoe company that sponsors the team. So unofficial visits are a big form of cheating and circumventing rules by providing student-athletes with what are essentially freebies. In some instances, students, family, and friends get to visit campuses, but the university, as well as the NCAA, have no idea who is footing the bill. We can ask who is paying for their visit, but a recruit may find the question insulting. And even if they provide an answer, there's no way to verify it.

But back to the official visits. The coaches will spend most of their time with the parents. We want our entire team to spend as much time with the prospect as possible. That's because when the visit is over, we ask the players for feedback on the prospect. We trust their insight. On quite a few occasions, we would step away from recruiting a prospect because players on our team said to move in a different direction. Sunday morning is checkout time. We generally gather for a two-hour breakfast and discuss what they learned during their visit, any issues they have, and how their son would fit into our team.

We ask the recruits questions, too. What did they do last night? What players did they get to know? What do they think of the campus? What are they interested in studying? What are their goals for personal development? We also take questions and try to leave a lasting impression. We want them to know Louisville is a program that is committed to player development, team building, and athletic and academic excellence.

This is where it got sticky with the enforcement staff. They kept going back to the questions I asked specific recruits on their visits. And really, what they wanted to know was whether or not I asked recruits pointed questions about what they had done the previous night.

My response was we asked kids to tell us what they did and if they had a good time.

A typical response would be, "We chilled and played a video game." Or, "We went to a party." Or, "We played pool and ping-pong and just hung out in Minardi Hall with the guys."

These answers were no different than the ones I got from my own teenage children when I asked them how they spent their weekend evening out.

But the enforcement officers wanted to know if I had asked pointed questions.

"Do you specifically ask the prospects, 'What did you do last night in the dorm?'" I was asked.

"Sometimes I will say, 'Did you have fun last night?' 'Did you go to a party?' 'Did you stay in?' But generally, more often than not, I'll ask the host, 'What did you do last night?'"

I should have added that I've been recruiting for nearly thirty years, and I've never thought of giving a recruit the third degree. It doesn't seem like a great way to get commitments.

They asked me about a number of players who made official visits to Louisville. Time and again, they'd say that someone reported "a strip-tease was provided to" player X, or "it was arranged for a woman to provide" player Z "with sex."

Then they would say: "Know anything about that?"

I was sickened by these reports. But I always answered no.

Again, they kept pushing. Did I press recruits for details?

Obviously, I knew why the enforcement investigators were pressuring me—because there was a scandal going on. But in three decades of recruiting, I never thought a staff member would run stripper parties. So I wasn't going to ask any recruits, "Did you see any strippers or ladies of the night?"

The investigators went back to asking about Andre. Was he responsible for recruiting? Did I know his friends? A ton of questions. I remember thinking that the investigators were fishing for evidence to prove that I ran some kind of loose recruiting program.

Nothing could have been further from the truth. I taught Andre McGee—as well as all the other assistant coaches—to live by the rules. He knew the rules. Our compliance department taught him the dos and don'ts of recruiting. We had daily meetings. We gave him the same handouts and forms we gave everyone else. We urged him to call our compliance team if he had any questions about anything. But we couldn't be in the dorm with him at two in the morning. If someone wants to break the law or cheat, they can do it, and try to hide and cover it up, which he did.

They asked if I monitored him and the rest of the staff.

"We meet at six forty-five to seven every morning during the season," I said at one point. "And we go over every single thing that we need to go over, including the roles of what we're doing."

The enforcement officers' questions came back to haunt me six months later, on October 17, 2016. That's when the NCAA filed a notice of allegations containing the following paragraph:

It is alleged that from at least December 2010 through April 2014, Rick Pitino (Pitino), head men's basketball coach, violated NCAA head coach responsibility legislation....Specifically, Pitino did not demonstrate that he monitored Andre McGee (McGee), then men's basketball program assistant (2010–11 and 2011–12 academic years) and director of basketball operations (2012–13 academic year through April 2014), in that he failed to frequently spot-check the program to uncover potential or existing compliance problems, including actively looking for and evaluating red flags, asking pointed questions and regularly soliciting honest feedback to determine if monitoring systems were functioning properly regarding McGee's activities and interactions with then men's basketball prospective and current student-athletes visiting and attending the institution.

Evidently, the investigators' questions about my supposed lack of specific questions and "monitoring" were designed to hit me with an infraction.

But the charges made no sense. They made no mention of specific red flags that I had missed. How could I evaluate a red flag if nobody had spotted one?

My staff monitored social media. We had dorm security. We had compliance meetings. We continually reiterated the importance of following the letter of the law.

As I readily admit, *I made a mistake hiring Andre McGee.* That was my fault. But I'm not sure what red flags I should have actively been looking for. Should all head coaches run spot-checks at 2:00 a.m. on Saturday nights? How about 4:00 a.m.?

And then there's my favorite failure: Not "regularly soliciting honest feedback." Is that opposed to me soliciting "dishonest feedback"? Did I ask for people to lie to me? Really?

In essence, the investigators decided to blame me for not knowing about a covert, potentially illegal operation that had been actively hidden from my entire staff. And for good measure, they also blamed me for failing to assume the worst about my staff—as if any management expert would advocate that—and for failing to identify "red flags" without offering a single example of what I should have spotted.

These ridiculous charges were an attack on my character and my career, and as such, they made national news. I started to prepare my defense. Scott Tompsett sent a letter to Nate Leffler, the Associate Director of Enforcement, asking for the details of the allegation against me:

Nate,

I hope you're well.

I'm writing to ask for clarification of the allegation that Coach Pitino failed to monitor Andre McGee. Specifically, it would help Coach Pitino and me to respond to the allegation if you would tell us:

1. Specifically what spot-checks the staff believes Coach Pitino should have been doing to uncover existing or potential compliance problems;

2. Specifically what red flags the staff believes existed, but that Coach Pitino failed to look for and evaluate;

3. Specifically what pointed questions Coach Pitino should have been asking and of whom; and;

4. Specifically how Coach Pitino should have been soliciting honest feedback to determine if monitoring systems were functioning properly.

Answers to these questions will help Coach Pitino respond fully to the staff's allegation and make sure that the COI has complete information to adjudicate the allegation.

Also, if there are key interviews the staff intends to use to support its allegation, we would appreciate you identifying those interviews to us.

We appreciate your continuing cooperation.

Scott

We never got any enumeration of the supposed red flags. We did get a response noting they had received our document.

The NCAA Committee on Infractions does not make it easy to refute charges against you. Yes, they give you ninety days to respond. But when it comes to showing you the interviews and "evidence" they've amassed, they make it very difficult—providing a link to "read-only" documents. You can't print them out. You can't cut and paste. You can only have one document open at a time, which makes any cross-referencing research very onerous. The agreement they make you sign before you get the link says taking a screenshot or photograph of a document on your computer is forbidden, too.

At any rate, Scott spent two months poring over thousands of pages of interviews and taking detailed notes of the vast amount of testimony that portrayed me as a detail-oriented control freak who consistently met with staff and urged them to follow compliance rules to the letter of the law. Again and again, my staff and team and many recruits exonerated me of any wrongdoing or knowledge of Andre McGee's transgressions.

In the end, Scott put together a sixty-eight-page response to the single charge against me. I think it is a document of concision, logic, and accuracy. Part of me wants to publish it as a stand-alone book.

Here are some highlights. This one addresses the absurdity of the "red-flag" charge.

The enforcement staff has not identified one single red flag that put Pitino on notice of McGee's illicit activities. The staff also has willfully refused to inform Pitino and his counsel of specifically what the staff believes Pitino should have done differently. That is because there is nothing that Pitino reasonably could have done to either prevent the violations or to uncover the violations.

Here, he addresses the NCAA's own guidelines with regard to coaches monitoring their staff:

The COI has stated that head coaches who set a proper tone of compliance and monitor cannot be charged with failing to monitor a staff member who secretively violates the rules.

He digs up this supporting quote from the guidelines:

"If the head coach sets a proper tone of compliance and monitors the activities of all assistant coaches in the sport, the head coach cannot be charged with the secretive activities of an assistant bent on violating NCAA rules."

And here Scott exposes how the NCAA Enforcement's findings against me fly in the face of logic.

Dozens of witnesses told the NCAA investigators that not only did Pitino not know about McGee's illicit activities, but also that he could not have known about them. The illicit activities were deliberately kept secret and out of view. The people who were trained and paid to watch the dorm while Pitino was sleeping did not know about the strip shows.

Full-time residents of the dorm—including one who lived across the hall from McGee—did not know about the strip shows. Friends of McGee did not know about his illicit activities.

Security guards, with security cameras and professional security guard training to detect security issues, had no idea that McGee was bringing strippers in to the dorm.

A full-time RA did not know about the strip shows. The RA's boss described him "as extremely ethical and very black and white, and if anything was warranted or deserving to be in an Incident Report format, he would have absolutely written one, and he knows that that's the expectation. He was trained very well and he goes to training every single year."

Yet according to the enforcement staff, Pitino should have known.

Later, we had a pre-hearing phone call with the enforcement team to go over any issues before we met with the NCAA Infractions Committee. During the call, Scott did most of the talking. Here's how he remembers it:

"I kept pushing them to address the red-flag issue. I said, 'Look, your allegation implies there were red flags. Will you please tell us what those red flags were?'

"There was silence on the other end of the line. Then Nate Leffler said something to the effect of, 'Scott, we're not necessarily saying there were any red flags. We're just saying Coach wasn't looking for them.'

"I was shocked. I said, 'So you're accusing him of a level-one violation for not looking for something that you admit never even existed in the first place.'"

A COMMITTEE FIASCO

On the morning of Thursday, April 20, 2017, I walked into the ballroom at the Westin Hotel in Cincinnati. For the first time in my thirty-year career as a college basketball coach, I was about to attend an NCAA hearing.

More than eighteen months had passed since I had first learned about Andre McGee's inexplicable antics. And now, finally, the NCAA had convened a panel of current and former college administrators, coaches, academics, and attorneys to weigh the charges filed by the NCAA investigators, ask questions of the principal players involved, and hear any rebuttals regarding the alleged violations.

The ballroom was set up with chairs and tables arranged in a U formation. In the center sat the panel members of the Committee on Infractions—the people who would decide our fate. Next to them, and directly opposite from our Louisville contingent, were the NCAA investigators who had grilled me repeatedly on "pointed questions." They had also interviewed scores of people, including my staff, to determine who, if anyone, knew Andre McGee hired strippers and prostitutes to entertain recruits and members of the Louisville basketball team.

As for the Louisville contingent on hand that morning, acting University of Louisville president Greg Postel was there. So was Elaine Wise, our Faculty Athletics Representative who is also an English professor and chairperson of Louisville's Humanities division. Tom Jurich and Kenny Klein were there, of course, along with assistant athletic director, Kevin Miller. Lastly, there were Louisville's two chief strategists, school legal counsel Leslie Chambers Strohm and Chuck Smrt.

Going into this meeting, I was really concerned with our lack of preparation in knowing who we were dealing with. We were about to attend the most important meeting in the history of Louisville's athletics department—a meeting that would not only decide our future but also had the ability to reach into our past and essentially try to rewrite history. That's what the NCAA Infractions Committee frequently does—retroactively change the results of seasons past, overturning victories and vacating championships.

To prepare for a game, my staff and I would spend countless hours discussing every possible way to achieve victory. We'd dive into analytics, we'd watch video, we'd study opposition tendencies, we'd weigh strategies. We'd even look at the calls made by the officials who are refereeing the game.

At Louisville, I attended one preparatory meeting in advance of our NCAA hearing with the Committee on Infractions. During this powwow, I asked for a detailed background on each committee member. I wanted to know their political views, what their likes and dislikes were. Basically, I thought we needed a detailed scouting report, just as I would expect from my staff if we were playing Duke. After all, this was bigger than any game.

But I never got any information beyond my own attorney, Scott, providing me with bios of the committee members. Going into the meeting, it felt like we were in the dark, as if we were about to play against a team from another country no one had ever scouted.

And never mind basketball metaphors. Think about anyone going to trial: they would want to know all about the judge, the opposing lawyer, the witnesses, and even the jury—everyone! We didn't have any of that kind of intelligence.

To say this aspect was frustrating would be a mild understatement.

Instead, we united around our rebuttal strategy: remind the committee that we had taken voluntary sanctions, that we had cooperated fully with investigators, that Andre McGee's actions were the work of one rogue employee who acted in secret, and that there was no hint of any wrongdoing according to dozens and dozens of witnesses with ties to the Louisville basketball program.

At 8:30 a.m., the meeting started. We exchanged pleasantries and got down to business.

The committee read all the charges—allegations, per the initial complaint, that McGee "acted unethically when he committed serious violations by arranging striptease dances and sex acts for prospects, student-athletes, and others, and did not cooperate with the investigation." They also detailed the charge against me—that I "did not monitor the activities" of Andre.

For Louisville, Chuck Smrt took the lead and gave his opening remarks. It was a strong defense of our program's compliance efforts with regard to NCAA guidelines.

The acting president Postel gave an eloquent defense of me, saying I couldn't have known about these wrongdoings and citing my well-documented history as a strict disciplinarian. He was followed by Elaine Wise, who delivered an outstanding, heartfelt speech about our values as an athletic department. Tom Jurich spoke about how more than a hundred people were interviewed about these incidents—and not one person had even suggested our coaches had knowledge of Andre's illicit parties.

Then it was my turn. I tried to explain once again that there were no red flags. I requested the committee ask the enforcement staff precisely what red flags they were talking about. Scott also pressed the issue. But we got nowhere. The committee did not address the enforcement officers as I had requested. And not once in the entire meeting were any red flags described.

I also told them that when I hired Andre, it was because I knew him as a hardworking ex-captain on my basketball team and a dean's list student. He showed no signs of any reckless behavior. I thought he was an exemplary young man based on my previous experience with him. I had never seen a single misstep on his part that would indicate he would ever dream of, much less carry out, the things he was found to have done.

Then it was time for questions. They were more or less what I expected. I tried to convey my pride in our program and our record of success. I mentioned my track record with developing assistant coaches and how many of them had gone on to achieve great things. One committee member who had been quiet all morning, a guy named William Bock III, who works as the General Counsel for the US Anti-Doping Agency, asked questions I found extremely odd. I don't have access to the transcript—the NCAA Infractions Committee keeps it under lock and key—but here's how Scott and I remember it.

"Did you ever ask Andre McGee if he watched pornography?"

"No."

Scott tried to interject and ask what possible reason there would be to ask such a question. But he was told to yield to Bock. The questions continued.

"Did you ever discuss strip clubs with Andre McGee?"

"No."

"Did you ever look at Andre McGee's computer?"

"Why would I do that?"

Bock seemed upset by my answer. "I'll ask you a second time: Did you look at Andre McGee's computer?"

I repeated my response. I couldn't believe what this guy was asking me—especially since he was a lawyer. Andre McGee's computer was his own private property. I had never inspected a staff member's computer in my entire career. Who does that?

Now my inquisitor got indignant. He said, "I'll ask a third time, did you look at McGee's computer?"

So one more time I replied, "Why would I do that?!"

"To look for pornography and gambling sites."

"No, I did not."

We broke for lunch. Scott told the Louisville contingent that he was shocked by the committee's relative silence. He said it was very common for the committee to ask the enforcement staff to clarify their findings. That morning the committee hadn't asked a single question from the investigators. He felt their minds were already made up.

Chuck urged us not to get distracted and to stick to our defense. As a former head of the enforcement staff, he was highly cognizant of how the committee worked.

I mentioned that I could not believe I was asked about whether I would sneak onto my assistant's computer.

That's when Lesley Strong, Louisville's legal counsel, chimed in. She said accessing another person's computer without permission is a felony in the state of Kentucky.

Now I was really in shock.

I wondered why Lesley didn't interrupt him and explain that. It felt like she had left me in a lurch. I was so upset, I got up and left the table.

On my way back to the hearing, I saw Bock in the hallway and had an exchange with him. I didn't like how he'd challenged me for not looking at Andre's computer, which would have been a felony in the state of Kentucky. And if anything bad were on that computer, there's no way Andre would give me permission to look.

I got a little heated.

Kenny Klein, aware there were photographers around, convinced me to go inside. I did get some satisfaction out of my interaction with Bock, though. He didn't say another word for the rest of the hearing.

The afternoon dragged on. It was made longer because now we all noticed the committee continued to accept the allegations and not ask one question of the enforcement officers.

Scott described the whole thing as surreal. Especially when, finally responding to our contention that the enforcement team had not found or noted a single red flag that would have tipped us off to Andre McGee's behavior, the chairwomen of the Infractions Committee weighed in, saying she thought the enforcement staff was really just telling us, "Look, this is your campus. It's your dorm. It's up to you to tell us what the red flags are."

"I made it clear that I disagreed with her," recalled Scott. "The enforcement division had the burden of proof, not us. It was nonsensical."

In the end, I wanted to be hopeful, but on some level the entire eleven-hour hearing felt like a useless formality—an excruciating, day-long charade on the part of the Committee on Infractions who were pretending this was some kind of legitimate due process when it was really a whitewash. It was hard to ignore a sinking feeling. The Committee on Infractions had a long track record of adding to self-administered penalties, not reducing them.

I prepared myself for the worst.

Two months later, the NCAA Committee on Infractions issued its report. They clobbered us. Our voluntary sanctions—the strategy pushed for by Smrt—added up to nothing. The committee piled on, vacating our 2013 NCAA men's basketball championship, 2012 Final Four appearance, two Big East championships, and an American Athletic Conference championship. The committee also ordered the U of L to return the money it made from the NCAA Tournament revenue sharing agreement from 2010 to 2015. Andre McGee was banned for ten years from working for an NCAA institution. The team was hit with four years of probation.

And me? As punishment for "failing to monitor" Andre McGee, I was suspended for the first five games of the 2017–18 season.

It was a paltry sentence. This is where the media and anyone familiar with NCAA rulings should have understood that the Committee on Infractions was essentially admitting I knew nothing about what Andre McGee was doing. If there was a shred of evidence or even a suggestion that I was somehow complicit in the allegations against Andre McGee, the committee would have had me drawn and quartered. Just prior to this decision, some other Hall of Fame coaches were hit with nine-game suspensions after facing charges for failure to monitor staff. In comparison, I got a hard slap on the wrist.

That said, I decided to do everything possible to win an appeal. It was still a false charge. Andre McGee was taught and monitored no differently than any other assistant I've ever had.

Louisville immediately announced plans to appeal the decision. I wondered if our appeal would contain some new information that broke on May 25, 2017, while the NCAA was still finalizing its ruling: a Louisville grand jury had decided there wasn't enough evidence for charges of prostitution and unlawful transactions with a minor against Katina Powell and Andre McGee.

In other words, the two people at the center of the scandal wouldn't be found guilty. They wouldn't even stand trial.

But Louisville?

Throw the book at 'em!

9

THE SNEAKER ATTACK

How shoe company money changed recruiting forever.

The good, the bad, the ugly.

▼

SOMEWHERE, CHUCK TAYLOR must be spinning in his grave.

For the record, I have been paid millions of dollars by Converse, Nike, and Adidas, but when I think about the power that billion-dollar sneaker companies now wield over college basketball recruiting—spending hundreds of millions of dollars to influence high school athletes' college choices and funding entire travel leagues where coaches sometimes steer players to certain universities in return for sponsorship money, and where agents and their runners lurk in the shadows, hoping to make piles of cash off a future NBA star—my head spins, too.

As a kid growing up in New York City and on Long Island, the most popular basketball shoe around was the Converse All-Star, also known as the Chuck Taylor, in honor of a gentleman named Charles Hollis "Chuck" Taylor. At the time, I had no idea who Chuck Taylor was. But I've learned more about him over the years. He was a born in 1901 and grew up in Columbus, Indiana. He played hoops briefly for the Akron

Firestones, a semipro team sponsored by the Ohio Tire Company. He went to work as a salesman for the Converse shoe company in 1922. Chuck played for the company's All-Star team, conducted countless basketball clinics as part of his job, and privately lobbied his bosses to make better sneakers. His passion was rewarded in 1932 when Converse created an ankle patch emblazoned with a star for its high-top All Star canvas sneaker bearing the words "Chuck Taylor All Star." For decades to come, the remodeled kicks were pretty much the world's go-to basketball shoes.

Converse and Chuck Taylor All Stars are still around. The venerable footwear firm was purchased by Nike in 2003 for $305 million—a sum that might shock any old-school shoe salesman. More stunning than that sale price, however, was the fact that Nike, which had only been in business for five years when Chuck passed away in 1969, was valued at $10.5 billion when it purchased Converse. Fifteen years later, in 2018, it was worth $119 billion.

That makes Nike the world's leading sneaker and sports apparel brand. Adidas, the number-two player in the basketball shoe business, had a market capitalization of $41 billion in 2018. And new kid on the block Under Armour was worth $9.75 billion. Not bad for a company launched in 1996 out of the basement in the home of its founder's grandmother.

Meanwhile, Puma, which has been a big player outfitting the soccer world and has a $9 billion market cap, just hired rap mogul Jay-Z as the creative director of the company's newly relaunched basketball division. The German-based company also made a splash signing the top two 2018 NBA draft picks, Deandre Ayton and Marvin Bagley III, to endorsement deals. It will be interesting to see what other roads Puma will take with regard to marketing strategies, including sponsorships and grassroots basketball.

Another reason Mr. Taylor might be rotating in his final resting place is that Under Armour agreed to pay UCLA $280 million over fifteen years to ensure the school's sports teams use Under Armour sneakers and apparel. That 2016 deal is, at the time of this writing, the most lucrative sponsorship ever for a college sports program. It pays the school $9 million annually in cash, another $1 million a year in marketing funds, provides an "annual product allowance" that ranges from $6.5 million to $8.5 million a year. And none of these numbers count performance bonuses for the various university teams winning conference championships or making it into postseason play. While the deal requires Under Armour to outfit all UCLA teams, you can bet that having the school's beloved basketball team decked out in the company's gear is viewed as the primary prize—a living, breathing, dunking advertisement to help sell basketball sneakers, the biggest sales drivers in the athletic shoe industry, generating an estimated $6 billion in the US alone. Yes, the constant roadwork of America's joggers means running shoes are the biggest-selling athletic footwear. But the price of those shoes is no match for the basketball sneakers branded with names like Jordan, LeBron, Kyrie, Kobe, and Curry that retail between $120 and $200. Football cleats, by contrast, don't come close to having the same mass appeal or, generally speaking, cost.

There have been many other astounding payouts in college sports, where basketball is a key driver. The University of Texas signed a $250 million deal with Nike for fifteen years. Adidas wrapped up the University of Kansas, paying out $191 million over fourteen years. The University of Michigan is getting $173.8 million in exchange for wearing Nike's Swoosh for fifteen years. Meanwhile, the University of Louisville inked a ten-year deal with Adidas for $160 million. Let me do that math for you: every year we were slated to get $16 million in cash, uniforms, sneakers, and warm-up suits. Even if Adidas accounted for the physical goods they provided at list price, the bulk of the deal still provided *millions* in cash to the university.

Collectively, the six schools with the top sneaker and apparel deals in the US stand to reap about $100 million per year in sponsorships. There are approximately 350 Division 1 men's basketball teams. It is difficult to determine precisely how much revenue the remaining 344 teams will receive annually from their schools' individual sponsorship deals. But in 2016, a minimum of sixty-five schools earned more than one million dollars annually from various sneaker deals with Nike, Adidas, or Under Armour. Those sixty-five schools generated over $200 million in annual funds—more than a *quarter* of the annual $797 million payment the NCAA receives from its $10.8 billion, fourteen-year agreement with CBS Sports and Turner Broadcasting for TV rights to the Division I Men's Basketball Championship. That TV payment, by the way, provides the bulk of the NCAA's operating budget; the organization has no claim to the popular televised bowl games that end the collegiate football season.

Of the remaining 285 D-1 schools, dozens more—particularly schools in high-profile conferences—are getting significant sneaker sponsorship cash. So it seems reasonable to assume the shoe companies are spending between $300–$500 million annually to lock in relationships with these schools.

To understand the landscape and big-money relationships and recruiting forces at work in college basketball, it may be helpful to think of college basketball as a pyramid. At the bottom of the pyramid are three companies: Nike, Adidas, and Under Armour. Above this sneaker trinity is grassroots basketball—frequently referred to as AAU basketball, the so-called "amateur" leagues of high school hoopsters that are funded by the three sneaker companies—and the coaches and lurking agents that surround these AAU teams. A sneaker company will spend millions of dollars at the grassroots level to identify potential stars and drive those players to the next level of the pyramid, the colleges and coaches who also have deals in place.

Now picture companies at the bottom of the pyramid pumping millions and millions of dollars upward, pushing the biggest schoolboy stars out of grassroots teams and into college, then out of college and into the top of the pyramid, the NBA, where finally, superstardom awaits and along with it…individual sneaker deals!

All that money has saturated the game of basketball for one reason: *shoe companies' insatiable quest for sales and market share.* That quest has defined the game's current power structure and changed the way college teams recruit players. It has increased pressure on the players and the coaches at the high school, AAU, and college levels. It has also introduced layers of potential corruption—as sports agents and their runners scramble for ways to connect with players and their families and win the players' future business.

Before we delve deeper into how all these things are connected, let me add that I have a personal interest in this subject. The prevalence of sneaker money in college basketball and a scandal involving sneaker money payouts to the families of recruits has been used as an excuse to fire me from a job that I poured my heart and soul into for sixteen years at Louisville. This is not to say the shoe business bears the full brunt of all that has happened to me. Not at all. As we'll see, there were plenty of other factors that led to my departure from Louisville, including some of my own bad decisions. But before we get to them, it is helpful to explore how college basketball has evolved to the point where sneaker money has complicated recruitment and laced up, if you will, everyone in the game—from players and their families, to coaches, to the universities themselves.

FROM PLIMSOLLS TO PUMAS

The sneaker evolved from an English invention: the plimsoll, a shoe made of a rubber sole and canvas upper, developed by the Liverpool Rubber Company in 1875. The shoe was a hit and became fashionable footwear for leisure activities. When, exactly, the plimsoll morphed into "sneaker" is anyone's guess. The *Oxford English Dictionary* indicates the "sneaker," as footwear, first appeared in print between 1911 and 1917. Here in the US, the Converse Rubber Shoe company, which was founded in 1908, unveiled a high-top model called the "No-Skid." In 1932, as I mentioned, the Chuck Taylor All Star was born, and from there, the development of sneakers—shoes designed in part to help athletes move quickly—slowed down considerably.

There were a few innovations over the next few decades. In 1949, Keds introduced PRO-Keds Royal Flashes, a new shoe designed for the basketball court. And four years later, the legendary George Mikan and the Minneapolis Lakers were all outfitted with Keds. But the NBA wasn't the multibillion-dollar enterprise it is today. And the league's biggest stars—Mikan, Wilt Chamberlain, Bob Cousy, and Bill Russell—were, in retrospect, marketing ball boys compared to the magnetic, brand-building giants Michael Jordan and LeBron James became.

In the 1970s, basketball kicks finally got sharper and more high-tech. Adidas launched the Superstar, Nike had the Blazer, and a company called Pony offered the Topstar. Suede and leather sneakers became fashionable. But the biggest change of all came from German sneaker maker and longtime Adidas-rival Puma,* which introduced the Puma Clyde in 1973. Named after New York Knicks all-star guard and notorious clotheshorse Walt "Clyde" Frazier, the Puma Clyde became one of the most popular basketball sneakers of the decade. And the secret of its success—naming a high quality, chic shoe in honor of one of the game's most stylish players, and having him wear the shoe on the court—was a revolutionary move. It may seem completely obvious now that this kind of endorsement could move mountains of sneakers. But, for whatever reason, nobody had done it with a basketball player since, well, Chuck Taylor.

One last thing about this elegant, revolutionary sneaker with the signature curved stripe that flows on the side of each shoe: It is still around and may be about to grow in popularity. Puma reunited with Clyde Frazier in 2018, signing the smooth-talking septuagenarian to a lifetime marketing agreement.

MARKETING MANIA

While Clyde Frazier unwittingly became the basketball shoe's second patron saint, a more low-profile operator, John "Sonny" Vaccaro, was getting ready to completely shake up the industry. A former schoolteacher from the Pittsburgh area, Vaccaro was an avid high school basketball fan and coach when, in 1965, he began organizing an annual all-star game featuring the best high school basketball players in the country. The game, the Dapper Dan Roundball Classic, was named

---

* Adidas and Puma were founded by two German brothers, Adolph and Rudy Dassler. A family feud led the siblings to end their shared enterprise, Dassler Brothers Sports Shoe Company, and form separate, bitterly competitive firms.

after a long-running Pittsburgh charity that got the proceeds from the event—after Vaccaro paid himself $5,000.

College coaches and recruiters quickly flocked to the tournament in the hopes of evaluating and identifying potential talent. But the tourney didn't just raise the profiles of top schoolboys, it also raised Vaccaro's visibility. He began another gig, one level up, guiding college players to a certain sports agent, but found his heart wasn't in it. He moved to Las Vegas, where he admits he did little more than gamble. In 1978, after three years of placing bets, Vaccaro decided a change was in order and offered his services to Nike, a running-shoe company looking to enter the basketball market. Vaccaro met Nike CEO Phil Knight and presented him with an idea.

"I told Phil that I could probably get all the major college teams in the country [to wear Nike shoes]," Vaccaro recalled to the *Washington Post*. "He looked at me very startled and said, 'How's that?' I said, 'Well, pay the coaches. Hire them as consultants.'"

The pitch was a slam dunk as far as Knight was concerned. He hired Vaccaro, who quickly set about putting the idea to work, striking private contract deals with college coaches and becoming—sorry, Chuck Taylor, Clyde, and Phil Knight—the world's greatest sneaker salesman. Most college hoops coaches were making five-figure salaries at this time, and a few thousand dollars of perfectly legal supplemental income was very welcome. The terms of the deals involved Nike paying coaches and providing each coach's team with free sneakers. In return for the payment and the swag, the coach's team would wear Nike sneakers during games.

On the face of it, these deals were win-win-win agreements. Colleges no longer had to pay for shoes, so an expense was eliminated. Meanwhile, coaches got a pay raise on Nike's dime, and Nike got a great marketing boost. The teams became living advertisements for Nike. And to fans, who may not have realized the company paid to outfit the players, it appeared the players were endorsing Nike footwear. Basically,

Vaccaro's mission was a shrewd extension of the idea Puma had hit on in the 1970s with their Puma Clyde and that Keds had tried back in the 1950s. Instead of having one player wearing its shoe—Clyde Frazier, in the case of Puma—Nike would now turn entire teams into live, often televised, advertisements for its shoes.

Vaccaro quickly signed up prominent coaches at major college programs, including Jimmy Valvano at NC State, Jerry Tarkanian at UNLV, and Lefty Driesell at Maryland University. The early deals were humble compared to the huge numbers that get floated today—back then the first consulting contracts paid a maximum of about $5,000. Other shoe companies followed suit. Converse was still an independent player at this time and they signed me to a deal at Kentucky. It was found money. As I said, at the time the deals seemed like wins for everyone involved, including the players, who loved getting free gear, too. It was a perk for them. Unlimited shoes just for the asking! That never happened when I was a player. Now it even happens on the travel team circuit for high school players.

It wasn't long before a few thousand dollars and free shoes would amount to chump change for everyone involved. Vaccaro's vision was in full swing. He signed up to twenty college coaches his first year and added sixty more the second. He also provided swag for the teams of twenty high school coaches.

Vaccaro wasn't limited to tossing money at colleges. He also helped set up the deal that launched Nike into another stratosphere. In 1984, he led the charge to convince Nike to sign the number four NBA draft pick—Michael Jordan—to a multi-year deal that would pay the Chicago Bulls star $1 million annually. The blockbuster deal hit on all cylinders for Nike and probably did more for the company's image and bottom line than all the deals that had gone before. But success with an NBA star didn't slow down its thirst for market share in college basketball.

In 1987, Vaccaro hit on a new paradigm. Signing one basketball coach was a great idea. But locking up every single sports program at a university was an even better one.

He cut a deal with the University of Miami to provide Nike gear to all of its teams. These deals expanded the shoe companies' reach in a number of ways. Now they weren't "just" outfitting basketball teams— they were marketing football, soccer, and swimming equipment, too. The deals also offered apparel companies an entirely new return on investment; the fine print often named the sponsor as the official provider of sportswear sold at the university and at games—an arrangement that generated huge numbers in clothing sales.

"They finally made a deal with the devil, me being the devil and Nike being the ultimate devil," Vaccaro told *The New Republic*. "We wrote the check to Miami, they paid the coaches… That's the day they became a commercial entity. That's the day they became a business partner to a business."

Four years later, after a falling-out with Phil Knight, Vaccaro was fired from Nike on September 15, 1991. But the marketing mania he set in motion continued to pick up steam. By April of 1993, the sneaker promotional budget had hit stunning new heights in college basketball. Nike cut a big new deal to have Duke wear its gear. The agreement paid Duke coach Mike Krzyzewski to switch his team from Adidas to Nike for a reported $1 million signing bonus and $375,000 a year for fifteen years. According to NCAA requirements, Coach K's agreement required the approval of school administrators.

RECRUITING REALITIES

While shoe money was pouring into college basketball, a radical change to recruiting policies instituted by the NCAA in 1982 shook up the college game even more.

Beginning in November 1982, the NCAA established an eight-day early signing period during which high school seniors could sign a letter of intent. Prior to that month, high school athletes couldn't sign to a school until April of their senior year. I asked Tom Konchalski, the writer and publisher of *High School Basketball Illustrated,* who is widely regarded as the most knowledgeable high school basketball scout in the country, to weigh in on the impact of this decision.

"What this did was push up and accelerate the whole recruiting process. It made the summers that much more important to colleges because now they'd have to target kids earlier in the year and sell [the schools] at an earlier point in order to get them.

"The November signing period made the summer camps more important, too. And, later, by extension, the grassroots basketball movement, which would have summer tournaments."

Those camps and tournaments became crucial to sneaker companies, as we'll see. But there was one other rule change from the NCAA that also changed recruiting. The organization announced restrictions on the number of days college coaches could go out during the academic school year to watch potential recruits play. The limits have been loosened over the years. But now each team still has only 130 "person" days when a coach or assistant can go watch players. If I go to a basketball tournament during the school year with two of my assistants, that day we are in the stands counts for three days. This stricture meant colleges had less time to find student-athletes.

I asked Tom Konchalski about the early days of recruiting players to college teams.

"In the fifties and sixties, recruiting wasn't very sophisticated," he said. "In general, schools recruited players from their own geographic area. They found players from schools in their backyard, in nearby high schools. Or if they were a state university, they would recruit from within the whole state."

As I've said, local recruiting consisted of coaches and assistant coaches chatting up their high school counterparts, the recruit, and his family. It was, in general, a low-key process.

Some college coaches did rely on scouts who were known as bird-dogs. The legendary bird-dogs from the New York area were my pal Howie Garfinkel, who sent people to NC State; Harry Gotkin, who helped Frank McGuire with his North and South Carolina teams; Mike Tynberg, who also worked with North Carolina; and Fred "The Spook" Stegmann, who was tied to Al McGuire at Marquette but also sent kids to small colleges and junior colleges.

These bird-dogs were lionized in Dick Schaap's 1957 *Sports Illustrated* article "The Underground Railroad." In true New York style, the story quoted the bird-dogs trash-talking their rivals. "The whole business is a rat race," said Gotkin. "There used to be only gentleman sportsmen in this scouting racket. Now there's a lot of bums around." For his part, Garfinkel confessed: "Gotkin hates me and I hate him."

Tom, who modestly refuses to count himself as a legend, was one of the last of the famous New York bird-dogs. As a young, self-described basketball junkie, Tom became friendly with Stu Aberdeen, who had coached his brother Steve Konchalski in Canada. When Stu landed an assistant coaching job at the University of Tennessee, Tom began steering players his way, including a Queens star name Ernie Grunfeld and a Brooklyn wonder named Bernard King. Both future NBA All-Stars ended up heading south and starring at Knoxville.

Most of these basketball maniacs did it for the love of the game.

"They weren't getting funded," Tom told me. "They were doing it as an avocation, just to be involved.

"Fred Stegmann would get some money for certain schools, mainly junior colleges, but not very much money. His wife, Claire, worked at IBM. Harry Gotkin had a baby-bib company, Niktog, which is Gotkin spelled backwards. Mike Tynberg had a wealthy family. He didn't work for years."

As for Garfinkel, he worked at his parents' garment business during his bird-dog days and liked to hang out at the family's digs on New York's ritzy Park Avenue.

Of course, money eventually tainted at least one of the bird-dogs. In 1961, the NCAA hit McGuire's UNC team with a one-year probation for violating recruiting rules after determining McGuire and Gotkin picked up entertainment bills and failed to report them.

Despite that smackdown, recruiting became more aggressive in the 1960s and coaches began to travel farther afield to find talent. But there was no sneaker money involved in the college game. There were no big TV contracts. And there were no million-dollar contracts for the players or coaches to look forward to in the NBA, either.

EARLY MONEY

In fact, there was relatively little money at all in college basketball. Let me tell you a story about the first time I ever saw "big money" touch the game. It will give you a sense of how quaint and untainted college hoops was, even in the 1980s.

As the rookie coach of Providence in 1985, I showed up at the Big East coaches meeting, which happens every year. We flew down to Puerto Rico. And Seton Hall coach P.J. Carlesimo and my old boss from Syracuse, Jim Boeheim, came by and gave me a pre-meeting update. They told me that the previous year, the league had a sponsorship deal to use MacGregor basketballs and each team in the league had received $3,500. This year, MacGregor only wanted to sponsor St. John's, Syracuse, and Villanova, which was coming off its amazing Final Four win over Georgetown on April 1, 1985.

Boeheim told me MacGregor had offered to pay the three teams $15,000, but Villanova's coach, Rollie Massimino, suggested a different deal: Give the three teams $12,000 each and give the other Big East teams $5,000.

Then Boeheim, who had hired me as an assistant coach for my second job ever, said: "I'm going to get $12,000, but I think we should all get the same."

P.J. and Boeheim said that Rollie really respected the pro game, and that, since I had just come from the Knicks, he would respect me. Therefore, according to their logic, I was the perfect guy to tell Rollie we should all get the same amount of money.

This sounded a little weird to me. "Why should the new guy do this?" I asked. "You guys know him better than I do."

P.J. reiterated the whole Rollie-loves-the-pro-game line and said: "Tell him, 'Look, you were champion last year, but this year it could be any of us. So we should all get seventy-five hundred.'"

I listened to their song and dance about how this would be a good way for me to establish myself and that they would back me up. When I thought about the fact Boeheim, who was initially set for fifteen grand and then twelve grand, actually said he believed we should all get the same, I thought he must be telling the truth.

When the meeting started, eight of the nine Big East coaches crowded into a small room. The only coach missing was St. John's legend Lou Carnesecca, who was running clinics in Italy. Georgetown's John Thompson chaired the proceedings—but he had a deal with Voit basketball, so he said, "I'm going to excuse myself from this discussion."

Rollie stood up. "Look, guys," he said. "MacGregor doesn't want everybody, but I cut a deal with them to make sure everybody gets something. They want to pay St. John's, Syracuse, and Villanova $12,000, and the other teams will get $5,000. Any questions?"

P.J. hit me on the leg and said, "Say something."

So I raised my hand and said, "Rollie, congratulations, first of all, on winning the championship."

"Thanks a lot. What's up?"

"We're all in this together. You won a brilliant championship, maybe the best-coached game I've ever seen. But next year it could be someone else in this room. I think we should all get the same amount of money."

I glanced at P.J. and Boeheim. They had their heads in their hands and they were looking down at the table. When I looked back at Rollie, I could see the rage rising on his face. "Who the hell you do think you are?" he said, clearly pissed off. "I got a deal for everybody—and they didn't even want the rest of you guys. I got you *found* money."

I looked over at Boeheim and P.J. for support. Now they were laughing their heads off, like this was the funniest thing in the world. I realized they'd set me up. They had known Rollie would blow a gasket.

I really wasn't sure how to respond. But Rollie's reaction was over the top so I decided to fight fire with fire. "Who the hell do you think *you* are?" I countered. "You don't have a lock on the championship."

Rollie was furious. Even though I must have been about twenty years younger than he was, Rollie launched himself over the table and we almost came to blows.

I remember looking over at cigar-chomping John Thompson. He was choking with laughter, but he eventually pulled himself together and suggested we table the discussion until Louie could be there at our September meeting in New York.

The next day, Big East commissioner Dave Gavitt organized a golf outing. Always a shrewd operator, he put P.J. and Boeheim in one cart, and booked me with Rollie. But I was so ticked off I refused to get in the cart. I didn't care if it was ninety-five degrees out. There was no way I was riding with Rollie. I ended up walking all eighteen holes.

Eventually, Rollie and I talked and patched things up. He realized I was set up by P.J. and Boeheim. But we didn't discuss the actual sponsorship money issue.

Months later, the coaches gathered to meet in New York, and this time Lou Carnesecca, who Boeheim and P.J. had briefed about their practical joke, was there.

"Rick, you say something," P.J. said with a laugh.

"How about, 'Screw you'?"

Rollie said, "We're all agreed on the MacGregor money. The top three teams get twelve thousand, the rest get five thousand."

Looie, as the New York tabloids used to call him, stood up and said, "Nope." Then proceeded to reexamine the deal in his signature "New Yawk" style.

"Look, guys," he said. "You come over to my house, and my mother cooks a great Italian meal for all of us. Now for dessert she brings out the apple pie. Is my mother going to cut three big slices and then five little ones? Or is she going to make sure we all get the same size?"

He looked around for a second, and then he finished his argument. I'll never forget it. "Leave the chandeliers, guys. There's enough in it for everybody. We're all in this together; we all get seventy-five hundred dollars. Everybody agree?"

Even Rollie had to raise his hand.

Leave the chandeliers!

That was big-time college basketball in the mid-1980s—nine teams fighting over a few thousand bucks in a single $67,500 deal. You could actually almost punch someone and live to tell about it.

Nobody discusses or fights over a few thousand bucks anymore at the college level. As I said earlier, shoe companies are spending at least $300 million annually on college teams. But their marketing sprees don't end there. They're also spending tens of millions on summer basketball camps and grassroots travel teams.

SUMMER LOVING

The summer basketball camp was the next big recruiting innovation.

When Howie Garfinkel launched his Five-Star Basketball camp in

1966 with his business partner Will Kline, he instantly upped his value as a recruiter. He now controlled access to the hottest potential recruits for a few weeks during the summer. The camp began as a moneymaking deal for Howie. As far as I know, every camper that attended Five-Star was paid for by either their family or benefactor. Some campers—including a kid named Michael Jordan—were able to work for a week at the camp dining hall to cover their costs.

I've already talked a bit about Five-Star and the great coaches who've worked there before they were famous: Kentucky's John Calipari, Wake Forest coach Dave Odom, Atlanta Hawks coach Mike Fratello, Hubie Brown, and Bobby Knight. But the players the camp attracted were even more impressive. Among the names that have been on the camp roster are Michael Jordan, Patrick Ewing, Dominique Wilkins, Isiah Thomas, Tim Duncan, LeBron James, Chris Paul, Kevin Durant, Stephen Curry, Carmelo Anthony, and Kyrie Irving—and I'm sure I'm leaving out plenty of other superstars.

So when the NCAA introduced the early signing period and limited coach visits, the importance of Howie's camp skyrocketed. There would be three hundred basketball coaches crowded around outdoor courts watching games. The access to players became such a concern that college coaches who didn't work at the camp began complaining to the NCAA about how camp coaches like me had a recruitment advantage because we were working with these kids. We argued that we were just former campers—which was true—and we had worked our way up the ranks. The NCAA, in its supreme wisdom, ruled against us and eventually college coaches were phased out at Five-Star. Did we have an advantage? Being on the court with kids did give us more contact, there was no question about that. But the camps were pretty frantic. It wasn't like I could take my five favorite players, buy 'em milkshakes (which would have been against NCAA rules), and charm them. Still, it was definitely a unique advantage.

Sonny Vaccaro took notice of summer camps while he was still working at Nike. In the early eighties, there were two other camps that college coaches paid attention to—B/C, a camp co-founded by former Ole Miss assistant coach Bill Bolton and a scout named Bill Cronauer, which operated in the South and out West, and Athletes for Better Education, an organization centered in Chicago that started running an All-American camp.

According to Tom Konchalski, the AFBE held a camp in Princeton, New Jersey. "Nike gave them $10,000 and Sonny flew in for one day," Tom said. "I remember picking him up at Newark airport and driving down for the day. The next year, I think Nike gave them $50,000. Then AFBE ended up in financial trouble and Sonny ended up taking it over, relaunching it as the ABCD Camp, which stood for Academic Betterment Creative Development."

With Nike's money behind it in 1984, Sonny's camp had something previous basketball camps lacked: swag. Five-Star handed campers T-shirts, Nike handed out thousands of dollars of sneakers, shorts, jerseys, and sweatshirts to campers. "Five-Star was more tamper-proof than ABCD," said Konchalski, noting the more money surrounding the game increases, the greater the chance of bad actors skirting rules and exerting influence.

I agree with Tom 100 percent on this. Anytime you get bigger and bigger pots of money, you've increased temptation. There's more temptation for schools to cheat. More temptation for AAU and travel teams to cheat. More temptation for agents to cheat. All because the money is so extreme.

ABCD quickly rivaled and eventually supplanted Five-Star as the major summer camp in America—although many players attended both events—becoming a must-attend showcase for every major college basketball coach in the country. The schoolboys who established themselves as stars there include Kobe Bryant, Kevin Love, Tracy McGrady, Paul Pierce, Kevin Garnett, and Stephon Marbury.

GRASSROOTS & WEEDS

The final and arguably most damaging development to the recruiting process, however, was the rise of grassroots basketball funded by shoe companies. Most people refer to grassroots basketball as AAU basketball, but that is not entirely accurate. While many of the teams are or were AAU, they play in leagues and attend tournaments that are paid for by the sneaker business and have nothing to do with the Amateur Athletic Union, which started over one hundred years ago to promote sports to kids.

Grassroots basketball is essentially made up of sneaker-sponsored travel teams—all-star outfits that gather the best high school players in a geographic area. Shoe companies sponsor these teams—and entire leagues—in part, to foster competition. The idea is to see the best players in the country playing against each other. Think of it as an on-the-court laboratory that runs experiments to identify each year's truly dominant players. Whatever other benefits grassroots hoops provides to its players—like coaching, travel, and life skills—the teams and leagues are created and paid for to yield results for the sneaker companies. The unspoken goals are the same for all three companies, but let's use Adidas as an example. Adidas wants to find top players, establish a relationship with them, see them guided to an Adidas-sponsored college team, and, if they leave college with NBA potential, sign them to an Adidas contract.

As for anyone who questions the wisdom of such long-term investments, since it could take as much as seven or eight years for a kid to go pro, and only a tiny fraction of grassroots players make it to the NBA, consider this: the top-ranked player on ESPN's recruiting database in the summer of 2018, R.J. Barrett, has over 200,000 Instagram followers, and the second-ranked player, Zion Williamson, has 1.5 million followers. In other words, these kids are already what marketers call "brand ambassadors."

Sonny Vaccaro knew about the power of teenage ballers before so-cial media platforms existed. To him, the players were the platform. "I used to say that Albert King at Fort Hamilton High School in New York City could sell more shoes in a day in the Fort Hamilton area than some NBA guy could sell playing the Celtics against the Knicks," Sonny said in a *Frontline* interview, "because no one gave a damn about the Celtics and the Knicks, but they cared about Fort Hamilton playing [some] major school in New York City. That was what the rivalries wore."

The travel game and its influence have increased in the last twenty years, but the last ten have been explosive. In 2010, Nike established the Elite Youth Basketball League (EYBL). It is now a forty-team league that holds an annual Peach Jam tournament in Augusta, Georgia, where the top twenty teams—plus four teams who are offered wild-card invitations—face off. (The wild-card invitations were added as magic "get into tournament" cards so that, if a major prospect's team doesn't actually qualify for the tournament, his team can still be invited to the big dance.)

Nike isn't alone in this field. Under Armour sponsors a twenty-eight-team league, the Under Armour Association, which stages a final tour-nament in July. The Adidas Uprising league has more than eighty teams and holds the Gauntlet, a multi-team summertime finale in Atlanta.

It is impossible to know how much money the big three sneaker companies spend on these teams. Since most of these teams are run as nonprofits, they are not required to divulge the source of the charitable contributions they receive on their 990 tax forms. But the league spon-sors are footing the bills for these supposedly nonprofit teams. And you can see that some of these organizations have budgets of over $500,000, which makes sense because the expenses of flying around the country to games, staying in hotels, and feeding everyone can easily cost tens of thousands of dollars.

One of the most famous and infamous AAU teams in history, DC

Assault, offers a prime example of how powerful and tainted grassroots basketball can be. Team founder Curtis Malone coached three eventual NBA lottery picks—DerMarr Johnson, Jeff Green, and Michael Beasley—as well as hundreds of Division 1 basketball players. Personally, I never had a problem with Malone, but it was well known that if you wanted to recruit anyone from the DC area, you needed to get his blessing. Or as local high school coach Mike Glick once put it: "He was the godfather of DC basketball."

That's probably why Sonny Vaccaro once signed Malone to an Adidas contract for $50,000 a year, according to a *Sports Illustrated* article, which also quoted rival DC AAU coach Rob Jackson saying Malone ran his team "as a business. He sold kids to schools, sold kids to agents."

Malone, whose program imploded when he was busted running a cocaine ring and sentenced to one hundred months in prison in 2014, according to the *Washington Post*, has denied profiting off his players. But his former star Michael Beasley once filed a civil suit claiming that sports agent Joel Bell funded Curtis Malone's program and that Malone returned Bell's favor by encouraging Beasley to sign with Bell when he went pro. Although Beasley eventually dropped the suit, Frank Martin, who coached Beasley for a year at Kansas State, told *Sports Illustrated* he was aware of an arrangement between Malone and Bell. "Of course I knew about it," he said. "Agents run the NBA, agents run grassroots basketball."

So AAU teams like DC Assault have become a plague for college recruiters. They are all funded with an unspoken, unofficial goal in mind: funnel the players to the right college and get rewarded. The unofficial logic, as far as Adidas is concerned, is that an Adidas travel team should send its best players to an Adidas-sponsored college team. I believe that same logic—and pressure—applies to any and all sponsored travel teams, including Nike and Under Amour.

But that's not the only negative impact. By creating these entities and identifying budding stars, you create more points of exposure for student-athletes. As the stories about DC Assault indicate, some agents do try to contact these players in the hopes of representing them when they go pro. They may offer enticements that bend or break NCAA rules—and, if you are an aggressive businessman, why not? Think about a star like one-and-done Karl-Anthony Towns, who played his freshman year at the University of Kentucky and then signed a four-year contract worth $25,720,035 when he arrived in the NBA as the number one draft pick of the Minnesota Timberwolves. His agent will get 3 percent of his contract earnings. That's about $771,000 over those four years. Not bad work if you can get it. And if Towns ever gets to a LeBron James level of marketing power—the King earned $55 million for one year of endorsements in 2017, reports *Forbes*—well, agents can get as much as 15 percent for some of those deals. And 15 percent of LeBron's endorsement haul is $8.25 million.

On the other end of the spectrum, a travel team coach is unlikely to haul down millions from his players' success—although a number of high-profile AAU coaches have been awarded personal contracts with sneaker companies. But generally, the livelihood of a travel team coach is dependent upon three things. First, his or her ability to recruit quality players. How is that done? Coaches can promise playing time, visibility, and sneaker swag from the team's sponsor. If the player is really special, he can promise to pay all the travel expenses. Anything else, of course, would violate an athlete's amateur status.

The second job-security issue is winning. The better the team, the more funding will be forthcoming from a sponsor. Winning also often makes recruiting easier, too.

The third and most important thing for a travel team coach, however, is making sure his stars choose the right college.

"There's tremendous pressure to keep your shoe contract," Tom Konchalski told me. "These are multi-year contracts, but there are always a couple of teams that get bounced from EYBL. So you've got to come up with the players. If you are an EYBL coach and too many of your players ended up going to Under Armour or Adidas college teams, obviously, your funding is not going to continue."

FOR RICHER OR POORER

The basketball world has changed—it is now a truly global industry and it is saturated with more money than ever.

In 2015, Steph Curry of the Golden State Warriors signed a sponsorship deal with Under Armour worth just under $4 million annually. He recently received an equity stake in the company as part of a contract extension that runs until 2024.

Michael Jordan now has his own division of Nike. Instead of making $1 million a year from the company, as he did during his first years in the NBA, he makes an estimated $100 million annually, according to *Forbes*.

The man who drove so much sneaker money into the game, Sonny Vaccaro, is no longer a player in the industry. He ran the ABCD Camp for Converse after Nike fired him in 1991. Then he ran it for Reebok and Adidas before shutting down in 2006.

Marketing in this day and age is a mega-billion-dollar universe unto itself. The ways a business promotes and sells its products have evolved in all kinds of obvious and odd directions. Television commercials, billboards, in-store placement, social media posts on Twitter, Instagram, and Facebook—these are some of the obvious channels for getting a message out and building awareness. But there are other off-the-beaten-path methods. Converse, for instance, owns a recording studio in the center of hipsterville, Brooklyn, New York, called Rubber Tracks. They record bands, singers, and rappers for free. There's no commitment from the artists required. It's just a public service to the world, apparently. No doubt, if one of the artists who recorded at Rubber Tracks scored a big hit, I'm sure Converse would love to outfit them for their video. In other words, Converse is using the studio as a grassroots music incubator to find new stars.

But a huge chunk of these companies' marketing budgets is now earmarked for endorsement contracts with top sports stars and college teams. These endorsements have become part of their corporate DNA, literally codified in corporate strategy. Look up Nike's annual 10-K form filed with the Security and Exchange Commission, which gives a summary of the company's fiscal performance. In one section covering potential problems facing the corporation, you'll find this headline:

Failure to continue to obtain or maintain high-quality endorsers of our products could harm our business.

Below this headline, the Oregon-based behemoth is completely up front about the dog-eat-dog promotional battles the company faces:

We establish relationships with professional athletes, sports teams and leagues to develop, evaluate and promote our products, as well as establish product authenticity with consumers. However, as competition in our industry has increased, the costs associated with establishing and retaining such sponsorships and other relationships have increased. If we are unable to maintain our current associations with professional athletes, sports teams and leagues, or to do so at a reasonable cost, we could lose the on-field authenticity associated with our products, and we may be required to modify and substantially increase our marketing investments. As a result, our brands, net revenues, expenses and profitability could be harmed.

Let's give Nike points for being honest.

And speaking of honesty, let's face some other facts. We are not getting shoe companies out of college sports. They are, in many ways, a positive force. The huge amounts of money they pay to sponsor college athletic programs help universities expand their own brands. Nike, Adidas, and Under Armour actually provide a marketing service to universities—they showcase our teams, our students, our campuses. We promote them and they promote us. So universities don't want the sneaker company money to go away. They are grateful and they should be.

I'm also grateful for grassroots basketball. AAU basketball—which is organized for young athletes to play within their state—is a noble institution. But pouring sneaker money into grassroots basketball, funding teams to travel to tournaments, effectively creates a microcosm of college basketball at the grassroots level. While this does save money and time for college recruiters and definitely makes it easier to evaluate elite high school players, it also creates a dangerous paradigm. Let's follow the thread one last time.

The shoe companies back travel team coaches to recruit the best players. Then they back those teams to get them to win and get them on the big stage. Then they use the coach's influence to steer the player to a Nike-, Adidas-, or Under Armour–sponsored college, where they can continue a relationship. Why? Because the connection may help them achieve the ultimate goal: signing a future NBA superstar to an endorsement deal and turning that player into a brand unto himself.

So where does this leave us? I believe we are overdue when it comes to figuring out a way to remove sneaker companies' undue influence at the grassroots level. In 2015, I met with members of NCAA president

Dr. Mark Emmert's staff. They asked me how we could make improvements to our system. I suggested two things:

1. Clean up the AAU/Grassroots situation.
2. Get the shoe companies out of the recruiting business.

We had a lengthy discussion on how to enact such ideas. I presented an option calling for the NCAA to develop an annual orientation program, organized over four weekends in July. The country would be split into four regions. High school coaches would instruct, the schoolboy athletes would be divided into teams to play, and the NCAA would educate players and parents on the rules around scouting, recruiting, and compensation.

The NCAA would now be in charge of all aspects of summer ball. This early education and intervention would help reduce the negative influence of shoe companies, the AAU coaches, and agents when it came to college basketball recruiting.

I never heard back from the NCAA about my suggestions.

Chuck Taylor, no doubt, is still spinning.

10

THE PRESS CONFERENCE

We identified the problem three years ago.

Here's the slo-mo replay.

▼

ON THURSDAY, OCTOBER 9, 2014, I held a press conference.

It was my first meeting with the media for the new season, an annual rite of fall for the University of Louisville Cardinals basketball team. Although I always preferred coaching and working with my players to talking to the press, I recognized it was an important event. One of my jobs as a coach was to instill confidence in my players, but another was to get our fans and the Louisville community at large excited and engaged. I wanted them confident and proud, too. Talking to the media can be an effective way to set expectations, stoke interest, and even send messages to my players.

We'd only held a couple of practices and were trying to get a feel for the seven new players on the roster. As you can imagine, there were a lot of unanswered questions about the team. So in order to have something concrete to share, I began the conference discussing the culture we'd been trying to instill at Louisville.

At one point I explained our vision for the team, revealing what I would always tell my players: "If you do everything humanly possible to have success with the name on the front [of your jersey], without question the name on the back is going to benefit." I said this for a number of reasons. First and foremost, I wanted my players to have a sense of humility. All these kids were stars in high school, but that status doesn't automatically carry over to the next level. Shedding ego, realizing you are not the Second Coming, and developing empathy are vital for personal development. The message also promotes an awareness of communal responsibility. Togetherness. I wanted our players to remember they are representing each other and a great institution. Finally, on another level, I was trying to apply a little pressure—by evoking the success of the players of the past.

But this Q&A session ended up being much different than previous kick-off conferences. Yes, the first question was a typical "state-of-the-team" query about the availability of Chris Jones and Akoy Agau, players who were returning from injury issues.

But then things went in another direction.

A reporter asked me a question about a Big Ten announcement that the conference would, for the first time, guarantee player scholarships for all four years a student attended one of their colleges.

I couldn't recall ever pulling a scholarship for a single one of my players unless it involved them violating school regulations. So I said it was rare for any college to pull a scholarship and that I thought the Big Ten would generate good publicity for something that was sort of a non-issue. Here's the transcript of my response:

"I think that's more PR than it is reality. We have so many other issues that we should be dealing with and correcting."

You've heard of a "leading question"? That was what I call a "leading answer." It led to this follow-up question.

"Anything in particular on your list?"

I didn't mince words. "I can't recruit a kid because he wears Nike in the AAU circuit," I said. "I've never heard of such a thing, and it's happening in our world. Or, he's on the Adidas circuit so the Nike schools don't want to recruit him. I never thought that shoes would be the reason you wouldn't recruit players. It's a factor. I think we need to deal with that. We need to get the shoe companies out of the lives of young athletes. We need to get it back to where parents and coaches have more of a say than peripheral people. That's easier said than done. I don't know how to do that."

I made these comments because I was fed up with the realities of modern-day recruiting. To reiterate quickly what I discussed in the last chapter, the best high school players in the country play on Athletic Association Union teams. These AAU teams, breeding grounds for future stars, don't just train and showcase talent; they have become conduits that can help drive a high school player to a certain college.

It took me a long time—too long, I admit—to fully realize how shoe company sponsorship money was tripping up our recruitment efforts.

By now I'd learned that players on Nike-sponsored AAU teams almost always end up playing for Nike-sponsored college teams. That arrangement was shrinking the pool of players we could realistically recruit.

As I told the reporters at the press conference, high school players never come right out and say they can't come to a school because of a sneaker sponsorship issue. But they are aware of the influence shoe companies have on their teams, and that if a player on a Nike-sponsored team goes to an Adidas school, it may hurt the AAU team's status with Nike. That's a lot of pressure on a teenager. "It's the outside influence. It's not actually the kid who cares," I said, noting that if an influential person in a young person's life says, "'Boy, you should really go to Kentucky, they're a Nike school,' he doesn't have to say a Nike school, he just has to say Kentucky. Everybody's in that court because you're all working for that shoe company. I think that's a bigger problem than whether you guarantee scholarships, but nobody wants to talk about that. Why nobody wants to talk about that is because it's money related …I think it needs to be cleaned up."

I also stressed that my alarm wasn't caused by any recent specific event. We'd seen a sea change over the last five years in just how competitive the shoe companies had become in the battle to get players. They were competing for these young kids—some not even fourteen years old—to get them on their AAU teams.

Then I admitted cleaning up the situation wasn't easy: "It's very tough to address because our pockets are lined with their money." At the time, I was talking from personal experience. I had an Adidas endorsement contract that paid me over $1 million a year, and my own school, as I've mentioned, got millions a year from Adidas, and every other major college basketball program in the country had a sneaker company sponsorship, too. But there I was, loud and clear, saying the system was broken—that companies like Nike and Adidas were a huge part of the problem.

That press conference made headlines across the country. PITINO: SHOE COMPANIES INFLUENCE RECRUITS was the headline in *USA Today*. RICK PITINO SHREDS SHOE-COMPANY IMPACT ON RECRUITING, chimed the *Indianapolis Star* website. And LOUISVILLE'S RICK PITINO ATTACKS NIKE OVER RECRUITING INFLUENCE, said *The Oregonian*. *The Sporting News* website ran an interesting take, too: PITINO'S SHOE COMPANY RECRUITING RANT A TOTAL FANTASY.

I don't think any other major college coach had ever gone on the record to publicly assail what had become business as usual in the recruiting world. And honestly, I'm not sure any other coach has really gone out on the limb since then.

I don't blame coaches for staying silent, though. In a sense, I was biting the hand that fed me. But I did not care. I realized the situation was out of control.

In retrospect, I did have one ironic exchange at that press conference. A reporter asked if I thought there was a relationship between sneaker money and high school players.

"I don't think there's anything illegal, but they're all getting shoes and apparel and the AAU programs are getting taken care of by the shoe companies," I said. "We all know that. It's out in the open."

Almost exactly three years after I uttered those words, a huge scandal broke and it involved sneaker money and illegal recruitment.

And when that scandal broke, I would become college basketball's Public Enemy Number One in the eyes of many.

It was as if my press conference had never happened.

11

BILLIONS

▼

SHOWTIME'S HIT TV series *Billions* is great fun to watch.

Here's the basic plot: Axe Capital, a hedge fund run by craven, narcissistic CEO Bobby "Axe" Axelrod, is suspected of engineering an illegal insider trading operation that generates billions of dollars. Chuck Rhoades, the United States Attorney for the Southern District of New York, is out to stop Axe's greedy money grab. His staff of US Assistant Attorneys deploys every tool in their legal arsenal to put Axe behind bars. Back and forth they go, using all their power, influence, and cutting-edge technology to combat each other for the ultimate prize—not justice—but victory.

Since September 26, 2017, when the biggest college basketball recruiting scandal in history broke, I've been living a real-life nightmare with the real-life Southern District of New York office. It is the opposite of fun. It's been terrifying, painful, and utterly frustrating. I've come to feel like I've been sucked into a *Billions* knock-off, one that isn't about insider trading or stopping individuals from amassing huge amounts of money. Instead, it's less a crime drama than an absurdist series about government investigators working with scam artists.

It's a frightening story, to be honest, about a manufactured scandal, misplaced priorities, abuses of power, and a mind-boggling lack of accountability. As of this publication, nearly a full year has elapsed since the complaint was released that essentially ended my tenure at Louisville. The case remains ongoing, and many threads of the investigation have not yet tied together publicly.

But here—according to court records, DOJ and SEC filings, a slew of published reports, and my own legal team—is how and why the lawmen of the Southern District swept me up in their investigation, used my name to generate big headlines, and then, having blown up my life, left me to pick up the pieces.

A CELLULOID ZERO

You've probably never heard of the guy who set college basketball's big scandal of 2017 in motion. I sure hadn't. His name? Louis Martin Blazer III.

Based in Pittsburgh, Pennsylvania, Blazer ran an investment advising and financial services operation called Blazer Capital Management. The company's bread and butter were NFL football players with ties to the Pittsburgh area. Acting as a financial advisor, Blazer got clients to grant him access to—and sometimes even control of—their money.

Around 2009, Blazer got Hollywood fever. Fueled by visions of generating big money profits by backing film projects, he tried to get his clients to invest in two movie productions—a sci-fi flick called *Sibling* and something called *Mafia the Movie*. When none of his clients shared his enthusiasm, he took matters into his own hands.

As described in coverage by ESPN, Bloomberg, *The Wall Street Journal*, and others, over a period of two years, Blazer scammed five of his own clients, including at least one NFL player, out of $2.35 million to help fund these flicks. He allegedly copied a client's signature to make unauthorized bank transfers. Then, according to the Securities and Exchange Commission (SEC), he would pay one client back using another client's money. As far as making his clients "whole"—the return on their unwitting investments wasn't so great. Blazer reportedly only paid $790,000 back to his bilked clients.

The movie projects ended up generating nothing but celluloid zeros. *Sibling,* starring actress Mischa Barton and the late *Green Mile* star Michael Clarke Duncan, was retitled *A Resurrection* and played in seventeen theaters where it grossed a total $10,730, according to the website Box Office Mojo. Meanwhile, *Mafia the Movie* was released straight to DVD as *Mafia.*

The Securities and Exchange Commission got wind of Blazer's Ponzi-like abuses and, eventually, a mountain of charges were brought against him—securities fraud, wire fraud, aggravated identity theft, and making false statements and documents. Blazer realized he might spend the rest of his life behind bars. So the failed and fraudulent movie mogul apparently offered lawmen a new, high-concept production: in return for possible leniency, he would help the feds conduct a sting operation and expose the rampant corruption infecting college sports. And as of this writing, according to a clerk in Judge Vernon Broderick's chambers, Blazer has still not been sentenced.

It's not clear who approved this idea or what kind of deal Blazer struck—the maneuverings and machinations of the SEC, DOJ, and FBI are a world unto themselves—but Blazer began cooperating with federal investigators in November 2014. According to insiders, he began by putting out feelers and letting it be known he was interested in meeting coaches who would direct college players to him. Working with the FBI, who were presumably coordinating the investigation with the US

Attorney's Office, Blazer became a "cooperating witness." Despite his background with football players, his forays into the underworld of NCAA scammers focused largely on college basketball. By 2016, he was traveling across the US meeting with assistant coaches, AAU team bigwigs, runners, and, eventually, Adidas representatives.

Blazer also roped in a former business associate, Munish Sood, a banker with his own investment firm. Sood began working with Christian Dawkins, an ex-AAU GM, to start their own agency, Live Out Your Dreams. After Blazer introduced Sood to a man named Jeff DeAngelo—a wealthy real estate investor—the budding agent set up a meeting with Dawkins where DeAngelo expressed interest in bankrolling their operation.

There was just one problem with this introduction. DeAngelo was actually a veteran undercover FBI agent.

DeAngelo actively pushed the Live Out Your Dreams duo to pay off college coaches to steer NBA-bound players to the budding operation, according to sources cited in a *Sports Illustrated* article.

Interestingly, a DOJ complaint—not yet fully adjudicated—indicates that's just what happened. On July 29, 2017, Dawkins, Blazer, and an undercover agent—presumably DeAngelo—met with USC assistant coach Anthony Bland, according to prosecutors. At the meeting—and as reported by the *Los Angeles Times*, *USA Today*, and *CBS Sports*—Bland allegedly took $13,000 provided by the agent to steer players toward Dawkins.

But there was a catch. The undercover operative then stopped working on the sting and went AWOL, spending time drinking and gambling, according to two published reports. This mystery G-Man who posed as DeAngelo is now said to be under investigation for misuse of funds, and, sources say, his behavior may compromise some of the cases he was working on.

The whole investigation was suspect from the very beginning, or at least built on a completely flimsy foundation—a con man setting up a sting operation for the government. Do runners try to steer players to agents? You bet. Do some families want cash up front to send their athletically gifted child to a certain school? No question. Do sneaker companies want top high school stars to play for the colleges they sponsor? Absolutely. But did every single college hoops corruption case filed by the DOJ in 2017 start because a desperate man facing serious prison time—Blazer—and a cash-flashing undercover agent stoked illegal activities? So far, that appears to be very much the case.

ROPING ME IN

Don't think for a minute I'm defending guys like Christian Dawkins, who lied about speaking to me concerning Adidas, or AAU team director Brad Augustine, who falsely claimed I had enormous influence on Adidas.

I knew Dawkins through his connection to Dorian's Pride, an AAU team out of Michigan. Only he wasn't a coach; he called himself the "GM." Whether that means Dawkins had delusions of grandeur or that AAU teams have gotten so sophisticated that they need a general manager, I have no idea. And I've only recently learned his father, Lou, coached Golden State Warriors star Draymond Green in high school. It's been reported that Dawkins got in trouble for working for two rival agents *at the same time*—something I learned after the complaint was filed. According to a 2016 suit filed in the US District Court for the Southern District of Indiana by Kurt Schoeppler of International Management Advisors (IMA), Dawkins was hired by IMA at $50,000 a year to help the firm recruit NBA prospects. At some point, however, Dawkins started directing players to sign with IMA rival Andy Miller Sports (ASM), as court papers charged in this way: "It became apparent that Dawkins was actually representing ASM's interests, not IMA's, when interacting with prospects, and he could no longer be trusted."

A 2017 investigation by the National Basketball Players Association determined that Dawkins used the credit card of IMA client Elfrid Payton of the Orlando Magic to charge *more than $42,000 in Uber rides* between 2015 and 2016. The DOJ complaint refers to Dawkins's employment at a sports management company where his job consisted of primarily "the alleged misuse of an athlete's credit card."

This is the person prosecutors seem to believe orchestrated one of the biggest college basketball corruption scandals in modern times? I'm not sure he could orchestrate a game of H-O-R-S-E. I think he has very little credibility. He got nailed for scamming IMA and for bilking Payton. It must have been child's play for Blazer and the FBI to spin him.

I've seen dozens of Christian Dawkinses in my forty-plus years of coaching, all the way back to Rodney Parker, one of Brooklyn's finest, who, depending on who you talked to, was either a street hoops Good Samaritan, a ticket scalper, or an under-the-table runner. You've probably known guys like this, too. Hustlers who always work in a cut for themselves in every scam they propose.

But these kinds of operators come in all shapes and sizes.

Take infamous booster Sam Gilbert, who greased palms and handed out perks to John Wooden's legendary teams at UCLA. As Seth Davis reports in his excellent book, *Wooden: A Coach's Life*, Gilbert got players summer jobs. He hosted glamorous parties for them. And he buddied up to some of the top collegiate players of the era, from Lew Alcindor to Jamaal Wilkes to Sidney Wicks to Henry Bibby to Bill Walton. And he frequently served as an agent or financial advisor to players once they left school. Wooden was so disturbed by Gilbert's influence on players he repeatedly voiced concerns to fellow coach Jerry Tarkanian and even went to UCLA athletic director J.D. Morgan.

"You coach the team and let me handle Sam," was the message Wooden got back, according to Tarkanian.

Gilbert's influence happened under the watch of the world's greatest college basketball teacher. I've been in Coach Wooden's company many times. He is a wonderful human being, great instructor, disciplinarian, poet, father, and husband. A man with incredible humility and grace. But for years and years, everyone in his program reportedly turned a blind eye until the NCAA finally investigated Gilbert. To some, Gilbert was just a very wealthy, UCLA-loving, overenthusiastic, over-aged fan. But Gilbert himself liked to encourage the idea that he had Mob ties. In 1981, after years of rumored violations, the NCAA finally slapped UCLA with two years of probation and a one-year NCAA Tournament ban for a series of misdeeds, including a charge that Gilbert cosigned a promissory note for one player's car purchase. Six years later, in 1987, he was indicted on racketeering and money laundering charges—by prosecutors who didn't realize the Bruins' biggest benefactor had died just four days earlier at age seventy-four.

Dawkins, of course, had nowhere near Gilbert's money or influence. The DOJ complaint—cited by news outlets from the *The New York Times* and *Louisville Courier-Journal* to *Sports Illustrated* and more— reported he "is not a registered agent." He was accused of conspiring to arrange payments of $100,000 provided by Adidas in order to steer high school star Brian Bowen to Louisville. He also allegedly schemed to arrange additional payments to the family of Florida high school star Balsa Koprivica to get him to commit to Louisville. And he was said to be involved in planning payments of $150,000 to entice a third player to sign with the University of Miami. In return, according to investigators, the plan was that the three players would retain Dawkins's "services"—presumably as an agent when they went pro.

According to the DOJ, Dawkins was allegedly caught on tape claiming to others that he had spoken to me about getting money to Brian

Bowen's family. He blatantly lied to co-conspirators, claiming he told me: "I need you to talk to Jim Gatto, who is the head of everything at Adidas."

The investigators obviously don't have me on a wiretap saying any of this. I can guarantee it with 100 percent certainty. Why? Because that supposed conversation never took place. So there you have it. A known scam artist quotes himself explaining to me who Jim Gatto is. Why would Dawkins have to explain to me that Jim Gatto works at Adidas? I've known Jim casually for years. After all, Adidas has paid me to wear its clothes season after season and has also sponsored Louisville's athletic teams.

The reason Dawkins would claim this conversation with me is because it's what a guy like Dawkins does—he spews B.S. to make himself seem like a player instead of a con man. Not only that, but Dawkins was always over-explaining himself. When he texted me, he would remind me who he was. That's not something that happens with people with working relationships. Here's an example of what I'm talking about:

1   iMessage: +1502*******
16   +1989******* Christian Dawkins
Coach- hope u are well. This is Christian Dawkins, used to run the grassroots team Jaylen Johnson played for. I know you already spoke to josh Jackson's mom, need to get u with Brian bowens dad soon. He's another kid that played in my former program. He's a 6-7 SG, ranked #6 in the 2017 class by ESPN. Stud. I told his dad today I want him to visit soon, let me know what game is good and I'll get them down.
Read   Unknown   2014/10/01   10/1/2014 7:23:4

Working with Dawkins was Brad Augustine, director of the 1-Family AAU basketball program in Florida. Augustine had coveted big man Balsa Koprivica on his team and he, as much as anyone, is responsible for damaging my reputation with his false bravado. But he also was the guy, apparently, who invited my assistant coach, Jordan Fair, for a drink at a Las Vegas bar and then invited him up to a hotel room where, according to the complaint—which did not identify Jordan by name, but called him "Coach 1"—Jordan was allegedly present for discussions about Koprivica.

Of all the quotes and "facts" revealed in the DOJ complaint—the culmination of at least two years spent actively stirring up wrongdoing—none made better copy or sounded more salacious than the words of Augustine, a man I barely even knew.

"No one swings a bigger dick than Pitino," Augustine said, talking about my supposed influence with Adidas, according to the FBI agent's testimony. "All [Pitino has to do] is pick up the phone and call somebody [and say] these are my guys."

Now, how the hell would Brad Augustine know how much power I have with Adidas? I have met him only a few times in my life and have no clue if he played basketball, coached basketball, or anything else about him. This is America, and I suppose there's a downside to free speech: anyone can talk trash about anyone else. But the fact that some wannabe big shot says something about me doesn't make it true. And as it turns out, Brad Augustine racked up more points in the liar category. As covered by the *Louisville Courier-Journal*, ESPN, the *Washington Post*, and *The Wall Street Journal*, although he was one of the ten men originally named as a suspect in the DOJ investigation, charges were dropped against him in February 2018. Why? Because sources close to the investigation say that Brad Augustine—allegedly caught on tape plotting a payoff with Blazer, Gatto, Code, and Dawkins on July 27, 2017, in a hotel room where he took an envelope from an FBI agent containing $12,700 earmarked to be given to Koprivica's mother—claims *he never gave her the money.* Instead, he kept it for himself.

If this is true, Augustine lied to other alleged conspirators—Dawkins, the Adidas guys, and the FBI agent. He was scamming them. And by not transferring the money earmarked as a payoff to the family of a recruit—in order, evidently, to enrich himself—he avoided any bribery charges. Apparently, there's no honor among thieves. Something about this whole scenario doesn't make any sense at all; it seems absurd. But I guess that's par for the course.

Of course, all this surfaced nearly half a year after the US Attorney's office repeated and broadcast Augustine's lies about me.

DIAL M FOR MISLEADING

There were a few other details in the complaint that seemed sculpted to inflict maximum damage on my reputation. One involved phone calls between me and Adidas Director of Global Marketing Jim Gatto. The complaint was written precisely to give the reader the impression that collusion was going on. Here's what the FBI agent in the complaint said:

> Based on my review of call records, I'm aware that on or about May 27, 2017 Jim Gatto had two telephone conversations with a phone number used by Coach-2. Based on the same, I am aware that on or about June 1, Gatto had a third telephone conversation with the same phone number used by Coach-2....Two days later, on or about June 3, 2017, Player 10 (Bowen) officially committed to University-6 (Louisville) in return for the commitment by Gatto and Company-1 (Adidas) to pay $100,000 to his family.

When you read that paragraph, you might easily think we were scheming together.

I'm sure that is exactly what federal investigators wanted readers to think. I'm not entirely sure why—but everyone I've spoken to in the legal profession says the US Attorney wanted to generate headlines.

This short paragraph was designed to implicate me. But it is filled with falsehoods and sinister-sounding circumstances. First and foremost, we already knew Brian Bowen was coming, as he had no other options but the University of Louisville.

Second, I didn't have three "conversations" with Jim Gatto. The first call was a voice-mail message and so was the third call. I gave recordings of these messages to the Department of Justice. So I might as well share them here, too:

Here's Jim's first message:

Coach. Jim Gatto with Adidas. Hope all is well. Sorry to bother you over the weekend, but I just got a call about a player I want to discuss with you. So when you get a chance, if you can give me a call at xxx-xxx-xxxx. Thanks, Coach.

Here's the second:

Coach. Jim Gatto. Hope all is well. Checking in. Heard the good news. Going to be great and I'm excited for you guys. Give me a call back, or I'll try you soon. Thanks, Coach.

As for the middle phone call, I was returning Jim's initial call. That's what people do. During our call, he asked me if I was recruiting Bowen. I said yes. And he said he might know some friends of the family, and he would put in a good word for me. I said that would be great. That was the full extent of our conversation. Any earlier conversations or texts I had that year with Jim involved two other things: lobbying on behalf of the Celtics' Terry Rozier, my former player who lost his Adidas sponsorship after a photo surfaced of him wearing some other company's sneaker, and repeatedly asking him to send me a pair of Lizard Yeezy sneakers—the limited edition shoes put out by rapper Kanye West.

I have never discussed illegal recruiting schemes with Adidas or anyone else, ever. So the reason there's no hard evidence about me plotting to violate recruiting laws is that there is none. Let me say for the thousandth time: in more than thirty years as a college head coach, I have never given any player or their family members a single inducement to play for me. Nor have I ever plotted or suggested doing anything like this. Never. Anything contrary to that statement is a bold, fat lie. But con men will say anything to sell their scam. And people will say anything to avoid jail time.

I'll also tell anyone who listens to look at my coaching history. I've established throughout my career that recruiting blue-chip, one-and-done players is not my primary focus.

As I've said, PhD athletes—Passionate, Hungry, and Driven players—are who I want on my team. Players like Terry Rozier and Donovan Mitchell. Those players weren't ranked in the Top 50 coming out of high school.

I've never really concentrated on recruiting one-and-done players, although at Kentucky I recruited five players who passed on going to college and playing with me, and left for the NBA. Four out of five of them, I believe, would have been one-and-done players. Understand that agents identify young players when they are in ninth grade. This practice has been going on for years. And their runners follow them as closely as the recruiters in college. And the most aggressive agents aren't sitting around waiting for players to announce they are turning pro. They want to lock up a commitment as soon as they possibly can.

Ultimately, I cherish the player development aspect of a young athlete and the fine-tuning of his abilities so he reaches his potential. Watching that development, working and sweating each day with him, is an extremely fulfilling process. The six-month experience of the one-and-done player was just not for me. But I certainly admire the coaches who can get these young, anointed superstars to play team defense.

Speaking of one-and-dones, the final sentence in the "phone call" paragraph of the DOJ report is also completely misleading. As far as I know, no evidence has surfaced that Brian Bowen was aware his father was requesting money to steer his son to any particular college. In fact, I sat face-to-face with Brian in the spring of 2017 while his family was present.

"How come you haven't decided on a school this late in the process?" I asked.

His response was completely believable. "I was leaning to Arizona but then [Arizona guards] Allonzo Trier and Rawle Atkins pulled their names out of the draft, so they will be starters there. Now that Donovan Mitchell looks like he's heading to the NBA and you might have a spot at the two guard position, it could be a perfect fit."

I certainly agreed. He played on the top-ranked AAU team in the nation and I was happy to have him be a Cardinal. But at no time did I think he was the type of person that wanted anything outside of a scholarship.

But that wasn't Dawkins's game. He wanted eventually to represent Bowen, apparently, and was working furiously trying to convince Adidas to come up with money to send him to one of their flagship franchises. The whole thing sickens me. Look at some of the damage Dawkins's scam caused: a terrific young man's life manipulated, innocent coaches fired, and a potential Final Four team left without the coach they came to play under.

PERSONAL FOULS

Other details offered in the complaint made it clear that the DOJ did not give a damn about protecting my identity. Here's how an FBI agent's testimony was used to describe "University-6":

"I have learned that University-6 is a public research university located in Kentucky. With approximately 22,640 students and over 7,000 faculty and staff members, it is one of the state's largest universities."

If you type "How many students attend the University of Louisville?" into Google's search box, guess what the answer was, as of May 2018? Bingo: 22,640. Given the complaint states that Coach-2 worked at University-6, anyone with a shred of common sense could have figured out my identity in a matter of seconds.

Thanks—or no thanks—to the allegations flying around as a result of the investigation and the subsequent actions of the University of Louisville, I have hired a team of lawyers to protect my interests and try to undo the damage of the DOJ complaint. The first person I retained was Steve Pence, the former US Attorney for the Western District of Kentucky who has also served as the lieutenant governor of Kentucky. As a former prosecutor, Steve was invaluable to me when DOJ charges broke. But when the University of Louisville used the bogus charges as the cover to fire me, I realized Steve would be consumed handling my suit against the board for wrongful termination. So I still needed representation to deal with the DOJ. Living in Miami, as I do, I'd become friendly with a guy named Armando Christian Pérez, better known as the rapper Pitbull. He called me and recommended I work with Marcos Jimenez, a lawyer who served as US Attorney for the Southern District of Florida for three years—at the same time, in fact, that Pence was the US Attorney in Kentucky. Now I had two former US Attorneys on my team.

As he familiarized himself with the issues, Marcos was stunned by the lack of discretion in the complaint. He told me he was amazed at how detailed it was and how much information prosecutors had disclosed about people who were not facing indictment. That information, as I just demonstrated, made it easy to identify many people who were involved in the investigation, no matter how tangentially.

"When you do that, you really expose innocent people to serious damage because you are essentially making accusations without charging people," Marcos said. "You don't have a way to really defend yourself. It's not like you can go to court and get a judge to rule on your case. There is no case. You're just being accused by a very powerful government entity of wrongdoing or who are quoting people who are claiming you are involved in wrongdoing. But you have no forum in which to air your grievances or defend yourself."

Marcos told me about the rules in place to protect citizens who are caught up in an investigation but who investigators have no intention of charging. They are supposed to protect identities, not divulge so many details that a third-grader can figure everything out.

The quotation that begins this chapter is taken from the US Attorneys' manual of official Justice Department Policy. The manual says that you should not name unguided or uncharged co-conspirators and should, in fact, protect the identity of individuals caught up in federal investigations. It refers to people like me as "unindicted co-conspirators," which is an unfortunate term. I am indeed unindicted. But I was not a co-conspirator. After three years of probes, where is the proof I conspired in any of these nefarious activities? It does not exist.

Marcos confirmed my impression that the complaint was written to make me look guilty. "I think that is really not what prosecutors should do. In fact, it's the opposite of what prosecutors should do," he told me. "Prosecutors are not there to convict and put notches in their belts. They're there to make sure that justice is done, and a lot of times justice means that you protect the innocent. There was no effort at all to do that in this case."

I don't want to put words in my lawyer's mouth, but I think the term he was politely avoiding was egregious prosecutorial overreach.

Marcos suggested approaching the team at the DOJ who had filed the complaint to try to clarify my status in the investigation. He also suggested that having someone with direct connections to the Southern District office in New York might be useful. I added Marc Mukasey, a former Assistant US Attorney at the Southern District who is now widely regarded as one of the top litigators in America.

Marcos and Marc began communicating with the DOJ. In one letter, Marcos made it very clear he thought the complaint had violated Department of Justice policy with regard to identifying suspects. He also noted that the prosecutor's job is to mete out justice and not just to obtain confessions.

A December meeting was arranged to take place in New York to discuss the case. I asked my legal team to determine if the DOJ considered me a suspect. If not, I wanted them to push for a way to clear my name. I'll be honest: I was furious at the DOJ. The false allegations spurred by this investigation cost me my job, career, and reputation. The prosecutors owed me more than an apology. They owed me a formal statement clearing me of any wrongdoing.

Before the meeting, I had been served with a subpoena to produce relevant documents to the case. I voluntarily handed over everything I had—all my text messages with the investigation suspects, all my voicemails from them, all relevant emails, and information about my telecom carriers—all at a great expense to me, so investigators could get whatever they needed from the phone companies.

ROUGH JUSTICE

Finally, Marcos and Marc met with two of the four DOJ lawyers who filed the complaint. They went through a timeline of the case. At one point, Marcos decided to state the obvious.

"Listen, this case is just Dawkins shooting his mouth off."

Marcos said the prosecutors reacted like he'd hit a nerve. "Like they were concerned it might be true."

But the conversation moved on. My guys highlighted some of the points about not identifying people who were not the focus of an investigation. At the end, Marc Mukasey didn't mince words:

"This is what's happened. You really have ruined this guy's career, and really caused him to be fired. You blew up his life. It was like a drive-by shooting. You shot him, he had no chance to defend himself, and you left him lying on the side of the road, almost dead. What do you have to say about that?"

"We deal with collateral damage all the time," said one of the Assistant US Attorneys.

When Marc relayed this remark after the meeting, I was shocked. "That's what he said? I'm just collateral damage? Did he express any regret? Any apology?"

"No." Then he described the Assistant US Attorney as a guy with no sympathy, no empathy—a rigid, hard-core prosecutor who could not care less about ruining someone's reputation.

I was beside myself. Collateral damage—that's how these prosecutors view the people who, for whatever reason, cross their path?

Later Marcos told me that the better phrase would be collateral damage without a remedy. "That's the tragedy," he said. "You have no remedy because you can't sue the government. They have immunity for their actions as prosecutors. You don't have a court case in which you can vindicate yourself."

In other words, I was screwed.

It's instances like this that show why something must change in our justice system. Prosecutors must take some responsibility for their actions. Giving them total immunity opens the door for abuses of power. I'm not sure how to change it, but this problem must be fixed.

After that first meeting, the prosecutors asked us to be more specific about certain things, so we put together a very detailed chronology on an Excel spreadsheet. Marc Mukasey presented it during a follow-up January meeting. Our hope was that by showing I had nothing to hide and was cooperating fully, they might release some kind of statement on my behalf. But after a few more exchanges with the DOJ, my lawyers determined the prosecutors weren't going to lift a finger to help me or undo the damage they created. And at that point, we realized talking with the US Attorney's Office was not going to vindicate me.

My team also felt some of the additional questions from the US Attorneys seemed like fishing expeditions, or as if they were still gunning for new suspects. And judging by new reports, they were probably right. Stories have leaked out suggesting a number of head coaches and major college basketball programs may be in trouble over various recruitment scams involving payoffs to athletes. But so far, the DOJ has added very little publically to its probe and seems to be having trouble prosecuting its cases.

Ten people had been named in the initial complaint. Manish Sood—Dawkins's alleged partner in crime—still hadn't been indicted eight months after the investigation became public. According to my attorneys, that's probably because the DOJ is hoping to flip him as a witness. The case against Brad Augustine, amazingly, has been dropped. I can't help wondering where the $12,700 he took from the undercover agent is. Meanwhile, some of the evidence against Dawkins may be compromised if the undercover FBI agent currently under investigation winds up facing charges of his own.

As for Marty Blazer, who pitched the probe to save his own neck, on August 10, 2017, the SEC ordered him to pay back $1.8 million to his victims and hit him with a $150,000 civil fine. He was barred permanently from working in the finance and agenting industries. One month later, on September 15, 2017—just ten days before the DOJ filed its sensational charges—Blazer pleaded guilty to securities fraud, aggravated identity theft, making false statements and documents, and two counts of wire fraud, as well as agreeing to pay restitution to his clients. He also broke down in tears. He has not, as far as I know, been sentenced yet.

There are more trials on the horizon. The eight other indicted figures will have their day in court, unless prosecutors can work out plea deals. Investigators—as reported by *The Boston Globe* and ESPN—also added another conspirator to the case, getting T.J. Gassnola, the former director of the New England Playaz, an AAU team from western Massachusetts, to plead guilty to conspiracy to commit wire fraud. Gassnola is said to have struck a plea deal, so he may implicate others. Christian Dawkins's old boss Andy Miller is reportedly cooperating with the feds, so who knows what will unfold down the line. It will be interesting to see if investigators ever uncover wrongdoing that wasn't instigated by Marty Blazer and his handlers. Perhaps Miller's office will yield a treasure-trove of information.

Of course, none of that will help me. Or Tom Jurich. Or our families. Or unwitting players like Brian Bowen who had his scholarship offer to Louisville revoked. Or the players that came to Louisville to work with me and my staff. Or the student body and faculty at Louisville, which will suffer from a shortfall in earnings for the athletic department as a result of these scandals.

You know, the collateral damage.

I'm sure some people will think I'm being melodramatic. Or throwing a pity party. But I'm not.

I'm just quoting a federal prosecutor.

Even now, after nearly a full year of waiting for clarity, I still don't get it. Was the acting US Attorney Kim Joon grandstanding for publicity when he announced this case in a press conference? Or did he truly believe he was going to clean up a plague of bad actors sullying college basketball? Or were he and his team conned by a crook who, looking for leniency, offered to expose people touted as big players but who turned out to be scam artists? I'm not playing stupid here. The whole thing is mystifying. Seriously, investigators spent at least three years and millions of dollars in resources to nab ten men suspected of disbursing or planning to disburse less than $500,000 in bribes—not exactly a future episode of *Billions*, is it?

I'm not exaggerating about the money spent to conduct the investigation. The FBI obtained a number of wiretaps, according to the issued complaints. The average wiretap costs about $40,000 to run. But the longer and more complex the investigation, the more expensive the taps can become. One of the issues with taping conversations—the kind of thing you never see in the movies—is that agents aren't supposed to listen to unauthorized information. If the FBI is investigating bribes, but the suspect being wiretapped has conversations about birthday party arrangements for his kid or about his mother's medical issues, those exchanges are not in the scope of the investigation and must be eliminated from the gathered evidence. Agents are instructed to "minimize" calls—in other words, they have to ensure that only relevant information pertaining to a case is recorded. Because the DOJ doesn't want agents sitting around all day waiting for calls to happen, they almost always outsource wiretaps and rely on contractors to "minimize" the gathered information. So investigators must have been paying a third party hundreds of thousands of dollars to conduct and manage a number of taps that went on for a considerable period of time.

Was that the goal of this investigation? To entice a few assistant coaches with easy money? To trick a wannabe agent into thinking he could sweet-talk a sneaker company into helping him cheat his way to millions? Is this a job for the FBI or for the NCAA enforcement branch?

Let's give some credit to the skilled men and women of the FBI and DOJ. If recent leaks turn out to be true, it's possible an enormous scandal will explode involving a number of head coaches and major universities and totally change the game forever. But if all they have are the charges they've already filed, then this investigation borders on the absurd. In an age of terrorism, at a time when opioid addiction is killing thousands of people and ruining the lives of so many Americans, is it worth millions of taxpayer dollars to stop a few shady payouts? As Vince Lombardi, famed football coach of the Green Bay Packers, would say: What the hell is going on out here!

I don't have the answers to those questions. But I can tell you that from where I sit, the Department of Justice exceeded its mandate and then some. Like the overreaching investigators on *Billions*, they had a scorched-earth policy as they boosted a scandal that didn't actually exist. And everyone who got singed or burned to a crisp as they marched toward filing indictments, well, you know what they were. But I'll say it one more time.

Collateral damage.

Shame on them.

12

History and conspiracy in a land where a contract is

not a contract.

▼

TO FULLY UNDERSTAND why Tom Jurich and I were forced out as athletic director and coach at the University of Louisville, you have to understand the almost inconceivable prominence of college basketball in the state of Kentucky. More than horseracing, more than bourbon, more than bluegrass music, more than any single aspect of life other than, perhaps, religion, basketball is the shared passion of the commonwealth.

You should also bear in mind that any company board can replace employees at any time. That's part of business. But if those employees have contracts, the company is required to honor those agreements and not try to smear the individuals they are replacing.

Finally, it helps to understand how the passion surrounding basketball can influence other aspects of Kentucky life. By this—and I realize this is hard to fathom for any out-of-state reader—I mean how the passion for Kentucky basketball can affect state politics. I know that sounds crazy. And, believe me, it is going to sound crazier as this tale unwinds, but as you will see, there is evidence that suggests my removal as coach of the Cardinals was influenced by the highest levels of the state government.

But I'm getting a little ahead of myself.

KENTUCKY'S OBSESSION

At the end of 2017, the editors of the Associated Press issued a top-ten list of biggest stories of the year in the state of Kentucky. It was quite a year in bluegrass country. The state's senior US senator, Mitch McConnell, presided over one of the most dysfunctional congressional sessions in history. As for the state's junior senator, Rand Paul, he was left with broken ribs after allegedly getting beaten up by his neighbor in a bizarre assault. Meanwhile—as covered by WKYT, the *Louisville Courier-Journal*, and other outlets—the Kentucky Speaker of the House was mired in a scandal over sexual harassment charges (and eventually resigned from his position in 2018); the state's pension fund was in crisis; and the state's budget was, too. Other major stories included a statewide opioid addiction crisis; a lawyer who defrauded the government of millions of dollars in bogus Social Security claims and fled the country; and a county clerk, once jailed for refusing to issue same-sex marriage licenses, who announced her plans to run for reelection.

But here is what the AP proclaimed was the biggest Kentucky story of the year:

1. UNIVERSITY OF LOUISVILLE: The University of Louisville endures a tumultuous year. Basketball coach Rick Pitino and athletic director Tom Jurich are fired after the school announces it's

being investigated in a federal corruption probe of bribery in college basketball. An audit uncovers mismanagement by the school's investment arm, and the school deals with a yearlong probation from an accrediting agency.

Despite this "honor," don't get the wrong idea. The Louisville Cardinals are not and never have been the favored sons in bluegrass territory. So why were Tom Jurich and I Kentucky's number-one story? Because, as crazy as it may sound, Louisville's basketball team is the arch-rival of the University of Kentucky Wildcats, and nothing—not Mitch McConnell, not Rand Paul, not the Kentucky Derby, not Makers Mark—is a bigger source of pride to the general Kentucky populace than the University of Kentucky Wildcats. Sure, Louisville is Kentucky's largest city, and the Cardinals basketball team has an impressive legacy of its own, but there is no comparison when it comes to which school is more popular.

I asked Tom Wallace, author of *The University of Kentucky Basketball Encyclopedia*, to describe Kentucky's passion for the Wildcats. "People out in the state are just 99.8 percent University of Kentucky fans," he said.

I'm not quite sure about that exact percentage. But you get the idea.

As for the difference between the two schools' fans, Wallace said, "Many Kentucky fans are from the eastern part of the state where they don't have anything to be proud of except Kentucky basketball. Whereas Louisville is a big city, more sophisticated. They'll accept a loss to Kentucky a lot better than Kentucky fans will accept a loss to Louisville. It kills them."

In other words, the state's basketball obsession and partisan attitudes made Louisville's basketball scandal a huge story.

THE RIVALRY

Depending on who you talk to, the animosity toward the University of Louisville and love for the University of Kentucky is rooted in any number of things: the dominance of Wildcats basketball, the history of the state, racism, and Kentuckians' vision of themselves as a rural folk as opposed to city slickers.

Let's stick to hoops for the moment. Over the last seventy years, the University of Kentucky basketball team has been the most dominant force in the college game. The team has the most wins (2,265 and counting) and highest all-time winning percentage (.764), according to Sports-Reference.com. Only UCLA has won more national basketball championships, eleven, than the Wildcats, who have eight crowns. The school has the most NCAA Tournament appearances, has played in the most NCAA Tournament games, and has the most wins in the tournament. The team has also made forty-three NCAA Sweet Sixteen appearances, and thirty-seven NCAA Elite Eight appearances.

I could go on and on about the Wildcats' success, since, as I've noted, I coached the Wildcats to the sixth of the school's eight championships in 1996. So I have firsthand experience with the team's legacy and the love that the Kentucky Wildcats generate—and the loathing its fans have for Louisville.

The Wildcats' legacy really took off with famous and infamous coach Adolph Rupp, who arrived on campus in 1930 as head coach and kept the job for forty-two years. In the 1940s, Rupp turned the team into a powerhouse. Under his watch, the Wildcats won the National Invitational Tournament in 1946, then won the NCAA Tournament in 1948, 1949, 1951, and 1958. These astounding achievements give Rupp, arguably, the most impressive coaching record this side of UCLA coach John Wooden's ten national championships, which included seven championships in a row.

Kentucky has never had a Major League Baseball team or an NFL team. So you can see how such a successful program would become the darling of the state. No matter how good other schools might have been—in Kentucky or even across the country—for decades they were the only team that mattered in the commonwealth.

Despite this long history of basketball glory, the rivalry between the Wildcats and the Louisville Cardinals is a relatively recent phenomenon.

"Kentucky and Louisville just didn't play because Adolph Rupp didn't believe in scheduling Kentucky schools," says Wallace, who speculates Rupp may have feared that a loss to Louisville would hurt the Wildcats' prestige. "If he'd play a Kentucky school, it was Georgetown College or Berea College. Somebody he knew he could beat."

In 1959, Louisville and Kentucky finally faced off in the Mideast Regional semifinal of the NCAA Tournament—and Rupp's great fear was realized. Louisville beat Kentucky by fifteen points, 76-61, and went to its first Final Four.

The teams didn't meet again for more than twenty years. Even without actual games, Kentucky and Louisville were still pitted against each other off the court. The most obvious difference between the teams centered on race. Under coach Peck Hickman, Louisville became the first Kentucky college to integrate its program by signing Eddie Whitehead and Wade Houston, the father of future All-Star Allan Houston, to basketball scholarships in 1962.

Meanwhile, Rupp's teams remained all-white and played in the SEC, the last college conference to integrate. On March 19, 1966, Kentucky's all-white reality stood out for the nation to see when it played—and lost—the NCAA championship game to Western Texas, a team with a white coach and an all-black starting five. *Sports Illustrated* writer Frank Deford was in the locker room at halftime during the Western Texas game. According to Deford, Rupp exhorted his players with racist language.

There is an ongoing debate about Rupp's racial attitudes. Some note he coached black players as a high school coach in Illinois; others say he was a fair man who was a product of his times—and of coaching a team in the segregated South. Rupp finally signed a black player to a scholarship in 1969, but the recruit, a seven-footer from Louisville named Tom Payne, didn't actually play until 1971 due to eligibility issues. Thirty years later, as I attempted to woo African-American recruits to my Wildcats program, I discovered the segregated past of Kentucky basketball still cast an ugly shadow on the school. Some of those student-athletes had parents who remembered Rupp and the school's reluctance to integrate. And some of those parents were dead set against their sons playing at the Rupp Arena. My insistence that institutions can evolve—which is something I wholeheartedly believe—didn't always win over converts, and I can understand why.

In 1982, another March Madness matchup between the Bluegrass State's basketball powerhouses finally happened. The media dubbed it the dream game—and it lived up to the hype when Kentucky's Jim Master sank a jump shot to send the game into overtime. The drama didn't last, however, as Louisville regrouped and won 80–68.

After that game, Louisville coach Denny Crum became more vocal about playing Kentucky. "He wanted a piece of the Big Blue," Wallace said. "But the ones who were really against it were Joe B. Hall, the Kentucky coach, and Cliff Hagan, the athletic director. They wanted, I guess, to adhere to Rupp's policy of not playing a Kentucky school. Or maybe they just were afraid of playing Louisville."

Crum thought the University of Kentucky may have had another motive for refusing to play. "They didn't want to give us any inroads in terms of recruiting," he said. "They had the advantage throughout the state and they wanted to maintain that advantage. If they never played us or acknowledged us, they'd be able to keep that."

After the dream game, the drumbeat for more Kentucky-Louisville games started to beat louder. The Kentucky governor at the time, John Y. Brown Jr., believed the two taxpayer-funded schools owed it to the state to play each other and that rivalries were healthy. Brown applied pressure to the then-UK Board of Trustees chairman Bill Sturgill, who also happened to be the Secretary of Energy in the governor's cabinet. He even added a mild threat.

"If you can't get it done, I'll come over there," Brown said. "I'll be over there by noon."

Eventually, the board voted 12–6 in favor of exploring the possibility of a Kentucky vs. Louisville basketball series. Two months later, Hagan and Louisville athletic director Bill Olsen agreed to a four-year series that would alternate games between Kentucky's Rupp Arena and Louisville's Freedom Hall.

The rivalry shifted to another level when I signed on to coach Louisville. Tom Wallace—who, of course, is a die-hard Kentucky fan— told a friend of mine, "Pitino went from being the God of Kentucky to, all of a sudden, Satan. Rick came in and he established those great Kentucky teams. But the big change, of course, was when he left Kentucky. Kentucky fans conveniently forget that he left Kentucky for Boston. In their mind, he left Kentucky for Louisville."

TOM JURICH AND THE LOUISVILLE RENAISSANCE

In 2001, Tom Jurich, faced with a program that had endured two losing seasons over the previous four years, made it a priority to return the Cardinals basketball team to national prominence. He did that. What the wins and losses don't reveal is the impact Tom had on the entire University of Louisville.

In 2001, the University of Louisville was still a large commuter school. As campuses go, it was in need of a makeover. Undergraduate life on school grounds was not exactly vibrant. In fact, my friend Hal Bomar, one of Louisville's biggest boosters, described the campus back then as "a ghost town." The dorms were run-down. The athletic facilities were ancient. Despite a legacy of great athletes—Johnny Unitas, Wes Unseld, Butch Beard, Junior Bridgeman, Darrell Griffith, Pervis Ellison—the Louisville campus was not going to lure top athletes, especially when other Division 1 programs, like Kansas and North Carolina, could wow recruits with state-of-the-art training facilities and grand landscapes.

At Louisville, Tom proved a master fund-raiser and builder. There are twenty-one sports teams at Louisville. During Tom's run, he oversaw the construction of brand-new facilities for twenty of those sports. As for the twenty-first sport, tennis, the Bass-Rudd Tennis Center was completely remodeled.

Tom also raised money for the University's $18.5 million Thortons Academic Center of Excellence, a spectacular 43,000-square-foot center designed specifically as a hub for the school's athletes to study and eat. With a thirty-six-desk computer lab, private tutoring areas, conference rooms, two-hundred-seat auditorium, and cafeteria, it is a crown jewel for recruiting—an inviting space that tells student-athletes the school is committed to helping them compete and excel in the classroom and in their chosen sport.

All this construction, as well as new dorms, new classrooms, and labs masterminded by school president James Ramsey, turned the University of Louisville into a first-class, modern institution of higher education. In fact, in May 2017, the popular news and entertainment website Buzzfeed named Louisville the most beautiful campus in Kentucky. Aesthetics are always debatable, but you'll get no argument from me on that selection. While U of L may not have quite the old collegiate elegance and acreage of the University of Kentucky, it is now its equal in every other way. The university that served the city for over two centuries had become a destination school for the whole state, with ever-improving academics and athletic programs and facilities that are second to none.

Tom also succeeded in raising Louisville's basketball profile in an entirely new way. He got us into the Atlantic Coast Conference beginning in 2014. The ACC is arguably the toughest division in college basketball. Members of the ACC include Duke, North Carolina, Syracuse, and NC State—in other words, some of the most successful and popular programs in history. For U of L, joining the division translated into huge ticket sales and increased TV revenue for each conference game.

These deals turned the University of Louisville into one of the most profitable sports programs in the country. For thirteen straight years, the Cardinals program was the top revenue generator of all basketball programs in the country, thanks to great sponsorships and TV deals, and, of course, devoted Louisville fans. Our supporters included 18,000 season ticket holders to Cardinals basketball games. Boosters also paid top dollar for luxury suites. Every fiscal year ended with our program in the black, with millions of dollars in profit. And the recent $160 million Adidas deal I mentioned earlier was put together to help the balance sheet even more.

There was one deal, though, that Tom Jurich did not want, at least initially, to see happen: The construction of a 22,000-seat arena in downtown Louisville. And that deal—which eventually became the KFC Yum! Center—would come back to haunt him. Big-time.

But arena controversy aside, Tom Jurich's initiatives earned him a reputation as one of the best athletic directors in the country and a promotion to Vice President of Athletics at Louisville. In the eyes of many, he was one of the most powerful men in the state of Kentucky. Through no fault of his own, that success made him a marked man.

THE GOVERNOR WHO WOULD BE KING

Kentucky governor Matt Bevin is much like Donald Trump, and whether that's a good or bad thing is up to you. Bevin is a big-business-loving member of the Republican Party. He also has a combative relationship with the press. "Part of Bevin's strategy is to simply ignore outlets and reporters he considers hostile," according to an article by Scott Jennings, a conservative Kentucky columnist and public relations strategist. "In his view, dealing with them never yields a better outcome so why bother?"

One noticeable difference between Bevin and Trump is that the governor comes across as a religious zealot with a puritanical streak. I have no problem with people of faith, as I am one myself. We've never met, but I wouldn't be surprised if he was upset by the fact I have been linked to two sex scandals—the Andre McGee-stripper debacle and my own stupid, brief, idiotic, extramarital indiscretion with a woman who was eventually convicted of blackmailing me.

There is speculation in Kentucky that Bevin isn't content to just be the governor. He appears to have national political ambitions, according to some political analysts, and sources have told me that he wonders if becoming a US senator from Kentucky—thereby raising his national profile—is his best path to the Oval Office.

It's not such a wild idea. Before he "settled" for the governor job, Bevin tried—and failed—to unseat Kentucky senator Mitch McConnell in 2014. And in early 2018, he aggressively sought out the national stage, appearing on MSNBC, Fox News, CNN, and NPR to weigh in on gun violence in America and claiming "guns are not the problem" while suggesting video games, music lyrics, and TV were partly responsible for the rash of school shootings plaguing America. McConnell's term ends in 2020. It's anyone's guess whether he will run again for Senate. And the same goes for Bevin.

THE ARENA OF INTRIGUE

In early 2016, a good friend of mine, a former Louisville athlete with a strong connection to the governor's inner circle, gave me a call.

He told me he shared a mutual friend with Bevin. This friend revealed that the governor was planning on getting rid of Tom Jurich.

Since this conversation took place not long after the McGee scandal had broken and my friend thought he had misheard, he asked: "You mean Rick?"

Bevin's buddy made it clear: Tom was in the crosshairs.

How did Tom become a target? Let's look at a long sequence of events surrounding Tom, U of L, Bevin, and the arena.

On May 23, 2005, the Louisville Arena Task Force, created by then-governor Ernie Fletcher, held its first meeting to discuss bringing a new, state-of-the-art arena to the city's downtown area. At that time, Tom let it be known that he would rather have a new arena built near campus or get money to redo the state-owned Freedom Hall, which is very close to campus.

Two locations for the new arena quickly surfaced: one on the Louisville riverfront and a smaller spot known as the Water Company. Tom and I voiced our immediate and obvious preference to have the arena on the riverfront. It was the clear choice in terms of size, location, and architectural grandeur. As school president Ramsey put it, it had the "wow" factor.

John Schnatter, a member of the Arena Task Force, and fellow Louisville businessman David Jones Sr., funded a study of the arena proposals for the competing sites and determined an arena built at the Water Company site would cost an estimated $120 million less than one at the bigger, ritzier riverfront site.

On September 26, 2005, the Arena Task Force approved the riverfront site. John Schnatter was the only dissenting vote. For the record,

Tom and the rest of the University of Louisville administration endorsed the plan.

Three months later, on December 16, Governor Fletcher announced the creation of the Louisville Arena Authority to oversee the design, construction, and operation of the new project. It was game on.

The LAA had an enormous workload. They had to plan for every aspect of the new complex—including how to pay for it. The LAA made a number of miscalculations and faulty income projections, according to a subsequent state audit. But in the run-up to the construction, the Authority made a deal with Tom. He was to handle the ticket sales and marketing of all Louisville basketball and volleyball games held at the arena. The university would earn about 88 percent of the sales of luxury box suites to Cardinals games. In return, the school would pay the arena between $1.3 and $1.8 million annually.

On April 19, 2010, the LAA announced the Yum! Corporation had signed a ten-year, $13.5 million deal for the naming rights to the arena—a substantial shortfall from the initial projections made by the LAA. As WDRB noted, the money was a "far cry from the $40 million minimum bid [LAA chairman Jim] Host originally said he would accept."

On October 10, 2010, the 22,000-seat arena, now known as the KFC Yum! Center, opened. Revenue issues surfaced almost immediately, as arena earnings and the Tax Increment Financing (TIF)—a portion of the sales and property tax revenue generated in the area around the arena that is used to fund a project—failed to match projections, resulting in cash shortfalls of millions of dollars.

In 2011, according to the *Courier-Journal*, the LAA had a net operations income of $500,000, which was $700,000 less than the $1.2 million budgeted amount, never mind the $3.7 million that was forecast in 2008.

Things got so bad by 2012 that Moody's Investor Services announced it didn't think the bonds that were issued to fund the arena's construction were solid enough to be investment-worthy securities. Then, in 2013, the company lowered its rating of the bonds again.

Matt Bevin announced on January 27, 2015, that he would run for Kentucky governor. By then the arena had been a political sore spot for years, one that had literally taxed the City of Louisville, as money had to be raised to make debt payments, and taxed the state coffers, too, because TIF sales tax money went to fund the arena instead of going to Frankfort.

On November 3, 2015, Bevin won the governor's race, in an upset victory beating Democrat Jack Conway. He inherited a state plagued with a number of headaches: budget troubles, a looming pension disaster, and a growing opioid crisis. And of course, the arena was a giant white elephant—a highly visible symbol of fiscal pain and long-term debt.

After only six months in office, Bevin suddenly showed a deep interest in the University of Louisville. He unilaterally fired the school's entire twenty-member board of trustees and announced that university president James Ramsey would resign.

Bevin explained his power play to reporters with this statement: "There have been a number of news stories—many of which you all have covered—that have been in the wind in recent months and, frankly, years as it relates to the University of Louisville that have shed less than the best light on the university and the commonwealth as a whole."

The move drew instant criticism. Bevin's executive order announced the new board would have thirteen members—ten appointments made by the governor and three representatives for students, faculty, and operations. But under Kentucky law at the time, the board was required to have seventeen members appointed by the governor. State law also dictated the governor could only remove board of trustees members "for cause"—after each member had had a hearing with an attorney before the Kentucky Council on Postsecondary Education. No such hearings had occurred.

Kentucky Attorney General Andy Beshear challenged Bevin's move, saying existing laws prevented his unilateral, blanket removal of the board. Circuit Court Judge Phillip Shepherd issued a ruling stating that Bevin "served as judge, jury, and executioner" of the board when he sidestepped state laws regarding the removal of board members. The Republican-controlled state legislature rewrote the law, however, basically handing Bevin control over the Louisville Board of Trustees. What initially had been an illegal maneuver was essentially legislated into a legal one.

Bevin claimed the board he fired was "operationally dysfunctional" and told reporters he wanted to "put the house in order." As for Ramsey's departure, he said there were many reasons behind the move. "Some have had to do with academic things," the governor said. "Some have had to do with administrative things. Some have had to do with athletic things."

Speaking of athletic things, a few months later, on October 18, 2016, Kentucky lawmakers voted to have State Auditor Mike Harmon audit the Louisville Arena Authority, due to ongoing concerns about the facility's finances.

Two months later, members of the Louisville's Metro Council took pot shots at the University of Louisville's lease agreement, and issued calls for the school to provide financial support for the Yum! Center. On December 6, 2016, Tom Jurich then told interviewers, "If they don't want us in there, just tell us—we'll leave."

In January of 2017, the University of Louisville's accreditation agency, Southern Association of Colleges and Schools, put the university on probation—and blamed Bevin for the move. Belle Wheelan, the agency's president, said Bevin's destruction of the board of trustees "demonstrates the board is functioning with considerable external control and influence," and the move jeopardized the board's "capacity to be ultimately responsible for providing a sound education program."

On June 20, 2017, State Auditor Harmon told lawmakers Arena Authority used flawed data as the basis for revenue projections. It was, apparently, nothing more than an innocent, multimillion-dollar mistake! According to Harmon, financial projections for the arena's TIF revenue used ten years of property tax data but sixteen years of sales tax data, which included a sales tax rate increase from 1990 that boosted expectations.

Harmon's office found TIF revenues had fallen as much as two-thirds below projections, according the *Louisville Business Journal*. The TIF revenue was $10.3 million in 2016, compared with a projection of $15.9 million.

But Harmon also ripped the University of Louisville for—are you sitting down?—profiting on ticket sales.

This had become a favorite refrain in Kentucky. And now Harmon was singing it, too. Tom and the U of L were guilty...of being good negotiators. He wrangled favorable revenue share agreements prior to arena construction. Was that Tom's fault? He was just doing his job.

I wonder if Harmon ever considered that the faulty TIF projections might have prompted negotiators to be more generous with Tom? Or if he examined whether the LAA botched projections on how much they'd need from U of L, too?

Bevin's appointee to the Arena Authority, Scott Cox, asked the university to give back $2.4 million each year. Tom balked at this. He felt he had lived up to his end of the contract and the faulty projections were not his problem. Furthermore, just producing $2.4 million isn't easy for a tightly budgeted institution. All the athletic department programs are allocated money. Pulling it back can be difficult. So Tom's reticence to come up with more funds was totally understandable from the point of view of a school administrator. But Tom's initial stance did not go over well in Frankfort, where the governor controls the purse-strings when it comes to funding Kentucky's state universities.

In July of 2017, after years of criticism and political pressure, the university approved an amended lease agreement with the Louisville Arena Authority to kick in an extra $2.42 million each year to help pay down the KFC Yum! Center debt. The school also agreed to release the arena from its commitment to hosting Louisville volleyball games so the Yum! Center could book more lucrative music concerts. At least two members of the Louisville Athletic Association told reporters they felt the department was being punished for its success and strong-armed by politicians.

After the deal was done, Tom Jurich noted that U of L was paying twice what the University of Kentucky paid to play its basketball games. The *Louisville Courier-Journal* confirmed Tom's statement, reporting the Cardinals agreed to pay an additional $2.42 million annually on top of the original terms for a total bill of about $4 million. Meanwhile, the University of Kentucky's deal to use the Rupp Arena for basketball games, which went into effect in 2018, calls for the Lexington school to pay $1.9 million annually—roughly half of U of L's bill.

So there you have it. The genesis of Tom's demise lies, I believe, somewhere in the events surrounding the KFC Yum! Center. But bubbling beneath these events, which I've tried to lay out in chronological order and which I believe also hastened my own exit, were many other agendas and complex relationships.

THE CONSPIRACY CAROUSEL

Also around this time, I heard another rumor involving the governor and his campaign supporter John Schnatter, the founder of Papa John's pizza. The former Louisville athlete told me Schnatter had arranged to fly Bevin to meet with Charles G. Koch and David H. Koch, the conservative billionaire owners of Koch Industries, who have spent millions boosting their business-friendly political agenda. I have no idea if this meeting ever actually happened, but I do know that in 2015, Schnatter teamed with the Charles Koch Foundation to bestow $12 million to the University of Kentucky's Gatton College of Business and Economics. (While Schnatter has also given millions to the University of Louisville over the years and owns the naming rights to Louisville's football stadium, his allegiance to the Wildcats has been well documented; in a 2013 TV interview, he called the coaching and athletic department of U of K "second to none.") A year after the bequest was made, news broke that Bevin had attended an exclusive weekend retreat in Colorado Springs hosted by the Koch brothers between July 29 and August 1, 2016.

I'm sure governors meet with political donors all the time. But these incidents further underscore Bevin's focus on becoming a national political figure.

For all his ambition, Bevin, who was born in Colorado, raised in New Hampshire, and graduated from Washington and Lee University in Virginia, nearly stumbled during his gubernatorial campaign, but he proved himself a fast learner. In May of 2015, he was asked on Kentucky Sports Radio to pick between me and John Calipari as his favorite coach. He picked me.

Anyone in the state could have told him backing me was a political mistake. A few months later, when asked to pick a team in the great Kentucky-Louisville basketball rivalry, he didn't hesitate to set his "record" straight. "I learned my lesson last time by trying to be diplomatic that it is important when speaking to Big Blue Nation to pull for Big Blue Nation," he said. "So I'd have to go with Kentucky."

In case anyone thinks I'm overstating the voting power of the

Wildcats fan base, let's take a minute to consider the political career of Richie Farmer. A former high school star from eastern Kentucky's Clay County High School, Farmer was a starting guard on the 1992 Wildcats team that lost to Duke on Christian Laettner's famous buzzer-beating shot. Eleven years later, in 2003, Farmer, then a financial investment advisor with zero political experience, decided to enter the race for state Agriculture Commissioner.

If Farmer's resume was a little weak, he did have the perfect name for that particular job—and it was one that would resonate with voters who remembered him as a Wildcats hero. He was elected with 55.2 percent of the vote. Four years later, he was reelected in a landslide, with 64 percent of the vote. Soon after, Farmer's star dimmed, as corruption rumors swirled around him. During his 2011 campaign for lieutenant governor, a Kentucky political scientist attributed the ex-Wildcat's political career to basketball.

"Richie Farmer owes his electoral success to his former career as a University of Kentucky basketball player," professor Don Dugi of Lexington's Transylvania University told the *Washington Post* in 2011. There can be no doubt Farmer's political clout came from his Wildcat past. He was a high school legend who reminded many people of the hardworking Jimmy Chitwood, the hero in the movie *Hoosiers* (who was based on Milan High School's star player Bobby Plump). He became one of Kentucky's favorite players, and I loved coaching him.

Farmer lost his bid for lieutenant governor. Soon after, the rumors that had surfaced turned into indictments for the misuse of state funds and abusing his position for personal gain. In 2013, he reached a plea deal for a twenty-seven-month prison sentence. Apparently, being a Wildcat star will only get you so far. I've kept in close contact with Richie over the years and will always love him for his work ethic and loyalty. I wish he had never entered the political arena.

At any rate, Bevin eventually soaked up the political importance of the Wildcats.

When Bevin told reporters he wanted to "put the house in order," he was alluding to a number of headline-grabbing issues—Ramsey's controversial multimillion-dollar compensation, the arena deal, and the optics of the Andre McGee disaster—but many were shocked by his singularly negative perspective on U of L. It was as if the school's amazing transformation had never happened. I've already covered the improvements to the campus and sports facilities. But as Louisville TV station WDRB reported at the time, the percentage of students who graduated within six years of starting school at Louisville rose to 53.6 percent in 2015—a 33 percent leap from 2002's graduation rate. The average ACT score of entering freshmen rose from 23.3 in 2002 to 25.5 in 2015. Meanwhile, research funding at the university, an important metric for higher-learning institutions, grew from $80.9 million to $179.3 million during the same period.

With so many positives, what was the real motive behind Bevin's moves? There are three theories.

The first, of course, is that Bevin's power play came from the heart and he truly believed his unilateral, arguably unlawful moves were in the best interests of the university.

A second theory I have heard is that this was a conspiracy by Bevin and his associates to get rid of one of the most powerful A.D.s in the country. According to this theory, Bevin's University of Kentucky–loving associates were driven by jealousy of a rival program becoming too successful and popular, and urged the governor to act—and send a silent message to Wildcat supporters across the commonwealth. Given the history of bad blood between the programs and the electoral pull of the Wildcat nation, this theory doesn't really seem completely far-fetched. As the former Louisville athlete with connections to Frankfort told me: "The way you become senator is you win the statewide vote.

The city of Louisville doesn't matter. So Bevin is focusing on winning the state." He also speculated that ardent Bevin-backer John Schnatter, who gave the maximum $2,000 donation to the governor's campaign, had pushed the governor to take aim at Louisville and thereby align himself with the Big Blue Nation of Wildcats lovers and consolidate his voter base.

"And to do that you cut the head off the snake, which is Tom Jurich and you," added my friend.

You could put some credence in this idea—especially the pandering for votes. With only 3.3 million registered voters in the state, having a calculated focus on the University of Kentucky—a school, by the way, that has a significantly larger student body than Louisville (U of K's total enrollment—undergraduate, graduate, and post-doctorate students—has outpaced U of L's by about five thousand students annually at least since 2005)—makes sense for almost every politician in the state. You will appeal to more alumni and therefore more voters. But I have a hard time believing jealousy of Louisville's success was the primary motivating factor.

Instead, I believe Tom's successful deal-making ruffled too many feathers. I suspect the decision to get rid of Tom—and by extension me—has its roots in a meeting between Bevin, Tom, U of L board chairman J. David Grissom, acting U of L president Greg Postel, John Schnatter, and Junior Bridgeman, one of the most popular and successful athletes in Louisville history, who was one of the original appointees to Bevin's ten-person board.

The meeting occurred soon after Tom told a gathering of boosters and administrators about the university's new $160 million Adidas sponsorship on August 24, 2017. Tom told me that during the meeting Postel claimed he didn't know about the Adidas agreement—apparently implying that Tom had forged the deal in secret.

Tom told me things got very heated very quickly. He vehemently denied anyone was kept in the dark and said any suggestion otherwise was a lie. In fact, he said, the school attorneys—essentially Postel's lawyers—read all the contracts and reported to all parties.

The governor turned to Postel and asked if this was true.

There was little Postel could say, according to Tom.

In the middle of this exchange, Junior turned to Grissom and said, "You are polarizing the city of Louisville and creating a cloud of division that is extremely harmful to our university."

"Maybe I should resign," Grissom said.

"No, we don't need that to happen," said the governor, who then asked Tom and Junior to leave the meeting.

It is my belief Tom was too strong a person to cave in to the whims of Bevin, Grissom, or Schnatter, and the contentious meeting just reinforced that reality to a trio of millionaires who are used to getting their way. They realized they would never have total control with Tom Jurich running the athletic department. In the end, Tom's triumphant Adidas deal—which was a huge improvement on the school's previous five-year, $39 million sponsorship with the shoe company—and the Yum! Center deal appear to have sealed his fate in the eyes of the governor.

As board chairman, Grissom has drawn fierce criticism. He insisted on a confidential search for a new university president—infuriating faculty members, who pointed out that the school's governance rules, known as the Redbook, hold that "in making the appointment of the president, the board shall consult with a faculty committee to be composed of one representative elected for that specific purpose from each" of the school's thirteen academic units.

A scathing editorial by a U of L student painted him as a dictator: "Grissom is a bully. He silences other board members and doesn't always do things by the book and made it clear that he's the board member that speaks to the media."

Why would an eighty-year-old man with limited ties to the University of Louisville take on this non-paying job? He had previously spent more than two decades as the board chairman of Centre College. And he has reportedly donated over $20 million to that private institution—a number that's in sharp contrast to the $128,407 he had given to the U of L as of January 2018.

As for Schnatter, he's made millions selling pizza. Other than that, I believe you'd be hard-pressed to find any other noble qualities with a search warrant. His widely reported remarks tying Papa John's disappointing earnings to the NFL's inability to handle the "controversy" over players who kneel during the national anthem to protest racial injustice serve as a sad example of his lack of nuance and decency. No matter where you stand on the issue, reducing it to whether or not you sell more pizzas is just clueless. According to *Forbes*, Papa John's stock prices dropped eleven percent after a disappointing third quarter in 2017, and Schnatter lost $70 million in one day. The cash hemorrhage came just months after Schnatter was added to the list of the world's billionaires—a list that no longer bears his name. Weeks after the valuation debacle and the ridiculous NFL comments another strange event happen: Papa John's announced Schnatter was stepping down as CEO of the company.

Both Grissom and Schnatter backed the governor with campaign contributions. The governor then destroyed the old board and installed Grissom and Schnatter as his chosen emissaries. Since then, stories appeared in the press smearing me and Tom—painting Tom as a bully and claiming I had kept millions of dollars of Louisville's Adidas sponsorship money, when in fact I had a completely separate deal.

All three of these men live by a "my way or the highway" credo. They share a disturbing pattern of quite a few leaders today: listen poorly, overreact, say anything to win, and, most of all, burn down anyone in your path.

Bevin's board of trustees moves seem even more calculated and cynical when you compare them to his appointments to the University of Kentucky's Board of Trustees. On August 12, 2016, two months after Bevin blew up the Louisville board, he appointed three new members to the Kentucky board, including Kelly Knight Craft—the wife of billionaire Joe Craft, the University of Kentucky booster who donated $6 million to build the Wildcats' practice facility that bears his name—who was a major fund-raiser for Bevin.

I have no argument with those appointees. I like Kelly and Joe, and it makes perfect sense to appoint board members who have a strong connection to the college they govern. In fact, as of 2018, fourteen of the twenty-one members on the University of Kentucky Board of Trustees had degrees from the school they serve. I applaud that. Which brings us to Bevin's newly installed members of the Louisville Board of Trustees.

Of Bevin's ten initial appointees, only two—Diane B. Medley and Junior Bridgeman, who resigned the board after only a few months—attended the University of Louisville as undergraduates. Two others, Grissom, who attended Kentucky's Centre College as an undergrad, and Tulane alum Ronald Wright, went to Louisville graduate programs. All the other new, governor-picked trustees—60 percent of his board appointees—have never attended the school they oversee. As for board vice chairman John Schnatter, who, as I mentioned earlier, teamed with a Koch brother to give millions of dollars to the University of Kentucky, he attended Ball State.

Why would Bevin load the University of Kentucky board with U of K graduates but stock the Louisville board with trustees who have no obvious connection to the school? Why name Schnatter, who is an openly partisan booster of the Kentucky Wildcats, to become a Louisville trustee and serve as vice chair of the board? Why appoint Grissom, chairman of a private investment firm Mayfair Capital and the Glenview Trust Co., which advises big money clients, to run the board in a secretive manner?

Tom and I were about to find out.

FLAGRANT FOULS

On April 12, 2017, board vice chairman Schnatter took a very public shot at Tom Jurich during a board of trustees meeting.

Charging "the leadership" of the athletics department is "invisible" to the university's governing board, Schnatter said, "The athletics thing scares me....Until you fix athletics, you cannot fix this university." He didn't mention Tom by name, but his target was obvious. It was an interesting statement for a number of reasons: It came from out of left field; it offered no specifics in his attack on one of the most profitable athletic departments in America; and Schnatter, at the time of his attack, was a member of the school's athletics association board.

So what was Schnatter's motive? By publicly tarring Tom's leadership and his department, was Schnatter laying the groundwork for further attacks?

As I recounted earlier, on June 17, 2017, the NCAA Committee on Infractions issued its decision on the Andre McGee scandal and announced penalties against the Louisville basketball program, including four years of probation and other penalties—punishments that would hurt the school financially. The moves would also hurt our recruiting efforts because the Cardinals TV and tournament exposure—something every player wants—had been taken away. The penalties were poised to destroy campus morale and turn the University of Louisville into a community of outcasts.

Postel immediately announced Louisville would appeal the penalties for being ridiculously harsh. He also singled me out: "This ruling is also unfair to Coach Pitino, who we believe could not have known about the illicit activities."

Eleven days later, I attended a board of trustees meeting at Tom's suggestion. He thought I should tell the board my strategy on how to frame the university appeal. I was given a light five-game suspension that made me believe I would win.

I distributed a twenty-six-page booklet to the board members at the meeting. My idea was to introduce myself and establish my reputation as a coach who has always run disciplined programs. It recounted my coaching career: 770 wins, 7 Final Four appearances, 2 National Championships, 16 first-round draft picks, and 15 seasons of 20+ wins. But the part of the booklet I was most proud of was the testimonial section, filled with appraisals from my former assistant coaches and players.

> *Besides my parents, there is not another person who has taught me more about the game, life, and what it takes to be successful.*— Billy Donovan, head coach, Oklahoma Thunder
>
> *Working for Coach Pitino, there was always a stern directive to follow every and all of the NCAA's rules. Every detail of how we did things had to be by the book. We were going to outwork everyone, but it had to be within the rules.*—Frank Vogel, head coach, Orlando Magic
>
> *Rick Pitino has been a part of my life since I was twenty years old. At that point, my life revolved around basketball and my playing career at the University of Kentucky. Before Coach P, I had played very little and probably deservedly so, because I was not very good and neither was our team. We had just accomplished something no other team had achieved in the history of Kentucky basketball...a losing season!*
>
> *Amid all the chaos and humiliation of probations, a once-proud*

program was on fire and burning to the ground. Quite honestly, the whole place was on the verge of extinction and never to be heard from again. As one of only eight scholarship players who were left, I can tell you self-esteem and morale were very low; if not nonexistent. Not only for the student-athletes, but for all the people of the commonwealth. The whole state was down and depressed. Our athletic director at the time was C.M. Newton, a man of class and character. He knew he not only needed a basketball coach with a tireless work ethic, but someone who believed in discipline and following the rules. The program, after all, was on probation. From day one, when Coach Pitino took over as the head coach at Kentucky, he gave everyone hope...players, administrators, and fans. He talked about working hard, being disciplined, completing with integrity, and living by the spirit and intent of the rules. Not just governing laws, but human decency. Treating people with respect. Being kind and helpful to one another, as well as personally sacrificing so a teammate could do more.

These were not just words. He demonstrated all these character traits himself on a daily basis. Coach Pitino encouraged and inspired us to heights none of us thought possible. He challenged us to go the extra mile, praised us in victory, comforted us in defeat, and helped us realize we were all valuable human beings regardless of our performance or the outcome of a game. He not only made us better players, but he made us better people.

When players, coaches, and people who have been around Rick Pitino for any length of time talk about him, they all speak of his incredible threshold for work, his dedication, and discipline to bringing out the best in others and his integrity to doing things the right way!

Coach's awareness and commitment to these core values of character is what have given him over thirty-five years of unprecedented *success and relationships that will stand the test of time.*—John Pelphrey, former Arkansas head coach (2007–11), current Alabama associate head coach

There were many more endorsements from my ex-players, including Reggie Theus, Peyton Siva, and Russ Smith, and from coaches Mick Cronin, Brett Brown, Tubby Smith, and others.

The board members looked at the booklet. "This is self-serving," one of them said in a voice dripping with contempt.

Of course it was self-serving! My reputation and the reputation of the school was on the line. But it wasn't fiction. I didn't make up those quotes. I didn't invent my career or my success or the impact others were saying I had on them.

After this exchange, Schnatter joined the proceedings via video conference. He started ranting about how the NCAA had charged my program with seventeen Level 1 violations, which of course wasn't even close to the truth. We were hit with three Level 1 violations and a Level 2 violation. Then he said: "I have a problem with coaches coming to trustees meetings. What's next, the women's volleyball coach coming in there?"

That was a pretty sexist remark. But his entire attitude was disrespectful and nasty.

He kept telling us, "I'm here with Peyton." He mentioned it a number of times. At first, I couldn't figure it out, because when I hear the name Peyton, I immediately think of my great Cardinal guard Peyton Siva, and I couldn't imagine the two of them hanging out. Then Schnatter finally indicated the Peyton in question was Peyton Manning. His behavior was bizarre and Tom and I looked at each other, as Schnatter kept walking in and out of the video conference screen. He seemed unhinged. We later found out that appearing at a meeting via video conferencing was a violation of board regulations. But why should that matter to John Schnatter?

By the end of the meeting, I realized these new so-called "stewards" of Louisville had absolutely no interest in establishing the truth, working with me, or defending the basketball program. It was clear they were not supporters of mine.

The next day I gathered everyone on the staff—from our trainers to strength coaches to assistant coaches to our administrative assistants— and I repeated my mantra: "Don't even think about jaywalking. These people are out to get me. Do everything by the book. If there's anything in question, call compliance." My staff was used to hearing this from me. But now I was adamant. Over and over and over, I preached compliance. They probably thought I was losing it. It was all I talked about: Every single detail had to be logged and every single regulation needed to be followed.

Unfortunately, on Tuesday, September 26, 2017, the board of trustees got the opportunity they'd been waiting for. The Department of Justice announced its slew of arrests. As soon as the alleged Louisville-Adidas pay-to-play angle surfaced, Acting President Postel and Board Chairman Grissom asked Tom and me to resign in separate meetings that lasted less than five minutes total. Since neither of us had done anything wrong, we both said: "Absolutely not."

Postel, who didn't ask about the details of the case or whether any of the allegations were true, said: "If you won't resign, you will be fired. You need to leave campus right now."

I said I needed to speak to my team. Postel told me to leave campus immediately after.

I went to see my players with what felt like a ton of bricks in my heart. I had brought them here expecting to coach them as I had so many other terrific players. And now, I was forbidden to be there for them. It was a very emotional meeting. I told the team I didn't know why I had been fired, because I had no part in any wrongdoing. Then I told them I loved them, I would be rooting for them, and wanted them to make me proud. Then I walked up the stairs to my office, wondering what I would take home with me after all these years.

A locksmith was changing the locks on my office door. It was a shocking sight. My job, a huge part of my identity, was being stripped from me. In fact, it was already gone.

I asked him to stop so I could get my personal belongings.

Joanne and I flew out of town that afternoon. We never returned to our house again.

Later that day, the board announced they were suspending Tom with paid leave. Then Postel, the guy who had defended me just two months earlier against the NCAA findings, announced the school had placed me on indefinite unpaid administrative leave.

In other words, we were both effectively fired with no investigation, no trial, no nothing. When it came to rushing to judgment, these guys could teach a master class.

Given the ensuing media firestorm, I could understand the intense pressure on the administration to condemn me and fire me. But there were strong reasons to keep both Tom and me at the school. For one, the DOJ complaints didn't accuse me of a damn thing and didn't even allude to Tom. For another, the school was appealing the NCAA sanctions after the Andre McGee case—which, to this day, have not resulted in a single criminal charge.

But few people in power at the university cared about this. My lawyers Steve Pence and Kurt Scharfenberger met with the board for an hour. They presented a letter certifying I had passed a polygraph test— administered by a respected ex-FBI agent who specializes in teaching polygraphs—that showed I knew nothing about alleged payments to recruits or their families, or any alleged scheme by Adidas. None of this made any impact on the university's decision makers. The U of L Athletics Association voted unanimously to fire me on October 16. Two days later, the Board of Trustees voted 10–3 to fire Tom.

By firing us—the two figures in the best position to defend the athletic program against NCAA findings—the board was effectively saying: "We don't care." Worse, they seemed to be sending a silent message to the NCAA: "Penalize Louisville, ban Louisville, destroy Louisville's reputation." Instead of defending the university, they were rolling over to be utterly decimated. They could have fired us at the end of the year and allowed us to help defend the case with the appeals committee.

There was another effect caused by my termination that I'm sure the Louisville board members never gave a moment's thought. Their actions impacted the lives and future of a number of players on the Louisville basketball team. In preseason polls for the 2017–18 season, the Louisville Cardinals were a top ten ranked team. Five of our players—Deng Adel, V.J. King, Anas Mahmoud, Ray Spalding, and Brian Bowen were projected as 2018 NBA draft picks going into the season. As of August 2017 ESPN had V.J. and Ray as high second-round picks with Anas going later. NBADraft.net had Deng as an early second-rounder. As for Bowen, Bleacher Report projected him as a late first-round pick.

Ten months later, when 2018 draft was held on June 21, only *one out of the five projected players*—was drafted. Ray Spalding was taken in the second-round with the 56th pick.

Of course, it's impossible to definitively say my presence coaching the team would have assured the players of landing in the draft. But playing within a stable, highly-ranked program would have given these players the kind of positive attention that can only help their draft prospects. And playing on a team that could receive an NCAA Tournament bid would have given them even more attention in increasingly competitive and pressure-filled situations.

It does not seem to be a huge stretch to say the board's decision to fire me likely robbed some of these players of their professional careers.

Were Tom and I fired as a knee-jerk reaction to the bad optics created by the misleading DOJ complaint and all the negative media coverage that followed it? Do you think either board knew about Marty Blazer and his save-my-butt FBI sting operation? Should they have looked into Christian Dawkins's scam-happy background before deciding Tom and I had to go? Or were the votes to banish us enacted to appease the powerful politician who had made the school his plaything? I doubt we will ever know for sure.

Look at what has happened to the coaches whose assistants were indicted by the DOJ. Auburn coach Bruce Pearl, who had Chuck Person working for him, received a five-year contract extension in June 2018. Just months before Arizona assistant coach Emanuel "Book" Richardson was indicted, his boss Sean Miller got a raise and contract extension through 2022, although the university reportedly has since amended the deal so that if Sean is ever hit with criminal charges or a major NCAA violation, he'll forfeit $1 million. As for USC head coach Andy Enfield, he got an extension months before the Feds busted his assistant, Tony Bland. Newly anointed Oklahoma State head coach Mike Boynton hasn't gotten an extension yet. But who knows? Before he got the job, he was a Cowboys assistant coach beside future ousted assistant coach Lamont Evans. Meanwhile, Jim Larrinaga, the other coach whose program was flagged in the same pay-to-play complaint that cited me, was given a two-year contract extension by University of Miami. Obviously, the universities involved here believe their head coaches had no knowledge of the activities of their assistant coaches. I was excited to see the leadership of these schools exhibit such loyalty toward the coaches who run their programs.

You really have to wonder if Bevin and his two board-controlling appointees had any interest in truly protecting Louisville at all. So far the rash decision has ended up costing the school millions to come to terms with Tom. And it will cost them millions more to defend my wrongful termination suit. And if they lose that suit, their rash act will cost at least another $37 million—the outstanding amount I had left on my contract, which was broken eight years and eight months before it ended. But I guess none of this matters to Bevin. And Grissom and Schnatter had their marching orders. They were out to destroy Tom, destroy me, destroy the legacy of sixteen years of great basketball, and maim a thriving, growing institution.

Why do that?

That's the question I come back to over and over again. Why would the governor, an avowed University of Kentucky supporter, fire the entire Louisville board of trustees and replace them with so many people with a scant connection to the school? Why condemn Tom Jurich? Why fire me when nobody from my program was indicted or even a target of the Department of Justice investigation?

Listen, I get that people blame me—especially for the McGee scandal. It was my program. I hired Andre and he did things that defied pretty much anyone's imagination. But he was totally instructed and educated on how to follow NCAA rules and be compliant to protect the integrity of our program. He was a mistake. My assistant coach Jordan Fair, who's been caught up in the FBI investigation? I hired him, too. Has he been charged with any wrongdoing? No. Did the FBI try to set him up? It sure seems like they did.

But if he is my mistake, I'll take full ownership.

In any profession, when a new CEO, president, or board is installed as the head of an organization, they have the right to change personnel and bring in their own people. But any decent company lives up to its contractual obligations to those they terminate. In my case, I was fired and Louisville effectively tore up a long-term contract and said, "So sue me." Well, I am. So far, the only thing the school has done was embarrass and humiliate me by offering to make a $1 million donation to the Daniel Pitino Foundation. I found their offer disgraceful and mean-spirited. Daniel's foundation is extremely important to my wife and me. The idea of buying off their inexcusable, nasty decisions with a so-called charitable donation disgusts me.

As for any actions that could have justified my termination, they don't exist. There is not a single shred of evidence that I conspired with anyone to have money funneled to recruits or recruits' families. That's because I never did. I've told friends for years, I wouldn't have paid five bucks to coach my favorite player of all time, Michael Jordan. It's not worth it.

So, why?

I've laid it all out here: history, rivalries, politics, voter influence, a thirst for power, and, frankly, an abuse of power. I don't have a smoking gun. But the strongman behavior of an ambitious governor with increasing power, the wealthy and politically connected elite, the callous disregard for due process, and the partisan mind-set of the Kentucky voter set the stage for these unfair, outrageous events.

Who will have paid the price for these events?

Tom and I have suffered immense stress and damaging hits to our reputations. Our families have endured extreme amounts of anguish, too. For me, the Louisville Board of Trustees' rush to judgement could be career-ending. The University of Louisville—the students, athletes, administrators, professors, and alumni who make the school what it is, and the entire city of Louisville, have been victimized, too. I firmly believe the city and the institution benefit each other, and when one suffers, so will the other.

13

THE FUTURE

The golden goose needs innovation to be saved.

I'm not sure it is going to happen.

▼

I AM EXTREMELY concerned about the future of college basketball. While nothing is etched in stone, I believe there is a very good chance the NBA and its players union will lift its one-and-done rule in 2020, removing the requirement that a player must be nineteen years old by the calendar year of the draft or one year removed from high school graduation. This will allow high school seniors to go pro when they graduate. It is a decision that will have dangerous implications not just for college basketball, but for a huge subset of kids going through high school.

I believe eighteen-year-old athletes should have the right to self-determination when it comes to whether they play basketball in college or professionally. There is no question in my mind about that. But the one-and-done rule has a number of positive aspects that get overlooked and I'd like to point them out.

In order to be eligible for a college scholarship, high school athletes have to focus on obtaining sixteen core required classes. They need to achieve a 2.3 grade point average in ten core courses and, depending on their GPA, they have to hit a certain score on their ACT or SAT exams.

Everyone realizes that the college freshman who will go pro after his initial season isn't getting much of an education. In my mind, that actually makes high school education even more important. High school is where the teaching begins, because focus, discipline, and guidance are all necessary to gain college eligibility.

If the one-and-done requirement is eliminated, what is there to academically motivate the thousands of basketball players who—rightly or wrongly—think they can make it playing some form of professional basketball? Today's youth—not unlike yesterday's youth—often overrate their abilities and misjudge where, exactly, they stand on the ladder of success. With one-and-done abolished, many young athletes will lose academic focus and decide they don't need to bother with those core requirements. Who can blame them—or stop them—from thinking, "Screw it, I'm going pro or play in the G league"? But kids who believe they can make that move and don't need an education are doing a real disservice to themselves. Top players, who inevitably will have huge amounts of money thrown at them, need to have a baseline education to thrive and grow in the world. Take away the one-and-done opportunity and its rules, and high school players will be disincentivized to study. And that same "who cares?" attitude will cascade down to students who won't make it at the pro level, and that is an even bigger tragedy.

When education loses—when young adults can't read or execute basic math skills—we all lose.

As for the college basketball game itself, if one-and-done vanishes and the NCAA does not change its attitude toward player compensation, the golden goose is in serious trouble. America's favorite tournament will be at grave risk.

Former Secretary of State Condoleezza Rice has been leading the NCAA's Commission on College Basketball, and she has been saying a number of things that give me hope. She has indicated she believes student-athletes should be allowed to profit from their likeness, just as Olympic athletes are. I truly believe that's the only way to save the college game. Players have told me they feel that profits are being made off their abilities. And I can see how family members may feel that taking inducements is not a form of cheating, as universities and the NCAA are making millions and millions of dollars off these athletes' talents while refusing to share even a fraction of the profits. There is no question players should be able to shoot commercials, take part in autograph signings, license their image, and become entrepreneurs. That is the American way.

I believe allowing these types of potential earnings will definitely help keep players in college longer. It will also get many of them to buckle down and study to obtain that high school grade point average and sixteen core requirements, which is a real relief to me.

If the Olympic model doesn't become a reality for college basketball players, the G league will blossom into a true minor league system. And when that happens, the talent pool in college basketball will decline precipitously. March Madness—God save us—will be void of a lot of talent.

With a decline in the "product"—mediocre players play mediocre games—it is likely TV ratings will decline and the NCAA and its member universities will see a dramatic loss of revenue.

Do I think the NCAA can avert this disaster?

I hope I'm wrong, but the short answer is no.

It will take bold, innovative thinking to save the golden goose. Based on its plodding, bureaucratic past, there is no chance of that. The organization has been under legal assault for years regarding its amateurism rules, and still clings to outdated thinking. In 2009, UCLA basketball star Ed O'Bannon was the lead plaintiff of a class-action lawsuit. A judge ruled that barring payments to student-athletes violated antitrust laws. That was the writing on the wall that the NCAA would have to change. But here we are.

It was encouraging, however, to read the Commission on Basketball's Recommendations. The new findings echoed a number of ideas I raised at my meeting three years ago with representatives of the NCAA, including my proposals that the NCAA develop an annual orientation program for high school athletes as a way to stop sneaker company influence and provide an alternative to the summer leagues that Nike, Adidas, and Under Armour sponsor.

Lo and behold, one of the recommendations is to "in cooperation with partners, establish NCAA youth basketball programs." No doubt, the success of that operation will depend on who, exactly, those partners are. But it's the thought that counts, right?

As for eliminating cheating, the Commission has proposed wielding a punitive sledgehammer to ensure nobody breaks the rules. They plan to "hold institutions and individuals accountable." At first blush, that doesn't sound like a big change from what the organization does now. But then the Commission turns up the volume when it comes to getting tough on infractions:

"Coaches, athletic directors, and university presidents must be held accountable for academic fraud about which they knew or should have known."

With all due respect, that is absurd.

Should university presidents inspect every student-athlete's academic schedule? Should they audit the classes that student-athletes take? Why should higher education be held to a higher standard than anyone else? For example, if a senator's aide takes a bribe to provide access to his boss, should the senator be held accountable for something his staffer did? Or imagine an FBI undercover agent abusing funds during an investigation in Las Vegas—should the Special Agent in Charge or the US Attorney overseeing the investigation be taken to task? The blame game is a difficult one to play. Trust me.

And penalties won't stop chiselers and con men from trying to grab a piece of what is a billion-dollar pie. That said, the Commission did mention one other good idea: implementing "independent investigation and adjudication of complex cases." That is very encouraging and overdue.

Of course, none of this will matter if mediocrity afflicts the game. Then basketball will become no different than many other sports at the collegiate level. A great sport with paltry revenue earnings. A game that generates some excitement and school spirit but isn't the way of life it is now. If that happens, the huge sneaker money endorsement deals—a great and vital revenue stream for so many schools—may not be so huge anymore. And football, which has already surpassed basketball in popularity, will be the only cash cow in collegiate sports. And you can bet that is not likely to change. Why? It's a long story involving, among other things, an antitrust lawsuit that went all the way to the Supreme Court. But suffice to say that the NCAA does not control college football.

Honestly, I pray the NCAA gets its act together and that Condi Rice can lead the organization forward. A great game and a magical tournament is at stake.

14

THE AFTERMATH

Repairing the damage and blazing a new path.

▼

WHY WOULD SOMEONE who has coached in seven Final Fours suddenly have to cheat?

Why would someone earning a multimillion-dollar salary—a matter of public record—jeopardize his livelihood by conspiring to bring in a player whose talents were unproven?

Why would someone hold a press conference about the negative influence of sneaker money on college recruiting and then actively participate in the problem he just complained about?

These seem like obvious questions.

Here's another: Given that assistant coaches from four other college teams were indicted as a result of the DOJ's investigation, why weren't my assistant coaches indicted? And why wasn't I indicted?

But nobody asked any of these questions in the media.

It wouldn't have been too hard for a reporter to contact any of the more than thirty head coaches who were once my assistant coaches and ask the million-dollar question: Did they ever witness me breaking recruiting rules?

Or, for that matter, they could have quizzed the hundreds of players I've coached and asked them if I ever broke any recruiting rules.

But those lines of inquiry didn't happen, either. If they had, the answers would have been, "No."

The coverage of the DOJ charges was brutal. It seemed like the entire reporting profession was in a footrace to win a rush to judgement against me.

I can't recall a single writer or commentator saying, "Let's wait and see! You remember that old American concept—innocent until proven guilty?"

The fact that I had publicly called on the NCAA to take an active role in fixing the sneaker money problem was only mentioned by a few local Louisville writers. The fact that I had pointed fingers at the entire sneaker sponsorship system wasn't given a second thought.

But as I said earlier, why let facts get in the way of a good story?

Here are some more facts:

No one from the University of Louisville basketball program has been charged with any wrongdoing regarding the DOJ investigation. Not by the DOJ itself and not by the NCAA.

My assistant coach Kenny Johnson, who met with investigators for nine hours, has a letter from the Department of Justice exonerating him from any wrongdoing in relation to the investigation.

David Padgett, another of my assistants, was found to be so squeaky clean, he was named the interim Louisville coach for a season.

Jordan Fair, my third assistant coach, was caught in a hotel room where scam artists were allegedly plotting illegal activities. He has not been indicted. And charges have been dropped against AAU coach Brad Augustine, who was allegedly caught on tape—after Jordan left the room—taking thousands of dollars as part of a scheme to pay the mother of one of his players. Augustine, as I've noted, reportedly says he never paid the mom. Instead, he just kept the money—which, apparently, means no crime was committed—or the DOJ doesn't think it has enough evidence to convict him.

So despite all the sensational headlines, it appears there will be no further sanctions or legal action against the University of Louisville or its former staff as a result of the DOJ investigation.

Strangely, that story isn't getting much ink.

I never expected reporters to hail me as a prophet for speaking out about disturbing, misguided forces swirling around the game. But I never expected they would turn on me and immediately pronounce me a crook, either.

Those negative reports had an instant effect. They set the court of public opinion against me. Furthermore, the outcry provided plenty of cover for the powers-that-be in Louisville to fire me. Now, they are currently running a smear campaign to justify their inexcusable failure to honor the contract they made with me.

Things were so bad, so negative and skewed that Pat Forde, who co-wrote *Rebound Rules* with me, banged out an article that said Louisville basketball should get the "death penalty." Rushing toward a worst-case scenario, his story for *Yahoo! Sports* was filled with the-sky-is-falling alarm:

> The program should be shut down, if the bombshell announcement of allegations Tuesday prove to be true. If that doesn't happen, the NCAA is useless.
>
> Hall of Fame coach Rick Pitino should be gone, a gilded career ending in disgrace. It seems highly plausible that he will take athletic director Tom Jurich with him, a man who lifted an entire department, and now oversees its ruination.

Pat wasn't the only one calling for my defenestration. With the exception of Dick Vitale and Jay Bilas, the entire fourth estate seemed to think I was guilty. The fact that there were no charges against me—or against my staff—didn't stop anyone from pronouncing me guilty without a trial.

Time and again, the media has lambasted me since the scandal broke. Supposedly even-handed accounts are filled with misinformation. *Pitino is under investigation. Pitino is a suspect. Pitino made phone calls to arrange payments.*

It happens all the time. Just this last May, I was sitting with friends getting ready to watch the Kentucky Oaks, which is the second biggest horse race run on the Kentucky Derby weekend at Churchill Downs. The announcer on TV mentioned a horse I co-own, Coach Rocks. He said, "This horse is owned by Rick Pitino who is under investigation by the FBI." Even on an exciting day that had nothing to do with basketball or sneakers, I couldn't catch a break.

It's been like a game of Telephone. The US Attorney whispered in the media's ear, and then the misreadings and misinformation snowballed.

I was so fed up with things that in the spring of 2018, I shared all my files—texts, call recordings, and emails—with a reporter for the *Washington Post.*

Through all of this, I have tried to take the high road. I respect the press. I have great friends who are writers. So I don't want to jump on Twitter and call out every reporter who gets something wrong. I don't want to explain to every sports radio host that the DOJ's negative portrayal of me is based on the lies of two charlatans who were encouraged to run scams by a convicted embezzler who was working with the DOJ so he could receive a reduced sentence. I just want people to get the story right.

Also, I understand reporters have editors, and some of those editors want to sensationalize things to generate sales or page views—running a media business is a profits, clicks, and numbers game now. Every outlet has been affected by the TMZs of the world. So battling with editors seems futile. It might work for a politician with a lot of time on his hands, but it doesn't work for a basketball coach.

Make that an *innocent* basketball coach. I have dropped my appeal of the NCAA Infractions Committee violation charges because the window to serve my five-game suspension has already passed. My attorney, Grace Speights of Washington, DC, advised me not to appeal; I'd be throwing money away, since the 2017 season is over. Still, I remain adamant—I had nothing to do with the Andre McGee shenanigans that resulted in my penalty. There was no evidence against me and there were no red flags I could uncover. The real travesty is that the NCAA Infractions Committee blamed the victim—the University of Louisville, which was violated and abused by the illicit on-campus activities of Andre McGee and Katina Powell.

And the idea the Infractions Committee would vacate Louisville's 2013 NCAA championship because a rogue employee arranged for strippers and sex—as horrifying as that was—is ridiculous. How is that an "extra benefit" to the team? How did those events help Luke Hancock score 22 points in the final? How did they impact all the years of hard work Peyton Siva and Russ Smith put in to get to that championship? Our team won because of the players' hard work, talent, and teamwork. Not because of anything Andre McGee did. And to suggest otherwise is an insult to those young men.

I was always proud of my players from the 2013 championship team. And I'm even more proud of them for fighting back by filing a suit in July 2018 against the NCAA that challenges the Committee on Infractions' decision to take away their much-deserved championship.

One employee's reprehensible behavior has nothing to do with what these players accomplished on the basketball court. A stripper party is no extra benefit. And while it is certainly reprehensible behavior, it has nothing to do with on-court performance. What that committee did to those young men is also reprehensible behavior. I hope and pray that the NCAA will seek to overturn the committee's inappropriate decision, as this team has been unjustly scarred by the ruling and robbed of a great achievement.

Meanwhile, I have mixed feelings about the University of Louisville. I love the school and the people of the city. A few members of the board of trustees and some of the administration are another story. They fired me without cause or even giving me a hearing. I am currently suing them, not just for the money they owe me on my contract—but to clear my name. And that will be accomplished through the depositions of my former assistant coaches, players, and staff members, including compliance enforcers.

I'm happy to report that, in May 2018, Louisville athletic director Tom Jurich, who was asked to resign five minutes before I was, negotiated a $7.2 million settlement with the University of Louisville. Without question, they settled with Tom because they knew he was innocent of any charges and feared Tom would file a wrongful termination lawsuit. Tom is no doubt glad this is behind him, but the settlement will never erase the smear campaign and the pain it caused him and his family.

On two separate occasions during the Andre McGee scandal, I offered to submit my resignation to Tom. The second time I brought it up, he cut me off.

"Do not ever mention that again. You've now mentioned it twice. Don't mention it a third time."

"But, Tom, it will just make things easier for you."

"You've helped us accomplish so much here. You've done it the right way. I have observed you running your program on a firsthand basis. There is absolutely no reason for you to resign. Don't do anything but continue doing what you've done for the last fifteen years here: run a clean program, ensure good academic discipline, and continue teaching basketball the way you've done it."

I have nothing but the highest regard for Tom. He is a visionary manager, shrewd negotiator, and driven innovator. When it comes to integrity, everyone can fall in line behind him. He supported me during the greatest crisis of my career and that meant the world to me. He deserves an unblemished reputation. So I was thrilled to read one particular clause in Tom's settlement—U of L will update his personnel file to read that his time ended at Louisville "without cause." For the chief architect of the school's rebirth, that is exactly as it should be.

ADVERSITY

Over the last three years I have struggled mightily to keep my faith in the face of so many lies and so much negativity. I could write a book on battling adversity. It makes people react in irrational ways. Some turn to drugs or alcohol. Some react with violence. I believe in beating adversity with motivation and a sense of purpose.

But it isn't easy, especially when you are down. I was utterly shocked when Pat Forde called for my termination. My first thought was that he knows me. He wrote a book with me. He must know I would never cheat to get a player. It was devastating to realize he thought so poorly of me.

For many, the first impulse when faced with adversity is to fight back.

This is not about fighting with your antagonists; it's about picking yourself pick up off the floor and embracing your passions.

For a person in the limelight, reading social media is like injecting poison into your veins. Reading and watching the regular media isn't always much better. Before I had a one-on-one interview with Jay Bilas on ESPN, a well-known preacher from Louisville called me to say God knows the truth, leave it in his hands. That hit home for me and I mentioned it to Jay while answering his questions. Soon after, someone sent me a piece by a popular writer who tore into me for bringing God into the conversation.

How did I respond? I laughed it off. If you can't turn to God during times of crisis, who can you turn to? This writer totally missed a fundamental truth. It was actually funny. And I realized I knew how to conquer adversity.

Here are six steps to turn the tide against misfortune.

Step 1—Laughter

The first step toward dealing with adverse conditions is getting in touch with your sense of humor. Laughter is the number-one gift we have for dealing with difficult times. Seek it out. With friends, with old memories, by watching TV or reading a book.

Step 2—Stay away from social media

I know many people enjoy their "community" on Facebook and Instagram. But there is so much negativity and poison that can surface on these platforms. Twitter, for example, often seems filled with anonymous insults. It's been said "misery loves company"—and that happens a lot on social media. Things can get ugly fast in that regard.

So for all the fun and information you can get from Twitter, proceed with caution. You'll need thick skin to endure the avalanche of negativity that could come your way. For every relevant point you make, somebody may come back at you and tear you down.

Also, for all the good cheer that social media tries to provide with "likes" and emojis, positive reinforcement easily turns into negative reinforcement when nobody responds to your posts or criticizes them. So do yourself a favor: don't feel you have to follow the crowd.

Step 3—Idleness is the devil's workshop

For the first time in forty-one years, I would wake up at 5:45 a.m. with nothing to do. No meetings, no player development, no staff luncheons, and no practice. It was an incredible void. If you want to feed the adversity monster, stay idle. I charted my day to the minute. At 6:00 a.m., I'd start a ninety-minute workout. Then I'd head to Starbucks and text or call family members.

I would then plan my day and fill up every minute with something to keep busy and bring about laughter. Obviously I'm blessed with a strong family and have great friendships. I relied on them to keep me strong. My assistant coaches and players have been great about reaching out. If it meant getting in my car and traveling somewhere to create a busy day, so be it. It's easier to sleep when you've had a productive day.

Step 4—Don't let rejection get you down

In the mid 1990s, I was offered coaching jobs with the Warriors, the Lakers, and other professional teams. Since leaving Louisville, my agent has reached out when NBA openings have surfaced. We couldn't even get an interview. I can't blame the general managers who turned me down. Louisville fired me so abruptly, it instantly created the impression that I must be guilty of something.

But you have to keep knocking on all the doors. Do not let anything deter you from getting a door open. Fulfilling dreams takes time and work.

Step 5—Take ownership for your dilemma

We all make mistakes in life. My biggest one occurred sixteen years ago. I shouldn't have been within a hundred yards of the woman who tried to extort me. That is and forever will be my deepest regret. When you hurt the ones that mean the most in life, it can be gut-wrenching when you realize what you have done. It creates a sadness that is unrivaled. But you have to come clean to yourself and to the people you hurt.

More recently, I've tried to rationalize when people say I must be responsible for the hiring mistakes I've made. My quick response is to name my thirty-plus ex-players and assistant coaches who have gone on to become outstanding head coaches. But the fact is, I hired Andre McGee and Jordan Fair. I have to live with the consequences of that decision and everything it set in motion.

Still, offering up excuses can seem like a sign of weakness... Better to admit your shortcomings and accept that bad breaks are part of life. Once you own up to things and accept the situation, you can learn from it.

Not only that, you can put it in the rearview mirror. That's partly why I've written this book. It's time to move forward.

Step 6—You must have faith

This is the last step to dealing with adversity and turning your life around. I don't just mean having faith in God, either. I also mean you need to put your faith in other people—the friends and family who will lift your spirits.

Sometimes you have to actively find these people. I've rekindled old friendships, reached out to ex-players from the past. When we get together, we laugh—which of course is step number one—and in doing so, forge new bonds that tie us to each other and give our lives meaning.

I've found I gather strength even from meeting strangers. Don't lose faith; it's there to get you through the toughest times.

Let me give one major example. I'm so appreciative of my old friend Dick Vitale. Since I was fired, Dick has called me three to four times a week. Not text messages. Not emails. He makes actual, live telephone calls, which doesn't happen much today.

With the exception of Dick's reminders about why I should have more college victories than Coach K if I had stayed at the University of Kentucky, his calls have been an absolute joy. He loves to talk basketball 24/7, and he frequently brings up the work I did at Louisville—he loved our style of play, our work ethic, our practices. I have known Dick for decades. We first met at Five-Star Basketball Camp and have been friends ever since. But he's a busy guy. For him to take the time to reach out, check on how I'm feeling, and lift my spirits with his excited, joy-filled voice is something I will always appreciate. How can you lose faith with friends like that?

ANCHORS

I have a small boat that I take out to the ocean. I find it calming to be out in the middle of a vast body of water, amid the beautiful, awesome forces of nature. And sometimes my mind just wanders. I know I advocate being busy. But there is grace in relaxing, too.

I went out recently, crossed the Haulover Bridge Underpass in North Miami, put the boat on autopilot, and just started thinking as the boat headed toward Fort Lauderdale.

I recalled the one and only time I had to get on Billy Donovan. It was the 1987 NCAA Tournament during the first half of our second-round game versus Austin Peay, who had upset Illinois. Billy was suffering through an awful half. Stu Jackson, my assistant coach, grabbed me. "I know you don't get on or yell at Billy the Kid, but you have to shake him up. He's out of it."

I couldn't remember ever yelling at Billy during the two years I coached him. He was the hardest worker and best teammate. Always early and eager to get better. But it was one of the worst halves I had seen him play. If he didn't snap out of it, our dream season was coming to an end. I went over statistical data with the team and then looked at Billy. "You know, I'm not too sure you deserve to wear a Friars uniform and I don't know if I should even play you in the second half. I may never call you Billy the Kid again." Then I walked out.

I felt pretty lousy about getting on him like that. But Stu had told me to strike a spark, and, boy, did Billy catch fire. We won in OT and headed to the Sweet Sixteen. After the game, I gave Billy a hug and said, "You're still Billy the Kid."

Then my mind wandered to winning the championship in 2013. The greatest week ever didn't just end with us beating Michigan to win it all. At four in the morning I got a phone message from President Bill Clinton that I've kept with me to this day. He said:

Hello, Coach, I'm in Abu Dhabi. I watched your game late in the morning and I'm so proud of you. You're a special man and a special coach. It was wonderful to see. Congrats on an incredible achievement.

I actually shed a happy tear and jumped in the shower. The president had called me! I headed down to the lobby for coffee, as I had to be on a morning show at 6:00 a.m. I was still buzzing. I was so proud of my team. They were a fun group. We laughed a lot. Just thinking about that crew makes me smile. But my heart is so heavy with the burden of the championship banner coming down. There's not a night that goes by when I don't lie awake thinking about how it has hurt my players, the University of Louisville, and the city.

Going up the coast, the halfway point from Miami to Ft. Lauderdale, I remembered some of the tougher moments of coaching.

I'm a big stickler about being early or, at worst, on time. Back at Boston University, two players missed the team bus going to our game in Cincinnati. It was the second offense for both of them. They were terrific young men who needed to understand that their time wasn't more valuable than the team's. I constantly reiterated that to my players—being late is a selfish act.

"Do you think your time is more valuable than other people's time?" I'd ask.

I made those two players run to our hotel after our game. One of them was Brett Brown, who is now the head coach of the 76ers. I don't think he's ever been late again in his life. He is a terrific leader who I believe will bring a championship to Philadelphia.

As I entered the Ft. Lauderdale channel, where the big cruise ships come in, I started thinking about one of my favorite players, Francisco Garcia. His freshman season he had awful body language on the court and constantly complained to officials during games. I had my staff put together a video tape of his behavior. He watched the tape and couldn't believe that was him.

I flashed forward to Francisco fouling out during a massive comeback against West Virginia in the 2005 NCAA Tournament. Instead of sulking on the bench, he started acting like a cheerleader. The cameras caught his positive behavior and Dick Vitale took notice: "Hey, look at Garcia! He's handing out water like a manager, jumping up and down like a cheerleader. He does it all!"

Another of my favorites, Terry Rozier, got in a scuffle with a teammate. I threw Terry out of practice.

"Man, you're a great player," I told him later in the locker room. "Protect your teammates and save that fierce competitiveness for our opponents." From that point on, Terry had everyone's back.

I docked the boat for lunch with my eldest son, Michael. I started to think about how my family members' lives had been turned upside down. My wife leaves her home of seventeen years without a goodbye, my daughter Jacqueline moves away from the town where she was raised. But family gets people through tough times, and I'm so lucky to have five incredible children and a wife who's been a Rock of Gibraltar for our forty-plus years of marriage.

After lunch, I headed back to the ocean and started thinking about the time I benched Donovan Mitchell before a nationally broadcast game against Indiana. Donovan was in a mini-slump and playing with little confidence. In the last five games, he'd shot just 16-for-54. I called him aside before the game. "I'm not starting you," I said. "And my reason is, I told everyone I had recruited a great player when you joined the University of Louisville basketball team. But you've been playing like someone who is afraid of failing."

When I substituted him into the game, I said, "Now show me you are a great basketball player." He exploded for a career-high 25 points and we beat the Hoosiers by fifteen. That was the last time he came off the bench as a substitute.

I spent hours just cruising. Speeding up, slowing down. I realized that wherever I happen to go, I'll always be accompanied by a lifetime of memories my players have given me.

Kentucky was Camelot. Louisville was real life. It was filled with ups and downs, great friendships and betrayals. I don't want to create a never-ending bitterness. It's time to let go. It's judgment time. I've told the truth in this book. Now the big questions are whether Andre McGee, Jordan Fair, or the people facing trials and possible jail time will tell the truth.

As I said earlier, Andre's lawyer, Scott Cox, has told Andre there is no statute of limitations and warned him to stay silent. According to Cox, the commonwealth attorney could at any time open a case against him. I totally disagree. Andre needs to apologize to the people he hurt and cleanse his soul for the actions that wounded his parents, teammates, coaches, university, and the city that stood behind him.

If Andre apologizes and admits his mistakes, there's no way that will result in the commonwealth attorney opening up the case. If anything, I believe that would help the healing to start and allow Andre to get his dignity back on track.

This may sound crazy, but I'm actually more upset with Jordan Fair than I am at Andre McGee. Andre's actions were inexplicable and so out of character that I sometimes wonder if he was a sociopath or being black-mailed. I have no idea. Jordan, on the other hand, was repeatedly taught to follow the absolute letter of the law with regard to recruiting regulations.

I found it incredibly ironic that a short time before the Las Vegas incident, Jordan approached me and asked, "Who were the best assistant coaches you've ever had?"

There are so many aspects to the job—recruiting, coaching offense, coaching defense, scouting, mentoring, managing, each with their own subsets of skills—that I found it an impossible question to answer. "In what area?" I asked.

Jordan cut to the chase: "I want to be your next Billy Donovan."

"You have a long way to go before you'll reach that status."

"What do you mean by that?"

"Bill never looked for credit with anything he did. He worked silently and selflessly. He also did every single thing by the book. When you gain that level of humility and discipline, you'll make strides to follow in his path."

There are no shortcuts to greatness was my message. You have to do the work. And because we were under the shadow of Andre's behavior, Jordan and other staff members were educated and cautioned about compliance rules at least ten times more than any other group of assistants I'd ever had. They needed to do the work and follow the rules. So the fact that he met with a roomful of scam artists is completely infuriating. Was he led astray by con men? Quite possibly. But he should have never been in that situation in the first place.

Like Andre, I'm sure Jordan's been advised to keep his mouth shut, for fear of getting caught in a DOJ dragnet. I'm also sure Andre's and

Jordan's minds are not focused on helping exonerate their former colleagues and coaches.

One day that may change. Time heals wounds and scars loosen up. When their time for asking comes about, I believe they will be forgiven. I hope they both will arrive at that point someday.

For years, I've taken bows for an amazing coaching tree: so many loyal and hardworking assistants who helped my team reach its potential. But I will adapt a line from Theodore Roosevelt's "Man in the Arena" speech: I did my best making hiring decisions and must take ownership of these decisions. But there is no effort without error and shortcomings.

As far as I'm concerned, I've always believed the truth will set you free. This book is a full accounting of the truth. Whether I coach again or not, I still must find a new passion in my life. At this juncture, I have no idea what that will be. But you can bet I will be knocking on doors until I find it.

It's never too late to teach an old dog new tricks, and I certainly after forty-one years of coaching would try different methods to make my product even better. But I don't think that opportunity will ever happen again, so it's now my time to share my methods with other coaches.

As I pulled my boat back into the dock and my daydream excursion came to an end, I arrived at a realization: that the buck stops with me and my coaching career is possibly finished. I need to let go of any bitterness. I'm not sure what I will miss most: the player development-practices, the late-night phone calls helping players cope with whatever obstacles stood in their way, the sideline X's and O's, March Madness, or all of the above. It is time to appreciate what my players and fellow coaches have given me—a lifetime of memories! Thank you, guys. I'll never forget any of you.

ACKNOWLEDGMENTS

HEARTFELT THANKS go out to:

Dick Vitale, for always reaching out and checking on me.

Marc Mukasey, for his generosity, support, and wisdom during very trying times.

Rick Avare, my business partner and great friend, for his honesty and loyalty.

All assistant coaches and players, for keeping my spirits high by reaching out so often and offering so much support.

And to JJ, who hurt along with me.

I'd also like to thank the following three individuals who were great innovators, administrators, and loyal friends. Thank you for giving me the opportunity to work with you:

Lou Lamoriello, for our terrific time together at Providence. It was there that I learned what was what possible with a terrific athletic director and a program with an amazing work ethic.

The late C.M. Newton, an athletic director with patience and polish, who made Kentucky great.

Tom Jurich, my athletic director at Louisville, who was bold, creative, and always principled.

ABOUT THE AUTHOR

RICK PITINO coached the Louisville Cardinals basketball team from 2001 to 2017. Prior to Louisville, Pitino was head coach for the Boston Celtics, the University of Kentucky, the New York Knicks, Providence College, and Boston University. He won two NCAA championships, is the only head coach to take three different schools to a Final Four, and was elected in 2013 to the Naismith Memorial Basketball Hall of Fame.

Seth Kaufman is the author of six books, including *The King of Pain* and *Metaphysical Graffiti*. He has written for *The New Yorker*, *TV Guide*, and many websites.